UTOPIAS AND
THE MILLENNIUM

Critical Views

UTOPIAS AND THE MILLENNIUM

Edited by
Krishan Kumar *and*
Stephen Bann

REAKTION BOOKS

Published by Reaktion Books Ltd
1–5 Midford Place, Tottenham Court Road
London WIP 9HH, UK

First Published 1993

Designed by Humphrey Stone

Photoset by Wilmaset Ltd, Birkenhead, Wirral
Printed and bound in Great Britain by
Redwood Press Ltd, Melksham, Wiltshire

British Library Cataloguing in Publication Data

Utopias and the Millennium. – (Critical Views Series)
I. Kumar, Krishan II. Bann, Stephen
III. Series
303.3

ISBN 0–948462–45–0
ISBN 0–948462–44–2 (pbk)

This volume was published with the aid of a subsidy from the
Centre for Modern Cultural Studies, University of Kent at Canterbury.
The Centre was established by the Faculty of Humanities in 1990.

Contents

Notes on the Editors and Contributors   vii

Introduction   *Stephen Bann* ✓   1

1   The Frontiers of Utopia   *Louis Marin* ✓   7

2   Formal Utopia/Informal Millennium: The Struggle between   17
Form and Substance as a Context for Seventeenth-century
Utopianism   *J. C. Davis*

3   From Robinson to Robina, and Beyond: *Robinson Crusoe*   33
as a Utopian Concept   *Louis James* ✓

4   Utopianism, Property, and the French Revolution Debate   46
in Britain   *Gregory Claeys*

5   The End of Socialism? The End of Utopia?   63
The End of History?   *Krishan Kumar* ✓

6   The Metamorphosis of the Apocalyptic Myth: From Utopia   81
to Science Fiction   *Vita Fortunati*

7   'Politics Here is Death': William Burroughs's *Cities of the*   90
Red Night   *David Ayers*

8   Utopia the Good Breast: Coming Home to Mother   107
Jan Relf

9   *McTopia*: Eating Time   *John O'Neill*   129

References   138

Select Bibliography   157

Index   161

In memory of Louis Marin (1931–1992)

Notes on the Editors and Contributors

KRISHAN KUMAR is Professor of Social Thought at the University of Kent. His publications include *Prophecy and Progress* (1978), *Utopia and Anti-Utopia in Modern Times* (1987), *The Rise of Modern Society* (1988) and *Utopianism* (1991); he is the editor of *Revolution* (1971) and *Dilemmas of Liberal Democracies* (1983).

STEPHEN BANN is Professor of Modern Cultural Studies and Chairman of the Board of Studies in History and Theory of Art at the University of Kent. His books include *Concrete Poetry – An International Anthology* (ed., 1967), *Experimental Painting* (1970), *The Tradition of Constructivism* (ed., 1974), *The Clothing of Clio* (1984), *The True Vine* (1989), and *The Inventions of History* (1990). He recently co-edited, with William Allen, *Interpreting Contemporary Art* (Reaktion Books, 1991), and contributed an essay to *The Portrait in Photography* (Reaktion Books, 1992).

LOUIS MARIN, who died in 1992, was Director of Studies at the Ecole des Hautes Etudes en Sciences Sociales, Paris, where he also directed the Centre de Recherche sur les Arts et le Langage. As a philosopher, semiologist and historian of representation, he published around fifteen books, the most recent of which to be translated into English is *Portrait of the King* (1988). He made a notable contribution to the study of Utopia with the collection of essays, *Utopiques: Jeux d'espaces* (1973: English translation, 1984), and he returned to this theme in his most recent publication, *Lectures traversières* (1992).

J. C. DAVIS is Professor of English History at the University of East Anglia. He has published extensively on utopian thought, in particular *Utopia and the Ideal Society: A Study of English Utopian Writing 1516–1700* (1981), and 'Utopianism' in J. H. Burns, ed., *The Cambridge History of Political Thought 1450–1700* (1991).

LOUIS JAMES is Professor of Victorian and Modern Literature at the University of Kent. His publications include *Fiction for the Working Man, 1830–50* (1963), *The Islands in Between* (1968), *Print and the People 1815–51* (1976) and *Jean Rhys* (1978), as well as numerous articles and broadcasts on Commonwealth literature and nineteenth-century fiction. He has lectured widely in the United States, Africa and the Far East.

GREGORY CLAEYS is Professor of the History of Political Thought at Royal Holloway and Bedford New College, University of London. He is the author of *Citizens and Saints, Politics and Anti-Politics in Early British Socialism* (1989), *Machinery, Money and the Millennium: From Moral Economy to Socialism, 1815–1860* (1987), *Thomas Paine: Social and Political Thought* (1989), and editor of *Robert Owen, A New View of Society and Other Writings* (1991), *Thomas Paine: Rights of Man* (1992), *Eighteenth Century British Utopias* and *John Thelwell: Political Writings* (forthcoming). He is co-editor, of *The Cambridge History of Nineteenth Century Political Thought* (forthcoming). His current projects include a volume entitled *Restoration British Utopias*.

VITA FORTUNATI is Professor of English at the University of Bologna, where she is also serving as Chair of the Modern Languages Department. She is the author of a volume on Ford's narrative technique, *Ford Madox Ford: Teoria e tecnica narrativa* (1975), and one on utopian literature, *Le letterature utopica inglese* (1979). She has published several articles on utopian literature, women's writing and literary theory. She has recently co-edited two books on utopian literature, *Paesi di cuccagna e mondi alla rovescia* (1989) and *Per una definizione dell'utopia: metodologie e discipline a confronto* (1992). Her study of Orwell's dystopia has appeared in *George Orwell's 1984* (1987).

DAVID AYERS is lecturer in English and American Literature at the University of Kent. He is the author of *Wyndham Lewis and Western Man* (1992).

JAN RELF is part-time lecturer in English Literature at the University of Plymouth in Devon and has recently completed a Ph.D. thesis on women's studies from 1960–1990 in the School of English at the University of Exeter. Her essay on the politics of separatism in women's utopias, 'Women in Retreat', appears in *Utopian Studies*, vol. II (1991).

JOHN O'NEILL is Distinguished Research Professor of Sociology at York University, Toronto and an External Associate of the Centre for Comparative Literature at the University of Toronto. He is also a Fellow of the Royal Society of Canada. He is the author of, among other works: *Essaying Montaigne: A Study of the Renaissance Institution of Writing and Reading* (1982), *Five Bodies: The Human Shape of Modern Society* (1985), *The Communicative Body: Studies in Communicative Philosophy, Politics and Sociology* (1989), *Plato's Cave: Desire, Power and the Specular Functions of the Media* (1991) and *Critical Conventions* (1992). He is presently at work on *The Domestic Economy of the Soul*, a study of Freud's principal five case histories.

Introduction

It would be an ambitious, and perhaps a self-contradictory, task to trace the boundaries of the modern study of utopia. Indeed, one of the most obvious features of utopia, as it has been understood in the twentieth century, is that it does not constitute an accepted field of study, divided and traversed by well-established disciplinary boundaries. Instead, it forms the concrete expression of a moment of possibility, which is however annihilated in the very process of being enunciated. This is partly because of the very history and etymology of the utopian project, which began, as is well-known, when Sir Thomas More described the detailed physiognomy of a 'No-place'. But it is particularly the case in our own period, when that 'No-place' has been subjected to a ritual of double negation. The 'End of Utopia' – colourfully expressed in Baudrillard's catchy declaration that 'the year 2000 will not take place' – is a concept that seems to suit our contemporary experience of society and politics on the world scale.

Yet the exchange of slogans and counter-slogans would not be enough to sustain a book of essays of this kind. If it be granted that the impending conjunction between utopian discourse and the approaching millennium gives this collection its timeliness, it must also be said that much has been done in the past few years to clarify the character and the direction of utopian studies. One particular scholar, the French semiotician Louis Marin, who died during the preparation of this volume, can be taken as exemplifying this new and productive turn. His collection of essays, *Utopiques: Jeux d'espaces*, was first published in 1973. His most recent collection, *Lectures traversières* (1992), contains a substantial section devoted to utopian themes. The fact that his contribution stands at the head of this group of essays is a tribute not only to his general pre-eminence in the field, but also to the fact that his presence at a symposium held at the University of Kent in November 1991 was a major catalyst for our other contributors.[1]

Marin's influence on Utopian Studies is perhaps most notoriously equated with his brilliant essay, 'Disneyland as a Degenerate Utopia'. At the close of this collection, John O'Neill's parallel 'approach to the idealization of place', entitled 'McTopia', differs from Marin's diagnosis only in that it treats with even greater irony, and to devastating effect, the logic of consumption as work. Yet Marin's analysis has also vastly expanded the range of types of 'place' which can be taken as falling within the distinctive category of 'no-place', and so fulfil a utopian project. Writing about the 'Jardin de Julie' (described by Rousseau in *La Nouvelle Heloise*), he notes the impulse to make the garden a place where time is suspended, a pure interiority with no representation, and no visible connections to the external world. Indeed, for Marin, Rousseau is the figure who draws together most tightly the two sides of utopia, as both practice and fiction: in the writing of his *Rêveries*, which describe his 'solitary' walks on a sequestered island on the Lac de Bienne, he shows how the promise of happiness conjured up in such a place is a function of its 'neutrality', its avoidance of the antithetical categories of self and other, subject and object, past and future.

As early as 1977, in an important article which has not been bettered as a clarification of Marin's thought, Fredric Jameson wrote about the significance of the category of the 'neutral' as Marin conceived it. Precisely because 'neutralization' suspends the logic of antithesis and contradiction, it offers to the imagination the opportunity for meditation and play. Indeed it goes further than this, for as Jameson emphasizes:

> To understand Utopian discourse in terms of neutralization is . . . to propose to grasp it as a process, an *energeia*, enunciation, productivity, and implicitly or explicitly to repudiate that more traditional and conventional view of Utopia as sheer representation, as the 'realized' vision of this or that society or social ideal.[2]

A sign that the shift recommended here is already taking place, even in the area where utopia seems to have achieved its most secure grounding in 'representation', can be found in the argument of Anthony Vidler's recent book, *Claude-Nicholas Ledoux: Architecture and Social Reform at the End of the Ancien Regime* (1990). Ledoux, the most illustrious representative of what has been called 'utopian architecture', has left many concrete realizations of his architectural ideas, and none is more remarkable than the Royal Saltworks at Arc-et-Sénans, in Franche-Comté, which incorporated much that was later expanded into his plan for the 'ideal city' of Chaux. But Vidler rightly gives no special privilege to the completed work, and emphasizes how, for Ledoux, the ideal city is generated by a series of writings which take the form of eighteenth-century travel romances. 'The Route to Utopia', as Vidler describes it, is in the form of a travel account that lies 'somewhere between Swift's *Gulliver's Travels* and Rousseau's *Rêveries du promeneur solitaire*': Ledoux, 'omnivorous reader of voyages, oriental tales, and utopian fantasies', prepares for the description of his architectural project by way of a narrative 'so picaresquely elaborated as the "plot" of *Joseph Andrews* or of *Tom Jones*.'[3]

'The Route to Utopia' is thus by way of a fiction. But the 'route' is not to be found through tracing the history of a formal genre: rather, it may be traced via the development over time of mixed genres, such as the travel account, which establish a form of discourse that produces new meanings in response to changes in historical circumstances. In this respect, Louis James is right to disregard, in his essay on '*Robinson Crusoe* as a Utopian Concept', the fact that this famous founding novel cannot strictly be classed as a utopia. If we cease to be preoccupied, as was once the case, with tracing an origin for the novel, then we can observe how a text such as *Robinson Crusoe* is itself a mesh of different discourses, to which the fiction of More's *Utopia*, engendered two centuries before, contributes its motif of the 'imaginary island'; more importantly, we can see how *Robinson Crusoe* itself generated a series of further elaborations of the island narrative, particularly after the work's utopian potential had been endorsed by that great patron of modern utopianism, Rousseau.

So it is in the very nature of utopian discourse that it should provoke both fictional and historical analysis. The list of contributors to this volume makes the point very clearly, being divided between those who specialize in literary studies and those who work in the historical or sociological field. For once we abandon the view of utopia as represent-ation – and no longer see a crucial distinction between what is 'fictional' and what is 'realized' – then it becomes clear that both types of specialists will be concerned with tracing similar discursive structures, as they emerge in the concrete circumstances of the historical moment. J. C. Davis addresses the central issue posed by this collection when he detects, in the context of the history of Britain in the 17th century, the 'struggle' between utopia as a formal prescription for the ideal society, and the millenniary ideal, dedicated to abandoning all constraints in its celeb-ration of unlimited divine power. Davis's techniques are those of historical analysis, and the significance of his essay lies precisely in the way in which he anchors this crucial debate within the context of Britain in the period of the Civil War. Nevertheless, it is worth pointing out the parallels with the issue of contemporary science fiction, as this mode of fiction is described in the essay by Vita Fortunati. Central to her own literary analysis is the presumption that utopia, as a complex genre, inherits both the cyclical, Greek notion of time and the more fluid, dynamic temporality of the Judaeo-Christian tradition. What, for Davis, forms the motivation for a conflict between warring sects, is for Fortunati a creative tension which links the fiction of Wyndham and Ballard to the speculative flights of contemporary theology. But, in both cases, the utopian idea is engendered by discursive formations which can be traced to the mythic sub-stratum of a heterogeneous Western culture.

It could be argued that, for this very reason, there is no position for the analyst to occupy, outside the endless recurrence of these aboriginal and conflicting trains of thought. Davis himself quotes the remark of Marin: 'As a figure in discourse utopia is written and imagined within the discourse that criticizes it.' Yet this would be an extreme and unnecessary conclusion. All of the contributors to this volume write, no doubt, as a consequence of the productivity of a utopian discourse which continues to invent commentaries on, and variations of, a well-worn group of themes. But they also write, to a greater or lesser degree, according to a contemporary agenda, and their critical force resides in the extent to which they challenge the specific formations assumed by the utopian idea in our own time. We are only a quarter of a century away from the decade in which liberated sexuality acquired a compelling utopian resonance, and the message of Marcuse has been echoed, in variants inflected with a more feminist tonality, in recent works such as Elaine Showalter's *Sexual Anarchy* (1991). Baudrillard has commented in a characteristically provocative way on this conflation of sexuality, and sexual politics, with the utopian theme:

The end of Utopias might be the end of masculine Utopias, giving way henceforth to feminine Utopias. But are there such things as feminine Utopias? It is man, in his naivety, who secretes Utopias, one of them being precisely woman. And woman, being a living Utopia, has no need to produce any such thing.[4]

It is not the way of our contributors to speak so aphoristically. Nevertheless, there is a real pertinence in Baudrillard's declaration if we relate it to the two essays which focus most immediately on the conjunction of utopia and sexuality. Jan Relf, in adopting a psycho-analytic viewpoint, is inevitably led to identify a 'progressive' and a 'regressive' tendency in her review of the feminist utopias contained in the fictional tradition. Of the various models which she uses in her classification – 'nurturing archetype', 'goddess', 'earth mother', 'phallic mother' etc. – none appears to satisfy the rigours of the psychoanalytic critique. So it is left to the fiction of Doris Lessing, with its characteristic witness of the 'lone, liminal soul', to escape the dangers of a 'return to the mother'. David Ayers's discussion of Burroughs's *Cities of the Red Night* might be seen as the other side of the coin, in the light of Baudrillard's remark: a utopian vision of 'Wild Boys' entirely eschewing female sexuality, which draws its strength precisely from the remarkable way in which it embroiders the pre-existing web of 'travel' and 'pirate' narratives. It is, in Burroughs's own words, a 'retroactive Utopia'.

If our contributors comment, in this way, on the contemporary form of the sexual utopia, the high point of which may have been reached during the 1960s, they are obviously not unconcerned with the radical crisis in the political discourse of utopia which has accompanied the collapse of Communism in Eastern Europe. Gregory Claeys looks carefully at the way in which the French Revolution stimulated the writing of utopian tracts in Britain, and finds evidence of the crucial debate about whether the small-scale values of the 'commune' can indeed be extended to the conditions of the modern nation-state. He suggests that, out of this debate, emerges the consensual decision to look for an ideal society not in the golden age of the past, but in 'a creative redevelopment of the present out of materials created by commerce and industry'. But he also concedes that this phase is now at an end, and he agrees with Krishan Kumar in locating socialism's present debate within 'a much "greener" emphasis'.

It is left to Krishan Kumar to confront most directly the clamorous contemporary issues of the bankruptcy of utopian thought, and the 'End of History'. For him, the spectacular and sudden effect of the collapse of the totalitarian regimes of Eastern Europe has indeed produced a temporary dazzlement, as a result of which (in George Steiner's words) 'California-promise' has become 'the concrete utopia in revolutions'. But this effect cannot but be an evanescent one: 'Capitalism needs socialism; if it did not exist it would have to invent it'. In positing 'the fate of the planet' as the new concern of utopian thought, Kumar is in accord with the overriding message of Andrew Ross's fine new book, *Strange Weather: Culture, Science and Technology in the Age of Limits* (1991). Ross, who is perceptive about the overwhelmingly dystopian effect of the recent 'cyberpunk' recruits to the genre of science fiction, sees it as essential that we disconnect the utopian tradition from its 'tradition of Marxist historical teleology, with its roots in the Enlightenment faith in scientific progress through technical mastery of the natural world's resources.' His option is a different one:

Indeed, my arguments resonate more with the traditional aim of utopian socialism, that of finding a credible language and imagery to represent the idea of a more radically democratic future; a horizon of expectations for *different* people to live by and act upon, with some measure and promise of real gratification.[5]

Here the challenge to be met is precisely that thrown out by Fukuyama, as quoted by Kumar: 'we cannot picture to ourselves a world that is *essentially* different from the present one, and at the same time better.'

Yet, of course, it is not exactly a matter of 'picturing to ourselves'. Nor is it a matter of that perfect representation of the ideal world which Fukuyama rightly sees as lacking. If, as has been argued here in line with Marin's emphasis, the discourse of utopia is about the achievement of a 'neutral' space – a space of 'interiority' but also of 'productivity' – then we should not be dismayed by the elusiveness of its concrete represent-ations. In the last resort, the production of utopia is the productivity of a language. That this is especially evident in the case of utopian socialism (and by contrast disavowed in the case of its Marxist successor) is beautifully demonstrated by Roland Barthes' account of Fourier in *Sade, Fourier, Loyola*: the utopian socialist appears, like the mystic and the reprobate who keep him company, as 'the founder of a language'.[6]

How much of Barthes' questing and anarchic spirit may have filtered through into *Utopiques*, published two years later, is a question which needs no answer here. It has been Marin's achievement to plunge utopian discourse back into the semantic texture of each particular period without for a moment denying the inventive powers of the individual writer. Yet what he proposes in this essay, on 'The Frontiers of Utopia', is an archaeology of the words and concepts that form the very precondition of utopian thought: notions of finitude and limitation, but also notions that give rise to a more expansive possibility, such as 'horizon' and 'frontier', which facilitate the engenderment of the 'neutral', the utopian space.

Words exist within history, as Marin reminds us. Walls disappear, and frontiers are moved – as the present state of Berlin displays with an unsettling and exhilarating clarity. But what does not change is lan-guage's disposition to retain, beyond the historical play of concrete forms, its figuration of freedom.

I

The Frontiers of Utopia

LOUIS MARIN

The title of my essay, 'The frontiers of Utopia', can be understood to refer to two possible issues: the frontiers that define and limit Utopia, if there are any such frontiers; and secondly, the frontiers that are created by the utopian imagination, if that imagination is indeed capable of such an act.

In any event, this theme, in its ambiguity, offers an opportunity to think about terms and words which appear to have some semantic affinities with Utopia and frontiers, such as 'horizon' and 'infinity', 'limit' and 'travel'. There is an immediate and (so to speak) unregulated affinity between frontier, limit and horizon, as well as between travel, Utopia and infinity. Let us consider then, the example of horizon and infinity on the one hand, and frontier and Utopia on the other: these plays on words and significations are useful in so far as they trouble the usual, reified lexical, logical and philosophical classifications in history, society and culture, in their representations as well as their ideologies. We must enter into these plays and games with language and meaning since they also, in fact, affect history – as plays of forces and powers; in this way we can grasp their practical, concrete efficacy and analyse the ideological significations which derive from their oppositions, proximities and even confusions.

The use of the term horizon is attested from the second half of the 13th century. At first the word signified 'limit', the limit of the gaze, the limit of sky and earth. In the 18th century, through metonymy, it came to designate the part of the landscape close to this line, and in the Romantic epoch 'horizon' meant the opening of vision to the 'extreme' of the gaze, the mystery of a remote space concealed from view, and, finally, the infinity of space. Oddly enough, 'horizon', which originally meant a limit, the power of circumscribing a place, came to mean immensity, infinity – such as the limitless horizon of the ocean. The conquest through the discovery of mountain landscape at the end of the 18th century, of higher and higher view-points, moved the horizon further and further back, until it vanished into infinity. In his essay, 'Utilité du Beau', Victor Hugo wrote:

Le sentiment de l'infini plane sur le monde moderne. Tout y participe de je ne sais quelle vie immense, tout y plonge dans l'inconnu, dans l'illimité, dans l'indéfini, dans le mystérieux . . . *L'idéal moderne,* ce n'est pas la ligne correcte et pure, *c'est l'épanouissement de l'horizon universel.*

The limitless horizon is one of the main characteristics of the Romantic landscape, and seems to be related to the attempt to display transcendence: at this extremity it seems possible to glimpse the other side of the sky, a 'beyond-space' which can be encountered through the poetic and rhetorical figure of twilight – through which a bridge is established between the visible and the invisible. Then beyond the horizon, in the imagination, appear Utopias. From the 16th century onwards these Utopias paradoxically attempt to define the infinite by an harmonious and rigorous totalization; they may be considered to be historical and philosophical 'plays' with the concept of the frontier, and they pushed that frontier towards its extreme limit.

The semantic value and historical status of the two words 'frontier' and 'Utopia' are quite different. 'Frontier' is a noun which entered into common usage in the 13th century; 'Utopia' is a proper name in, so to speak, two senses: first as the title of a book written by Thomas More and published in 1516, and second, as the name of the island described in Volume 2 of the book *Utopia.* The word was fabricated by More as a Latin neologism from a fictitious Greek word '*ou-topia*' or '*eu-topia*'. But this toponym quickly became a common noun, and as such was admitted into dictionaries in the 18th century at the very moment, it may be observed, when the 'horizon' was becoming 'infinite'.

A strange frontier exists between the terms 'frontier' and 'Utopia' – and I recommend this frontier as a subject for further study. My essay seeks to be a journey through this lexical and historical zone, between the well-defined semantic and historical loci of dictionaries, an anchorless voyage and one that passes between limit and infinity in order to discover the equivocal frontiers of Utopia.

Frontier as a Polemical Notion and as a Locus of the Neutral

In the 16th and 17th centuries, the notion of frontier was first of all understood to indicate a 'front' opposed to intruding enemies: 'Frontier means the extremity of a kingdom that enemies encounter in front of them when they invade it.' But this was the period in which the great national monarchies were being constituted, and the defensive front of the 'Frontier' was immediately displaced from the interior to the exterior by the dynamic thrust of expansion. To take the example given in a French dictionary: 'By his conquests, the King has expanded and moved forward the frontiers of his kingdom.' The frontier defines a state of equilibrium and balance between the opposing forces of expansion and resistance. This is clear in a recent admirable film by Angelopoulos, *Le pas suspendu de la cigogne*, which is entirely devoted to the notion of frontier (military, political, ethnic and emotional frontiers), and which portrays a wedding ceremony that is celebrated on the two sides of a frontier river, in between the two patrols of a police car. Similarly, in order to celebrate the marriage of the King in 1665, Le Brun constructed the whole scenography of the Kings of France and Spain meeting on the border of the Pyrenees, precisely on the Ile des Faisans on the Bidassoa river, an island crossed by the frontier between the two kingdoms. Thus the frontier is the limit which separates two states from each other. The limit is the abstract notion of the frontier, its juridical meaning.

The limit is just a line, the boundary line between domains and territories. But even as a mere line, the limit makes manifest an interval between contiguities and vicinities. The Latin *limes* signifies, in its etymological origin, a path or a passage, a way between two fields; the *limes* is the distance between two edges, like the '*chemins creux*' that pass between the fields in Brittany without trespassing upon the enclosures of their hedges, or like the cartage way for waggons on top of the Great Wall enclosing the Chinese Empire – or like, in the above-mentioned film by Angelopoulos, the deserted river between its two banks. The 'limit' is a way between two frontiers, a way that makes use of their extremities to make *its* way. The limit is at the same time a way and a gap. Often in the 17th-century dictionaries (Furetière, Académie Française), the 'moral' or 'figurative' sense of 'limit' appears in sentences which negate the word itself: 'la bonté de Dieu est sans limite'; 'l'ambition du Prince est sans limites' (that is, 'without any measure'); 'être déraisonnable, c'est sortir des limites de la raison'. In sciences, when mathematics deals axiomatically with infinity, the limit is a magnitude which another magnitude indefinitely approaches without ever surpassing it, as if (to take the example of the *limes*), one of its edges was tending towards the other without ever attaining contact. The way of the *limes* does not move indefinitely towards the infinite horizon. Constantly, at every moment of its travel, it maintains the difference between the two edges of the limit.

I would like to say a last word on these notions of frontier, interval, limit: I suggest we look at the term 'selvage' (used for textiles), or edge (for a wood or a village), which are combined in the French *'lisière'*. This term no longer signifies a way, but rather a no-man's land, the fringe of an edge. The *'lisière'* is the space of a gap, but uncertain of its limits, as when a land, an estate, a forest have simply their own edge, with no other limit in front, just a wild or an undetermined space. Here again, examples in 18th-century French dictionaries trace a remarkable network of significations: this is no man's-land, a limit blurred by destructive or wild forces: 'les champs qui aboutissent au grand chemin ont souvent leurs lisières mangées par les moutons'. 'Les bêtes fauves endommagent fort les terres qui sont des forêts'; 'les ennemis voulaient entrer dans cette province, mais ils n'ont ruiné que ses lisières.'

My semantic journey adrift on the term *lisière* (edge, fringe, selvage), points out a notion I will call *a neutral place*, a locus whose character-istics are semiotically negative, whose specificity consists in being neither the one nor the other, *neither* this edge *nor* the other: it is the place where two kings meet to make peace after having been at war with each other for many years, a neutral place where they negotiate on an island which, in the middle of the Bidassoa river (one bank of which is French and the other Spanish) is the 'common-place', the locus of a peace. Other examples are the raft that was the site of the meeting between Tsar Alexander and Emperor Napoleon, or the ship off Malta, and the 'island' of Iceland, which were the places where the American and Soviet leaders met one another. The island was on those occasions the neutral place *par excellence* in between the two halves of the world. Today, the separating gap, the neutral place, the interval structure, is in the process of becoming a *lisière*. It is becoming a fringe-structure which has on the one side a well-determined edge, and on the other side an edge fraying so as to become a chaos, an *apeiron*, an infinite *chôra* as ancient Greeks would have said; this is, perhaps, the advent of a new horizon. These three terms seem to me to be related to each other nowadays: *'lisière'*, the 'indefinite', 'horizon' . . . This network may soon constitute the chance of Utopia, just as in the early modern period the structure suddenly manifested itself between a newly discovered America and an old, tired Europe, between the opening of the Western space of a New World, and the terrible confrontations – national, political, religious – of the Old World.

This is the merging place of Utopia: a neutral place, an island in between two kingdoms, two States, the two halves of the world, the interval of frontiers and limits by way of a horizon that closes a site and opens up a space; the island Utopia merging into the 'indefinite'. As I have already mentioned, the term 'Utopia' was coined by More in about 1516 to name the island he describes in the second book of his work. *Outopos, Outopia* is a paradoxical, even giddy toponym, since as a term it negates with its name the very place that it is naming. If we translate the Greek term, it does not mean a place which is nowhere, that is, an island which only exists in More's imagination or a place which does not exist: the term as a toponym designates a no-place. Furthermore, the term designates *another* referent, the 'other' of any place. When More says 'Utopia', this name performatively creates that 'otherness'. In this sense, Utopia is the neutral name, the name of the 'neutral'. It names the limit, the gap between two frontiers or two continents, the old and the new world; it names the 'way of the *limes*', travelling between two edges which will never join together as an identical line.

Utopia, at the dawn of our modernity, could be the name of the horizon which, as we have seen, makes the invisible come within the finite, all this by a strange nominal *figure* of the frontier (horizon, limit), that is to say a name which would constitute a distance, a gap, neither before nor after affirmation, but 'in between' them; a distance or a gap that does not allow any affirmation or negation to be asserted as a truth or as a falsehood. *Ne-uter*, this is the radical of the frontier (limit, horizon) as well as that of Utopia. As I write, in 1992, suddenly in Eastern Europe there has opened up the immense emptiness of the end of a certain Utopia, an end that does not cease to end; it is precisely today, at the end of a millennium which sings out loud the end of ideologies, when the end of frontiers seems to be accomplished in a universal totality – when (in a recent debate) there is confusedly and loudly forecast, in the manner of Hegel and Kojève, the end of history, no longer however in the extreme and alternative terms of material animality or abstract formalism, but as the universal mode of high-tech, democratic hyperliberalism – it is precisely at this moment, while new, or very old and frightening, frontiers appear or reappear, those of nationalistic, racial or religious exclusions – precisely at this moment that it is worth recalling the fiction of an island that appeared at the dawn of a period for which our present time would form the twilight.

In the case of the island of Utopia, the frontier is the infinity of the Ocean, its border, a boundless space. Utopia is a limitless place because the island of Utopia is the figure of limit and of distance, the drifting of frontiers within the 'gap' between opposite terms, neither this one nor that one. Utopia is the figure of the horizon. If in the functioning of a city, in its structure formed by streets and dwellings – if in the functioning of a landscape, in its partition between nature and culture, forests and fields, waters and rocks – space cannot exist without limits and frontiers, Utopia develops and displays a virtual or potential spatial order: it offers to the beholder-reader an ambiguous representation, the equivocal image of significations that are contrary to the concept of limit. On the one hand, it offers the synthetic unity of the same and the other, of past and future, of this world and the beyond – and the frontier would be in this case the place where conflicting forces are reconciled. On the other hand, it offers the active tracing of differences, the indefinite fight between opposite forces – and in this case the frontier would open a gap, a space 'in between' which could not exist except by the encountering of violent and resisting forces.

Some years ago, I attempted to tackle the immense questions raised by Thomas More's island, through what Kant constructs, on the border between sensibility and understanding, as the schematism of the transcendental imagination. Utopia could be envisaged as a scheme of pure, *a priori* imagination, here displaced into ethics and politics, into aesthetics and religious matters. As Kant wrote, 'the scheme is produced by a mysterious art, hidden in the depths of the human soul, an art whose secrets would be difficult to elicit and reveal by *pure knowledge* alone.' 'Image', Kant wrote, 'is produced by the empirical faculty or reproductive imagination. On the other hand, the scheme of sensory concepts (like spatial figures) is a product and somehow a kind of 'monogram' of the pure *a priori* imagination, through which and from which images are at first possible . . .' In the Kantian scheme, Utopia is not an image or a representation. It does not belong to a definite ideology. It is the monogram of the art of pure fiction on all these borders and frontiers that human thought sketches out so as to achieve a knowledge shared by several human beings; that human will marks and displaces so as to become a collective power and to accomplish itself in common action.

As 'horizon', moreover as a scheme of the horizon, Utopia does not transform the sensible into the intelligible, or reality into ideology. Utopia is the infinite work of the imagination's power of figuration. Utopia is the infinite *potentia* of historical figures: it is this infinite dimension, this 'work', this *potentia*, that the Greek negation 'ou' allows to be understood as a prefix to the name *topos*. Utopia is the plural figure of the infinite work of the limit or frontier in history.

Totality and Infinity: Utopia at the Horizon of a Voyage (Travel)

It seems worthwhile to call Utopia back, as such, into the philosophical field. In order to deal with the return of Utopia, it seems opportune to think about the epistemological conditions of that coming back. It will be useful tentatively to grasp Utopia in *its process*, what I called some years ago, in a homage to Ernst Bloch, its 'fiction-practice', rather than to treat it as an icon or as an image, in its monumental formalist organicity, in its architectural system, in a word, in its representation.

As a representation, Utopia is always a synthesis, a reconciling synthesis. It decodes its image, it deciphers its icon. It stands as a perfect idea above any limit; it asserts an originary or eschatological projection beyond any frontier, and gains a universal validity by making all details explicit. Utopia as ideology is a totality; and when political power seizes it, it becomes a totalitarian whole. The utopian representation always takes the figure, the form of a map. In the complex unity of its ensemble, with its names, numbers, coloured fields all exactly coded according to the rules of representation, it gives a location to all journeys, all itineraries, all voyages and their paths: all of them are potentially present because they are all there, but implicitly it negates them all. The eye that sees it is an abstract eye, since it has no viewpoint: its place is everywhere and nowhere. Utopia as representation defines a totalitarian power, an absolute, *formal* and abstract power.

But at the very moment that I look at the map – when I follow with my finger the route of a road, a contour-line, when I cross here and not there a frontier, when I jump from one bank of a river to the other – at this very moment a figure is extracted from the ground and the map, the figure of a projected journey, even if it is an imaginary one, a dreamed one. With that figure, a narrative begins, with a before and an after, a point of departure and a point of arrival, a happy coming-back or a final permanent exile. The locus has become space: directions, speeds, travel-timing give motion to the map with the tracings of various routes. With all these temporal processes, these potential action-programmes, with all these proximities and distance, space 'awakens' to narrative, and loci open up to various practices which change and transform them through variations, transgressions, etc.

All narrative is a space narrative, said Michel de Certeau. All narrative is a travel narrative; all travel consists in going from a place to a no-place, a route to U-topia, from a starting point which, in a narrative, always describes a peaceful order of things and loci, of co-presences regulated by the laws of a kinship system, a local organization, a geographical articulation, a political system. Narrative proceeds from a place and a moment that narratologists call the 'schema of incidence', that is, the trespassing of a limit, the crossing of a frame, of a threshold. This is the way in which narratives demarcate space; travels, as departures and passages, beginnings and crossings in the narrative they produce – and by which they are produced as well – determine frontiers which they trace upon encountering them in order to cross them in some of their parts. As Michel de Certeau has superbly shown, the travel narrative authorizes frontiers to be established and displaced, founded and trespassed over. Travels and voyages, as a result of their movements, are 'located' in the gap of the limit, on the *limes-way* and trespassing over its double edge. Travel would be the 'work' of the horizon, the neutral space, the space of limits and frontiers they trace or demarcate while crossing them: this is the typical form of the Utopian process.

From the time of More's book, Utopias have tended to begin with a travel, a departure and a journey, most of the time by sea, most of the time interrupted by a storm, a catastrophe which is the sublime way to open a neutral space, one which is absolutely different: a meteoric event, a cosmic accident, which eliminates all beacons and markers in order to make the seashore of a land appear at dawn, to welcome the human castaway. In fact, even if the travel does not end with a storm and with arrival in an unknown land, the process of travel may be a way of displaying, just in front, a utopian space (or the utopian *chôra* as Plato would have said). Any travel is, first of all, a moment and a space of vacancy, an unencumbered space which suspends continuous time and the ordering loci.

The ideology of travel implies a departure from a place and a return to the same place: the traveller enriches this place with a whole booty of knowledge and experience by means of which he states, in this coming back to the 'sameness', his own consistency, his identity as a subject. The utopian moment and the space of travel, on the contrary, consists in opening up in this ideological circle, in tracing out its route, and *nowhere*, a place without place, a moment out of time, the truth of a fiction, the syncopation of an infinity and paradoxically its limit, its frontier.

When Peter Giles, More's friend, introduces Raphaël, the traveller and narrator-descriptor of Utopia, to Thomas More, he narrates precisely Raphaël's travels; he tells More of Raphaël's motivation to travel, his desire to visit the world; he informs More on the subject of Raphaël's travels, his departure from Portugal, his participation in Amerigo Vespucci's expeditions. Raphaël's travels, in fact, would have been very similar to Vespucci's if, during the fourth journey, instead of coming back to Portugal, he had not been one of the twenty-four men left at Cape Frio, on the Brazilian coast. Fiction, in this location on the American shore, is exactly tangential to the geographical routes on the maps of the time and the 'real' world. This place is, in a sense, a minimal space at the limit between what is unknown. Giles draws our attention to this point, he locates the sailors' fortified camp *ad fines postremae navigationis*, at the limits of the 'last' voyage. And on this frontier, which is also an initiating threshold, human abandonment, the desire of travelling and the encounter with death merge together. Giles and More sum up all these notions with two classical mottos: Raphaël, while happy to be left on the extreme edge of the world, is less concerned with pursuing his travels than he is with finding a tomb where he can definitely rest. He is in the habit of saying that 'sky is a tomb for the one who is deprived of an ultimate dwelling'; he says too that 'from every place in this world there is a route that leads to the heavens'.

The horizon, as edge of the world, joins on to another edge, that of the other world, and on this limit between the two, a space, a gap is opened up, which belongs neither to the one nor to the other, a gap between the interior space which is enclosed by the routes of travels, the *terrae cognitae*, and the unknown outer space: this is the indiscernible gap which is the imaginary site of the voyage. Raphaël, the hero of More's *Utopia*, is the figure of that imaginary site on the frontiers, on the limits, on this gap. The narrator of *Utopia* displays the very space wherein the imagination will create the mysterious island and bring it into the world.

Nevertheless, Raphaël's story is less concerned with narrating travel than it is with displaying a map, but a map whose essential characteristic consists of not being another map. Or being in maps, it cannot exactly be found in them. This means that Raphaël, and only Raphaël, can travel to Utopia. As a Utopia, travel cannot be repeated; while as an ideology, as an ideological representation, it imperatively demands to be repeated. The story that Giles tells Busleyden about the geographical location of the island is well known. At the very moment when Raphaël gives More that information, a servant comes up to More and says something to him, whilst one of the members of the party who has flu coughs so loudly that Giles cannot catch the traveller's words. Thus in the ironic fiction of an accident, the possible inscription of the island on a map disappears completely.

But should Utopia not already be on the existing maps? Giles does not come across it either among the ancient cosmographers or the modern. Maybe it exists under a name other than its Greek name *Utopia, Nowhere*? Perhaps it is an 'unknown' island? This would not be surprising when today (that is, in 1516) everyone knows that many new lands which the Ancients did not know are being discovered? If so, the island map is caught up in a displacement process within the mapping representation: constantly, unceasingly displaced, about to be inscribed at the very moment when it is about to be erased amidst all the real islands that travellers register when they find them, among all the potential islands which other travellers will discover. The island which exists at the frontier of all travels, as their dream or as their hidden figure.

If the name of the island, or its map, can be condensed within the term that introduces it into the universal map of all the places that are known and into the dictionary of their names, then the name of the utopian island, in its turn, is going to be named, inscribed and erased in terms of the displacement of the letters that compose the name: *Outopia, Eutopia, Oudepotia* – three names which circulate in the surroundings of More's text or from Giles's foreword to Budé's letter to Lupset; three terms in which the 'e' of happiness (*eutopia*) is substituted for the 'o' of nowhere (*outopia*) to cross the infinitely small and infinitely great distance which separates a geographical fiction from a political and social one; or where the permutation of a 'p' and a 't' (potia/topia) makes time and space equivalent. Displaced letters, displaced names (displacing their significations) – a displaced map displacing all maps and really finding none – Utopia as process is the figure of all kinds of frontiers, displacing, by the practice of its travels, all representations, secretly duplicating any kind of real geographical voyage and any kind of historical and temporal change.

In the term invented by More to name the best possible republic, in his fiction of the perfect state, we can read today, in 1992, the limits or frontiers of any state, of any institution – I mean what it is that limits their totalitarian desire for absolute power: in Utopia, we read the unfigurable figure of Infinite Liberty.

2

Formal Utopia / Informal Millennium: The Struggle between Form and Substance as a Context for Seventeenth-century Utopianism

J. C. DAVIS

If early modern England was a seminal location in the development of Western utopian thought, it was also a period of intense millennial expectation. There are useful things to be learned from the contrast between the two, particularly in relation to issues of formality and informality. This essay begins with a depiction of some early modern English concerns about formality and its absence, before endeavouring to show how these might illuminate utopia and millennium in the same period. There is no attempt to universalize a model of utopia that might only be appropriate to the closed, monistic utopias of the early modern period,[1] but we may, nevertheless, take Darko Suvin's definition of utopia as a starting point: 'sociopolitical institutions, norms and individual relationships . . . organised according to a more perfect principle'.[2]

Formality/Antiformalism/Informality

On 9 August 1650 the Parliament of the Commonwealth of England, known derisively as the Rump, passed an ordinance against blasphemy and atheism, the so-called Blasphemy Act.[3] The Rump, a broken and purged form of the Long Parliament, was itself a breaker of forms. It had erected a High Court to try the King, had engineered his pseudo-judicial death, had abolished monarchy and the House of Lords, and had declared England's first and only republic. If there was an English revolution, this was its powerhouse and its instrument. In its revolutionary imperialism, it swept aside the problem of multiple kingdoms which had brought Charles I into crisis, conquered Ireland, inaugurated the process of transportation and settlement, reduced Scotland to an occupied nation and, in fury at the rejection of Anglo-Dutch union, waged successful war on the most powerful maritime nation of mid-seventeenth century Europe.[4] The English republican tradition shaped by Vane, Milton, Sidney and Ludlow was to invoke the greatness and triumphs of this exceptional body, just as the classical republican tradition invoked those of republican Rome.

Admirers and enemies alike saw the Rump as an extraordinary assembly, but it was surely unexceptional that, as the spearhead of a godly revolution, it should legislate against blasphemy and atheism. And yet there is a notable oddness about the ordinance of 9 August 1650. First, it relaxed, or at least moderated, the rigours of earlier enactments against blasphemy. Secondly, it was designed to suppress not only blasphemy and atheism, but also 'Prophaneness, Wickedness, Superstition and *Formality*'.[5] At the heart of the revolution, then, there was a struggle against, amongst other things, formality.[6]

This is illustrated by the republic's war against Scotland in 1650–51 – a war undertaken with heavy hearts because it was a war against brothers in Christ, a fellow godly nation. Sir Thomas Fairfax, commander of the New Model Army, resigned his commission rather than undertake it. The final justification for Cromwell's invasion of the northern kingdom was the formality of the Scots, their attempt to annex the 'Spirit to outward formalities', 'Legall Dispensation' and 'Carnall Administration'.[7] Most vividly, however, we can see the struggle against formality, on the eve of regicide and revolution, at the Whitehall debates of December 1648. Aware that the ancient constitution was doomed, these debates were focused on the issue of a new constitution, and the debaters had before them the Levellers' constitutional proposals, their second Agreement of the People. Two arguments ran through the debates, intertwining and finally producing deadlock. The better-known issue is that of religious liberty, but more critical for the nature of the English Revolution was the debate over the appropriateness of any form of constitutional provision. Faced with the Levellers' constitutional proposals, Joshua Sprigge argued that any form of constitutional provision was inappropriate: 'God will bring forth a New Heaven and a New Earth. In the meane time your work is to restraine, indeed to restraine the Magistrate from such a power.' Philip Nye also thought that God would punish them if they erected new formalities. The debate was clinched when Thomas Harrison urged the setting aside of the Levellers' Agreement, since a true Agreement could come only from God and not from men. God's providential determinings in pursuit of His millennial plan, however obscure that might be to human observers, were overthrowing human forms – Monarchy, Lords, Church. In such a moment, it was obviously impious to erect fleshly formalities anew. No constitution was formally adopted to replace that overthrown in 1648–9. When, at last, Cromwell adopted the Instrument of Government in December 1653, it was greeted by the saints as his great apostasy. Gideon had lost his way. The Lord Protector, having put his trust in fleshly instruments and carnal formalities, could no longer enjoy status as an instrument of providence.[8]

Associating formality with the indictable offence of blasphemy in 1650 summed up one of the persistent anxieties of England's revolutionary decades. Formality deceived the godly because it was the sin of the seeming saint; because it bore the face of outward reformation. It was godliness perverted into a preoccupation, negative or positive, with externals; a placing of form above substance. The hypocrisy of outward piety masking inner corruption; the maintenance of formal observance, and the neglect of substantial practice: these were the hallmarks of the formalist. The reformation aspired to get beyond outward conformity, formality, to inner conviction, the reformation of the heart, mind and will, and thence to conscientious action. Since God was not a god of stasis but a dynamic, perpetually intervening providential presence and millennial prospect, forms were at best ephemeral things, and a preoccupation with them revealed a kind of idolatrous diversion from the task of making one's self available as an instrument of the Almighty's changing will and unfolding purpose. At best forms were childish things, at worst, insistence on them, formality, was unchristian.[9] Like blasphemy and atheism, formality should be swept away by a godly revolution.

Formality and Early Modern Society

Formality, then, possessed a highly negative value for the godly vanguard of the English Revolution, and its legal proscription in 1650 is perhaps intelligible in these terms. But we can also see that formalistic structures and behaviour played an integral role in early modern society, and I shall argue that they were a key feature of early modern utopia. In the last fifteen to twenty years historians have rightly become more interested in the role of symbolic representation and behaviour as a means of understanding the social cohesion and adjustment/readjustment of early modern society. Decoding images, buildings, gardens, costume and human social performance in rites, processions, street theatre, carnival, skimmington and all forms of ritual observance has become a major means of advancing our understanding of the nature and articulation of early modern society. In some respects we can see that society as a series of interchangeable forms which could be used to assert, invert, sustain and adapt existing social categories. But, even in the most satirical or burlesque exploitation of these forms, the key is the recognized form of orthodox anticipation. The power of a mock trial comes from appreciation of the anticipated form of an orthodox trial. To get the joke in a riding's satire of marital or domestic relations gone wrong we have to know the expected form of a good or true marriage. The anticipation of shared expectations of social form is one key to both early modern social cohesion and critical release. Even in the challenge of riot or charivari, formalities had to be observed. A pattern of formal order could therefore be anticipated even in the invocation of disorder, in the rites of riot and the world turned upside-down.[10]

In dress, speech, labour, rest, in the round of daily, weekly and annual routines, in the life-cycle *rites de passage*, we expect a society to be bounded and, at least in part, to be identified to itself by its behavioural forms. In early modern society power was much exerted by means of formalities at Court, in judicial courts, in Council, assemblies and in progresses and processions. Rankings of dress, diet, precedence, function, proximity and distance – the fine, symbolic details of display – had to be carefully negotiated and observed if formality was to do its work of imposing order upon chaos and of sustaining power in its appropriate location. The use of violence in the punishment of the miscreant, in the suppression of disorder and in war itself had very marked and distinctive formal rites, ranks and observances, and these were anticipated by both the perpetrators and the victims of violence.[11] Even for the apparent contingencies of violence scripts also existed and were expected to be observed. In short, formality was indispensable to the early modern world – as it is to some degree to any society – if the reality and the anticipation of order was to be maintained. The spread of neo-Stoic ideals and attitudes amongst the ruling elites of the sixteenth and seventeenth centuries served to reinforce that appreciation of formality.[12]

Millennial Informality

A cursory glance at an already daunting literature on the sumptuary, gastronomic, processional, aural, theatrical and ritual formalities of the early modern period should be enough to persuade that my point here is devoid of all originality. I am uttering a commonplace. Early modern society's prized values – such as honour, magnanimity, justice, status, and liberty – were bound up with the self-conscious observance of forms, with formality. Those who attacked formality were inevitably associated with disorder. The defence of those antiformalists who struggled to liberate the English Revolution was that service to a cataclysmic, millennial God involved abandoning human forms in order to embrace divine flux. It is the freedom of God Almighty which is at issue in that revolutionary struggle. Its freedom fighters sought, above all, to submit to the role of instrumentality in the hands of a restless, wilful and, given the limits of human comprehension, an apparently arbitrary God. The worst crime of tyrannical magistracy was, according to John Lilburne, that it usurped the right of a sovereign God to rule 'by this will and pleasure'.[13] Faith in the millennium meant embracing the dissolution of all human social contrivances, the destruction of all formalities. Scenting an apocalyptic moment in 1651, Joseph Salmon observed, 'The formall world is much affrighted, and every form is up in Arms to proclaim open wars *against it selfe*.'[14] In the millennial dawn formality would self-destruct.

Formality and the Ideal Society

If millennium and formality were antithetical, where might we locate utopian aspirations with respect to these issues? Setting aside the concerns of antiformalists, for the moment, and looking again at a society limited both in its coercive power and in its capacity to absorb mass energies in consumption, we can see formality as one of the key ligatures of social cohesion. But a society bound together and ordered by its formalities, may, obviously, still be perceived as a far from ideal society. The question is how, out of the socializing experience of such a cohering network of formalities, could shape be given to visions of a complete and alternative society. What I have called the perfect moral commonwealth represents, in this sense, no alternative, since it simply calls for existing formalities to be better observed. The reformation of substance, the perfecting of our second natures, leaves form intact. Arcadia and Cockaygne assume away the basic premise on which all social constraint is based: nature's inability to meet all our needs or satisfy all the wants we are capable of conceiving. Unlimited substance overwhelms form. We revert to our, variously conceived, first nature. The millennium, unlimited divine power, imminent and immanent, finds human form irrelevant and brushes it away. Our nature is transcended and redeemed. But as the millennium, contemptuous of fleshy contrivance, is antiformalist, informal, so utopia responds to a world of deficient formality with improved and perfected form. In the millennium, transcendent substance withers form. In utopia, flawed and recalcitrant substance is constrained, ordered and harmonized by formality.[15]

Utopia responds to a society whose forms are deficient by prescribing formal perfection. But as Louis Marin has observed, 'As a figure in discourse utopia is written and imagined within the discourse which criticizes it.'[16] What I am suggesting is that we should locate early modern utopianism within the key contemporary discourse of formality and antiformalism, of form and substance. What might we observe when we contextualize utopianism in this way?

First, we may note the numerous ways in which early modern utopians build on the formalities and formalizing aspirations of their own social milieux. Second, we might discern a linkage with contemporary perceptions of the relationship between legal formality and liberty. Finally, I would argue, we may locate utopia more cogently in relation to a changing discourse of human liberty. These are the three tasks attempted in the second half of this essay.

Utopian Formality

Just as early modern society was perceived as a form analogous to a variety of other forms, so early modern utopia was imagined as a formal structure. 'The necessary action or life of each thing is', according to James Harrington, 'from the nature of the form'.[17] Consequently, his *Oceana* is meticulously detailed about the forms of an Equal Commonwealth. The forms of government, the scaffolding of *ordini* within which the fabric of utopian life is imagined, must be exactly prescribed and observed.[18] The institutionalism of utopia is no more than a handbook of ritualized bureaucratic behaviour. The ultimate expression of formal performance was, as Zamyatin realized, its mathematization: 'It is necessary to say that in this instance, even as in all things, we have no room for any chance happenings whatsoever – nothing unexpected can eventuate.'[19] Prior to this, the analogy was more likely to be mechanical rather than mathematical. Oceana could be compared to a mechanical contrivance driven by cats who could do nothing but operate the machine to prepare and cook a meal.[20] Utopia is 'a frictionless social machine'.[21] It expresses the utopist's love of balances, accounts, measurements, equations, uniforms and civil codes, culminating in what Gilles Lapouge has described as an 'automatic system' which 'organises the informal'.[22] Like the theatrical play we choose to attend, we know that the utopian social performance will be the same tomorrow night as last night and tonight. However willing we are to suspend our disbelief in the utopian thought experiment, it is the sense of a performance, in all its following of prescribed formality, which tugs awake our scepticism. As Marin says, 'Utopia knows nothing of change'.[23] It is, to quote Krishan Kumar, the millennium which 'forcibly introduces the elements of time, process and history'.[24] In doing so, it undermines utopian formality.

In utopia the already formal is reduced to unruffled ritual observance. In law,[25] in its depersonalizing rotation of office, in its frozen consumer preference schedules, the ritualized consumption of uniform dress, housing, communal dining and controlled leisure, endlessly recurring cycles of behaviour displaced the unordered contingencies of social interaction. Innovation via science or technology also had to be controlled or eliminated.[26] Utopia formalized space in its architectural uniformities, its city planning, its urban and rural zoning. A recent exercise in this vein can visualize the 'ritual geometries and signifying forms' of the architect's dream as comparable to the function of musical notation in the orchestration of a piece of music.[27] In an anonymous utopia, written in about 1700, the cities and towns were likened to a stage set, 'built square, all the streets straight, broad and equal; so that there should be no lanes nor Allies, but the Streets should be alike.' All houses were to have piazzas and identical gardens; 'All unnecessary Persons should be obliged to remove to some other place.'[28] If purity required no matter to be out of place, then the purely formal required no person to be out of place.

But utopian order also required actions to be formally located in time:

The first thing that shall be done in the morning (after our People have washed and are ready, and have been at their private Devotions, which shall be done at Six of the Clock, there being an hour allowed for that and their dressing, being called up to rise at five of the Clock at farthest; and then just at six of the Clock, a Bell having tolled) they shall repair to the Common Hall, where there shall be made a Publick Prayer, and one Chapter shall be read in the New Testament, after which every one shall also prepare for Work, and shall Work three or four hours, or more, as it shall be best determined. Then the Bell shall toll again, and every one shall wash and clean himself; and all things being disposed of, and the last signs of the Bell being given, all shall repair to the Hall again, where the whole Service shall be read, and after that, a portion of some Book of Devotion. Then will follow the Dinner before and after which, Grace shall be said. And after some Conversation after Dinner, there shall be sung a Spiritual Hymn, before they return to work. And thus shall they spend their time. They may dine about one, and sup about seven. Immediately also before supper, the service shall again be read. And at Night, the last thing that shall be done in Publick before they part, shall be to Worship God by Prayer and Devotion.[29]

The formalization of work, leisure and devotion, of time, that is documented in this quotation is paralleled in works such as Harrington's *Oceana* by the formalization of public time, of the actions of civic participation.[30] Elsewhere, in Campanella's *City of the Sun*, the events of physical intimacy, the fortuitousness of sexual contact itself, are reduced to order: 'the rules regarding procreation are observed religiously, for the public good and not for the good of private individuals.'[31] In Andreae's *Christianopolis* the rhythm of public ritual was matched by the physical regularity of the city, the illumination of the night, and the opening out of every private space to civic scrutiny. 'It is', Andreae concluded, 'a public show.'[32]

For the public show to work, the private had to be ordered, the informal reduced to formality. In More's *Utopia* the organization of the household is regularized. There must be no fewer than six, no more than ten, adults in every household, and transfers between households take place to ensure observance of these limits.[33] The vagaries of kinship and cohabitation are replaced by regulation. Like the city, language could be planned and formalized in such a way as to control the understanding of utopian citizens. Descartes imagined a future language so regulated that by it peasants – whether they wished to or not – would know truth more readily than today's philosophers. 'But', he warned, 'do not ever expect to see such a language in use. That presupposes changes in the way things are ordered converting this world into an earthly paradise.'[34]

Education in utopia was not only designed to internalize the formalities of the utopian social construct, and the knowledge which underpins them, it might even be a means of formalizing perception and imagination: 'a training in perceiving and imagining, a training in applied physiology and psychology, a training in practical ethics and practical religion, a training in the proper use of language, and a training in self-knowledge. In a word, a training of the whole mind-body in all its aspects.'[35] The identification of civilization with the internalization and outward observance of such formal values has had potent consequences. The colonial utopia was preoccupied with formalizing perceived native informality.[36] The common anxiety about immigrants to utopia was that they might not have been formalized appropriately.

Despite its educational drive towards the internalization of its social forms, Utopia is also formal in the early modern sense of being willing to settle for outward reformation. To reach the perfect moral commonwealth there has to be a change of heart, mind and will. Socially harmonious behaviour is personally authentic. The values of social harmony and the behaviour indispensable to it have been internalized. By contrast, utopians distinguish between those of their citizens who have internalized the ideal society's values, those who are capable of outward reformation only, and those who are potentially or actively deviant. Vivian Carol Fox has persuasively demonstrated that it is in this sense that deviance is integral to the utopian construct.[37]

It is no surprise then to find that contemporary institutions which constrained their members to formal obedience and predictability exerted a strong imaginative pull on utopian writers. Pre-eminent amongst such institutions were, of course, the monastery and the emergent standing armies of early modern Europe.[38] But just as contemporary society was marked by its symbolic rituals, its formalization of order and dissent, so too early modern utopians deployed festival, ritual and process not only as symbols of utopian order but as essential to the forming of utopia. In Bacon, Gott, and Harrington ceremonial is meticulously observed, and festivals and processions are witnessed in extraordinary detail.[39] In *Antangil*, a French description of utopia written in 1616, institutional descriptions alternate with detailed depictions of the ceremonial functioning of those institutions. Underlying the whole is the ranking, dress, drill, decorum and discipline found in the early modern military model. Bacon, too, drew upon the metaphor of military formality. When his scientists, the Fellows of Salomon's House, processed through the streets of New Atlantis, the spectators stood in such order that Bacon's narrator could truly compare it to 'battle array'.[40] More instructive still is the formality which Bacon invoked in describing the processes of scientific enquiry in the ideal society. Three Fellows – the Lamps – draw up directions for experiments. That task then passes to three other Fellows – the Innoculators – who carry out the experiments. Three more Fellows – the Interpreters – then take the results of those experiments and raise axioms from them. It has all the flavour of an elaborate ceremonial ritual performed before the altar of science, and, sure enough, Bacon immediately goes on to describe what he calls the 'Ordinances and Rites' of the House of Salomon.[41] In his *City of the Sun* Campanella had gone a stage further, making scientific enquiry an entirely past ceremony commemorated on the theatre of the city's concentric walls.

Formality, Nature and Second Nature

In all of this then we may observe three patterns. Some of the formalities of existing social life – aspects of ritual or processional – were reproduced or elaborated in the early modern utopias. Some of the existing formalities of contemporary social life were realigned. For example, in dress, food and housing what had been aligned vertically in a ranked hierarchy might be realigned horizontally to establish an equality of consumption patterns. Finally, new areas of life – space, time, bureau-cracy – might be formalized. But in all this there was no reversion to a perfected first human nature, no invocation of a prelapsarian humanity. The objective was rather, through elevating formal observance to the level of custom, to give form to second, or fallen, nature and out of it to create a harmonious society. We might pause to illustrate this by considering three contrasting examples.

In 1657 Henry Carey, Earl of Monmouth, published his translation of Paolo Paruta's *Politick Discourses*. It may be read as a contribution to the debate, inaugurated by the publication of Harrington's *Oceana* the previous year, as to whether formal institutional contrivances could rescue England from its chronic instability. The true form of government was not one cast on the play of providence, or in its pagan form *fortuna*, but that 'by which people living in peace and union, may work righteously and obtain Civil felicity'. Harrington had, however, sug-gested that civil felicity could be identified with undisturbed formality, and Paruta/Monmouth were not inclined to disagree. The issue was this: how were forms to work in relation to what men had become accustomed to, their second natures? For Paruta the suitability of forms was relative to the age and its social circumstances: 'in a well-ordered City, the Laws ought to be confirmed by the Manners and Education of the Citizens, the which is of more force to make men honest, then is the fear of punishment; nay for hence Actions arise according to true Honesty and Vertue; for they proceed from a vertuous Habit, which is only acquired by Exercise.' To orchestrate and formalize such exercise 'good institutions of life' were necessary, and it was the utopian's function to devise them.[42] Paruta recognized the inherent value of society's existing customs and manners. His endeavour was to build on these conventions, reshaping and adding only as necessary. Harrington had begun from a different perspective. The material preconditions, in the sense of the distribution of real property, for the erection of an ideal commonwealth were present in mid-seventeenth century England. But the political habits with which the English were imbued were so corrupt that no reliance could be placed on them. It was necessary for the political nature of the English to be reprogrammed by the institutions and formalities of 'a well ordered commonwealth'. Since 'we are certain never to go right, while there remains a way to go wrong', it was necessary for 'the orders of a well constituted state' to 'make wicked men virtuous, and fools to act wisely'. So that in a 'commonwealth rightly ordered' the people 'can have no other motion than according unto the order of their common-wealth'.[43] The premise is different; we may place no faith in existing manners and customs. But the solution is similar; the reordering of social conventions can achieve social harmony and stability without retributive violence.[44]

In George Psalmanazar's description of an idealized Formosa (1704), the basic assumptions are once again varied. Customs must be reformulated but that process must embrace the formalities of public violence. In this utopia, capital punishment is the automatic penalty for theft, as well as for murder and for a second offence of adultery. Husbands had capital authority over wives. The penalty for false witness was the removal of the tongue. Blasphemers were burned alive. Those who struck their mother, father or anyone else in authority had to endure the amputation of their arms and legs and were then cast with a stone around their necks into the sea or a river. The penalty for striking a priest was burial alive after the arms were burned off. Those who struck the King or a magistrate were hung by the feet until they were torn to death by dogs. The result, according to Psalmanazar, was 'a profound Peace'. Alongside the penal horrors, he lovingly described the elaborate ceremonies, the formal distinctions of dress, housing and diet, the rituals which encompassed and channelled the public life of Formosa.[45]

Beginning from contiguous but differing premises Paruta, Harrington and Psalmanazar had more or less faith in the customary formalities of the societies they began with; more or less need of recourse to formal violence. What they had in common was the desire to use formal regularity in their utopian institutions to customize people to utopian order: to recreate a second nature appropriate to an ideal social order. To create such a second nature was not an aspiration that died with the Enlightenment. In the ideal order of Bulwer Lytton's *The Coming Race* (1875), 'Obedience to the rule adopted by the community has become as much an instinct as if it were implanted by nature.'[46] Such 'system design' has been implemented in the workplace, and in communities large and small, in the service of ideologies of both the right and left throughout the twentieth century.[47]

Utopian Formality, Liberty and Authority

It may be worth remembering that the subtitle of More's *Utopia* was 'A Truly Golden Handbook'. Such handbooks formalize the world. For them, 'Corruption' is another word for 'informality'.[48] Their function is therefore to formalize the informal,[49] to eliminate spontaneity and chance.[50] But chance was also seen as the enemy of law and freedom in early modern England, and to that connection we must now turn.

In contrast with twentieth-century attitudes, it was not assumed in early modern England that authority and liberty were antithetical.[51] In terms of civil liberty a congruence between liberty and law was sought in order to defend the subject from will and power.[52] It was, John Lilburne contended in 1653, 'impossible for any man, woman or child in England to be free from the arbitrary and tyrannical wills of men, except those ancient laws and ancient rights of England for which I have contended even unto blood, be preserved and maintained.'[53] For Freeborn John it was a matter of *Legall Fundamental Liberties*. That the essence of freedom was to live under known rules and not to be subject to the arbitrary wills of other men was a commonplace formulation of the seventeenth century well before John Locke gave his own utterance to it. Exploring the meaning of true freedom in 1651, Isaac Pennington Jr found that 'It consists not in licentiousness, to do what you will, nor in having no Taxes Layd upon you (this may be necessary for your safety)', but in four things: good laws, suited to one's state and condition; a good 'method of government' (by which Pennington meant government that ensured benefit of the laws, and cheap, easy redress for its subjects); good governors faithfully overseeing the execution of the laws; and, fourthly, a clear, settled way for parliament to amend, alter or add to law.[54] We need not labour the point. To talk of civil liberty was immediately to talk of law.

What held authority and liberty in a complementary relationship within this framework was law duly or formally observed. Due observance of the forms of the law was what the Petition of Right sought to reassert, what the 'freedom fighter' Lilburne struggled for in his interminable battles with Star Chamber, the House of Lords and extraordinary tribunals, and it was what Charles I claimed was at stake and threatening all his subjects' liberties in the illegal trial for his life. The due observance of the formalities of the law constrained authority from tyranny and liberty from license. Civil formality reconciled liberty and authority, hedging against arbitrary incursions from either people or governors. Both license and tyranny arose when will was elevated above law; they both represented arbitrary incursions on the rights of others. I have argued more fully elsewhere[55] what I am simply asserting here: that, without the formal constraints of the law, civil liberty was barely imaginable to seventeenth-century Englishmen, and that formality reconciled liberty and authority.

In utopia, formality not only reconciled liberty and authority, but also eliminated the arbitrary and contingent from social life. In the seventeenth-century sense (if not, it should be noted, in the twentieth-century sense) utopian formality guaranteed and extended the liberty of utopian citizens.[56] In submitting to its standing rules they freed themselves, as John Locke might have said, from the inconstant, uncertain, unknown, arbitrary wills of other men.[57] Allowing for the radical redefinition of liberty in the past two centuries of Western history, we can see that pre-modern utopia is about freedom in a pre-modern sense. A primary function of the early modern ideal society was to prevent arbitrary incursions upon its citizens. In Arcadia it would never occur to its moderate citizens to behave in such immoderate ways. In the Perfect Moral Commonwealth they restrain themselves from such incursions. In Utopia, the formalization of institutions, *ordini*, bureaucracy, socialization, space, time and consumption prevent them. Utopia is about freedom as the absence of the arbitrary and the contingent. Its order and predictability, its formality, bestow such freedom in abundance. Should freedom, however, be conceived as human autonomy, a willingness to risk the contingent, then utopian formality becomes a prison, absolute in its confinement.

We have then an early modern triad, reconciled one to another and capable of relating to utopia: the triad of authority, liberty and formality. Collective submission to an authority that has been formed so as to be entirely predictable may represent an ideal freedom. But, in a society preoccupied with godly reformation, how does this relate to submission to a God who retains some of the characteristics of an arbitrary despot, ruling by awe-inspiring and mysterious providences, by judgements not only before the event but before the beginning of time, judgements against which there was no appeal, a God not so much of law as of will? What could liberty – or indeed formality – mean in the service of such a God?

Divine Freedom, Human Submission

'Eye not man', Isaac Pennington Jr advised those considering liberty, 'no not in those things wherein he appears as the main agent. Consider who it is that doth all, especially in such great changes. It is not the wit of man the will of man, which manageth these things but one above man.'[58] In that service, that submission, which is perfect freedom, men must be careful not to inhibit the submission of others, nor to erect barriers to God's freedom to act.[59] 'Let my people go, *that they may serve me in the wilderness* . . .'[60] Modern liberation movements have tended to adopt the first phrase of this text from *Exodus* while dropping the second, but in the seventeenth century it is the second which is vital.[61] Liberation was the precondition of a far from token submission, for it was submission in the service of a demanding God. Man's way is easy and attractive; God's way is a hard way, and man, like a wilful child, rebels against it.[62] Richard Baxter had often been tempted to separation from the lawfully established church, but one test held him back. It was 'too easy a way to be of God'.[63] Seeking that harder way of public promptings of conscience involved a series of rigorous public exercises: Fast Days, Days of Humiliation, endless scrutiny of the scriptures in public and private exercises, searching for the Divine Will to which submission must be made. The Blasphemy Ordinance of 1647 called, under the shadow of providential chastizement, for a day of public humiliation in which the nation could search for a right discernment of the will of God to which England must submit.[64] In a 1648 list of such things it was specified as blasphemous to say that God was not present in all places, or did not know and foreknow all things, or was not almighty.[65] With such an omnipresent, omniscient and omnipotent deity, what could human freedom mean?[66] In one crucial respect it meant the absence of external obstacles or internal impediments to the conscientious submission of every individual, and the nation, to God's will. William Walwyn identified liberty of conscience with the liberty *to serve and worship* God according to one's conscience.[67] *The Agreement of the People*, as debated at Putney, found matters of religion and God's worship 'not at all entrusted by us to any human power, because therein we cannot remit or *exceed* a tittle of what our consciences dictate to be the mind of God without wilful sin.'[68] The issue is not self-determination, but the avoidance of wilful sin in the eyes of the Lord whose servants we all are. Gerrard Winstanley's early confidence was in a rising spirit of righteousness to which all should submit.[69]

Conscience keeps us in the closest communication with the Divine Will. Its free operation and understanding was a prerequisite, not of antinomian liberation, but of effective submission. Sir Henry Vane Jr distinguished three models of conscience: natural, which was the best that reason could do; legal, which observed the letter of God's law; and, best of all, evangelical, which recognized *God's freedom* to direct and redirect us.

> For now's the Father's 'pointed time
> which he did fore-intend
> to set up Freedom, and pull down
> the man which did offend;
>
> This time, I say, it is now come
> in which the Lord will make
> All tyrants servants to the Son
> and he the power will take.[70]

The denouement in this Digger hymn of 1650 is not man's freedom but God's. Earthly authorities and individuals must be prevented from doing anything which might appear to infringe God's liberty. As Joshua Sprigge exhorted, 'your worke is to restraine, indeed to restraine the Magistrate from such a power.'[71] Those who did obstruct God's freedom, by the relaxation of discipline or excessive formality, would be punished.[72] There was a sense in which any form of fleshly or worldly authority or freedom could be seen as a usurpation of God's freedom and rule. As early as 1642 John Goodwin announced that 'the time is coming when Christ will put downe all rule, and all authority and power.'[73] A ceaselessly intervening providence, a God of apocalyptic shakings and overturnings, was a deity of awesome power and awesome liberty. The lurching transitions and switchback fortunes of the 1640s and 1650s underwrote that sense. Texts such as Isaiah:24, with its image of a mighty, unfettered and almost capricious God laying waste, making empty, turning upside down and scattering, were texts to ponder. All governments not based on submission to Christ and his word must cease or be swept away.[74] Freedom from the arbitrary authority of a civil power might only be a preliminary to subjection to the arbitrary power of an overwhelming divine authority. 'NO KING BUT JESUS', was, for John Canne, the slogan which epitomized the Good Old Cause.[75] An anonymous advocate of Presbyterian-Independent unity in 1648 urged the two groups not to set up a worldly government which might get in God's way.[76] Throughout the 1640s and 1650s the godly were seeking to discover the current generation's work in God's overall scheme. All obstacles to its performance must be removed.[77] Reviewing the history of the previous nineteen years in 1659, Christopher Feake enumerated in sequence the 'interests' which had distracted the nation from submission to God's will.[78] Our immediate obligation, he argued, was always submission to that which represented the fullest, albeit imperfect, submission to that will.[79] John Cook, prosecuting attorney at the king's trial, was later to argue that monarchical government had been against the mind of God. The essential function of the magistrate was to act 'as a good steward of the grace of God under penalty'.[80] Like other regicides, Cook's final justification was his submission to the will of God:

... not only for the Priestly and Prophetical Officers of Christ Jesus, but for his Kingly also; the peculiar Light and Work of this Generation being to discover and oppose the Civil and Ecclesiastical Tyrannies intended upon the Nations by the Popes *Leger demain*, to exalt Christ as Lord and King over mens Consciences, to magnifie and make the Law of God honourable and authentick every where and to give Justice and Mercy the upper hand.[81]

The thing that was wrong with a tyrannical civil authority was not that it deprived its subjects of their liberty or humanity in some secular sense, but that it could prevent their agency under God; it got in the way of Christian subjection. With an active, interventionist, engaged God, the true end of Christian liberty was its self-immolation in submission to the Divine will. The theme runs through Richard Coppin's much misunderstood writings. The 'wisdom of man is folly, and confounded with the wisdom of God.' So, Coppin complained, the Rump tried to keep the populace in bondage and subjection to themselves when the people should be subject only to Christ. God is the only governor, and to Him full submission must be made. No sacrifice is better than obedience.[82]

Conclusion

Seventeenth-century English society was gripped by a tension of an intensity that was unparalleled even in the Europe of the general crisis. On the one hand, there was a social consensus on the value of law and its formalities as a guarantee of freedom and as a protection from the arbitrary, the wilful and the tyrannical. On the other hand, society was infused with a desire to submit, in an apocalyptic moment, to the unknown, apparently inconstant and arbitrary will of a God whose service required the casting aside of fleshly formalities and carnal institutions. Between utopian formality and millennial informality there could be no compromise. There is a story to be told, a history to be written, of how we have travelled from that epic conflict to a situation in which we despise formality but have no God; in which we seek liberty but are suspicious of law; in which we demand protection but distrust authority; in which we see utopia as a disposable vehicle of protest, but fear apocalypse, if not the millennium. There is a story to be told but — you will be relieved to hear — it is not mine to tell.

3
From Robinson to Robina, and Beyond:
Robinson Crusoe *as a Utopian Concept*

LOUIS JAMES

For A. L. Morton, Defoe's *Robinson Crusoe* (1719) was 'the character-istic [English] Utopia of the early eighteenth century', and constituted an expression of the conflict between progressive idealism and squalid individualism that lay behind the Glorious Revolution of 1688.[1] Other critics, as we will see, have also viewed *Crusoe* as a utopian narrative, although they have differed widely in their interpretation of its meaning. Further, Defoe's tale created a considerable subgenre of derivative works or 'Robinsonnaden' throughout Europe and in the United States – works defined by Ben Fowkes as 'Utopias on the lines of Defoe's *Robinson Crusoe*'.[2]

Yet if *Crusoe* is to be regarded as a utopia, it lies outside the formal conventions of the genre. It is true that Defoe created an imaginary island isolated from many complicating factors of human life, where ideas could be worked out – an island which was, like Thomas More's Utopia, both 'a good place' and 'no place'. But while utopias characteristically portray a political *society*, Crusoe's island is a community of one, and when Friday arrives, he is little more than an extension of Crusoe's identity. Utopias usually exist as a 'given' world explored by an alien visitor: Crusoe progressively *creates* his island world. Furthermore, the utopian form generates an often ambivalent tension between the viewpoint of the intruding narrator and the observed utopia: Crusoe's island is seen only by Crusoe himself. For these and other reasons, *Robinson Crusoe* cannot be classed as a utopia on strictly formal grounds.

There are, however, other approaches. One definition of utopia, suggested by Ruth Levitas, is that it is not a prescribed fictive formula, but rather an objective expression of human desires.[3] Another method is suggested by discourse analysis. By focusing not on the structural entity of a work, but on its discursive practices, meanings emerge that are invisible to a single predictive approach.[4] These approaches are particu-larly useful when looking at a mixed narrative such as *Robinson Crusoe*, where the utopian elements are complicated by other forms of discourse. I wish to argue here that *Crusoe* introduced a genre of discourse which was to become a dominant strategy for expressing utopian ideals in the two centuries which followed.

On Interpreting Robinson Crusoe

In *The Origins of the Modern Novel, 1600–1740*,[5] Michael McKeon questions Ian Watt's formal account, in *The Rise of the Novel*,[6] of the emergence of a specific narrative form in the work of Richardson and Fielding, neither of whom consciously created 'the novel'. McKeon instead identifies earlier types of discourse – such as the religious allegory, political debate, prose romance – and shows how these forms intermesh in the narrative practice of the mid eighteenth century. These genres, McKeon argues, often have utopian elements. For instance, the progressive narrative which bears directly on the form of the 'novel' as written by Fielding was indebted to *Don Quixote* (1605–15) on one hand, and to *Pilgrim's Progress* (1678–84) on the other. Both these works placed their human action within utopian perspectives, on the one hand that of Quixote's chivalric fantasies, and on the other, Bunyan's vision of the Celestial City.

The genre of the travel narrative also lent itself to utopian ideals. By the eighteenth century the first phase of global discovery was over, and explorers such as James Cook (1728–79) were about to engage in a scientific investigation of the habitat and life-styles of alien peoples. The travelogue became an obvious method of exploring different views of society, and by implication, of criticizing one's own. As McKeon writes:

Following the tradition of their most famous predecessor, Thomas More's *Utopia* (1516), the imaginary voyages of the late seventeenth and early eighteenth centuries often combine a recognizably progressive critique of contemporary social stratification with a nouance of conservative doubt concerning the practicality of attaining utopias through the exercise of industrious virtue.[7]

McKeon, like John Richetti in *Popular Fiction before Richardson* (1969),[8] discusses a number of quasi-utopian travelogues. One such is the cheerful Republican idyll by John Neville, *The Island of Pines* (1668), which was translated into several European languages. The brief tale recounts how one John Pine found himself wrecked on an island off Australia in the company of four women. Free from the restraints of Church, society and money, he set about populating the island, and dies in perfect happiness amid an extended family of over seventeen hundred descendants. A contrasting example is Mary de la Rivière Manley's anonymously published *The New Atalantis* (1709), a series of scandalous stories which John Richetti describes as offering a dystopian view of a society dominated 'by a masculine spirit of lust and selfish possession, both in an economic and a sexual sense'.[9] Utopias were also embedded in other forms of narrative. McKeon, for example, takes Aphra Behn's account of the Surinam Indians in *Oronooko* (1688) as potentially utopian, although Behn is too sophisticated to fully idealize a pastoral community.[10]

Defoe's *Robinson Crusoe* offers a complex case. A. L. Morton sees the work as 'single-minded almost to the point of naivety',[11] and contrasts it with the complexity of Swift's utopian/dystopian vision in *Gulliver's Travels*. On the contrary, however, Swift's work is unified around the progressive disintegration of the narrator and main protagonist, Lemuel Gulliver, while the comparatively 'naive' artistic structure of *Crusoe* creates an unstable and sometimes conflicting authorial perspective which produces, in Bakhtinian terms, a 'polyphonic' narrative,[12] full of tensions and ambivalence. Instead of detracting from the work, this complexity, if largely unintentional, lies at the root of *Crusoe*'s continuing power to challenge and to inspire imaginative derivations.

Debate about the work's real meaning began within a year of its publication. Defoe was anxious to defend himself from accusations of fabrication or 'lying', and in his *Serious Reflections . . . of Robinson Crusoe* (1720), he asserted that the story was an 'emblem' of his own life and spiritual pilgrimage. Like Crusoe, Defoe had offended against a happy acceptance of 'the middle way'; like Crusoe he had been shipwrecked by bankruptcy (in 1694), and had arrived at a state of acceptance through Divine Grace. In *Crusoe*, God's consolation comes after despair.

But now I began to exercise myself in new thoughts; I daily read the word of God, and applied all the comforts to my present state. One morning, being very sad, I opened the Bible upon the words, *I will never leave thee, not foresake thee*; immediately it occurred that the words were for me.[13]

The passage reads like a devotional reflection by Defoe himself.

Any spiritual interpretation, however, was contemptuously dismissed by Charles Gildon in his pamphlet *The Life and Strange Surprizing Adventures of Mr. D—— de F——. Hosier*,[14] in which he declared that *Crusoe* was a complete fabrication which, if it did reflect Defoe's life, revealed only intrigue, vagabondage and deceit. More recently, critics such as Ian Watt have argued that Crusoe's religious protestations are contradicted by the book's overwhelming materialism, since whatever gestures Crusoe may make towards piety, the book's concerns are with exploitation and material gain.[15]

Watt's perspective, however, is not necessarily an eighteenth-century one. McKeon draws on Weber's arguments in *The Protestant Ethic and the Spirit of Capitalism* to argue that:

... in the historically transitional territory of early modern Protestantism, spiritual and secular motives are not only 'compatible'; they are inseparable, if ultimately contradictory, parts of a complex intellectual and behavioural system.[16]

This complexity is both moral and political. Defoe had spent much of his life in political intrigue and pamphleteering. He earlier had written *The Consolidator* (1705), a political allegory of contemporary England, set on the Moon. *Crusoe* is more direct. Crusoe's activity embodies the ideals that motivated the Whig landowners who were enclosing and developing the open spaces of old England. Crusoe, too, briskly set about enclosing his fields with hedges and barracades. He even parodies English legal protectionism: 'So I took up [the shot crows] and served them as we serve notorious thieves in England *viz.*, hanged them up in chains for a terror to others.'[17]

Yet while Crusoe acts like a landowner, his sturdy individualism and simplicity of taste identify him with the English commoner. This duality of class outlook is reflected in the two homes Crusoe inhabits on the island, his humble cave and his carefully built 'country seat'. Both these attitudes were to be found, too, in Defoe's life. As a commoner, Defoe barely escaped execution for his part in the Monmouth rebellion against James II in 1685. Yet the upwardly mobile Defoe acquired both a city 'cave' and country 'seat', had a coat of arms painted on his coach, and in 1695 had 'De' added to the family name of Foe.

Crusoe is not only a landowner, he is also an island despot. As Defoe has Crusoe return to England immediately *prior* to the Glorious Revolution of 1688, Defoe may be mocking the Stuart style of absolutism, although the scene is cosy enough:

It would have made a stoic smile to have seen me and my little family sit down to dinner; there was my majesty, the prince and lord of the whole island: I had the loves of all my subjects in my absolute command. I could hang, draw, give liberty and take it away, and no rebels among all my subjects.[18]

With this in mind, Crusoe's extraordinary appearance, his 'great, high' hat, elaborate weaponry, and dandified moustachios – 'I will not say they were long enough to hang my hat upon them but they were of a length and shape monstrous enough'[19] – has a parodic resemblance to the style of the Stuart court.

In the 'landowner' reading, then, Crusoe is provided with most things he wants from the wreck, including money (which in fact he can't use) and a virtually inexhaustible supply of pen, ink, gunpowder and bullets. Yet this is in direct contrast to the utopian significance that two centuries of readers were to take from the book. This is the account of Robinson Crusoe as 'natural man', alone on the island and using his ingenuity and resilience to create an ordered life from a wilderness. This is signalled when, after coming to accept his situation on the island, he wrote in his journal that 'I . . . was now reduced to *a meer state of nature* . . .' [my italics].[20] He has to make a spade, pots, and a boat with his bare hands, and he produces loaves of bread starting from seed. He writes: 'Tis a little wonderful, and what I believe few people have thought upon, *viz.*, the strange multitude of little things necessary in providing, producing, curing, dressing, making and finishing this one article of bread.'[21]

This aspect of Defoe's portrayal shows Crusoe as Natural Man, practical, self-sufficient and self-fulfilled. He is an Adam without a serpent or an Eve in sight. This evoked Defoe's most compelling writing, and was to lie at the heart of the utopian subgenre that his story was to bring into being.

The 'Robinsonnaden'

The term 'Robinsonnade' was coined by J. C. Schnabel, whose *Die Insel Felsenberg* (1731–42) was the first European work to be inspired by Defoe's narrative. It is significant that it emerged not in Britain, but in Germany, where the story was read with a utopian emphasis.[22] Schnabel's work was written for children. This as we will see became a common feature of the genre, but not all retellings of the *Crusoe* story were about or for children. In America, James Fenimore Cooper was indebted to *Crusoe* in drawing the hero Leatherstocking and the American Indians in his frontier tales,[23] and Cooper explicitly developed Defoe's story in *Mark's Reef, or the Crater* (1847). This tells how Mark Woolstone, an enterprising New Englander, is wrecked off a Pacific island with the sailor Bob Betts. 'I see no other hope for us, Mr Mark, than to Robinson Crusoe it awhile', declares Betts.[24] They 'Robinson Crusoe it' with success, transforming a reef and a volcanic mountain, which successively rise from the sea, into a fertile Eden, and in time Mark becomes Governor of a utopian colony. The community however disintegrates when 'the devil, in the form of a "Professor", once again enter[s] Eden'.[25] A lawyer, a newspaper editor, and four nonconformist ministers join the community and disrupt it, encouraging the colonists to sue Mark for possession of the land. After a return to the States, Mark and Betts come back to find the colony has sunk without trace under the sea, in a just retribution.

The hero of Jules Verne's *The Mysterious Island* (1875) is also an energetic New Englander. Verne was fascinated with Crusoe, writing that 'the Robinsons were *the* books of my childhood and they remained a permanent memory with me. Frequent reading has only strengthened their appeal to my mind.'[26] Verne's novel shows how Crusoe might have developed his island with later scientific knowledge. Captain Cyrus Harding is an engineer, in Grant's army, 'a true northerner . . . courage personified'. He escapes the siege of Richmond in a balloon together with Neb, a freed slave and his devoted 'Friday'; a young Crusoe, Herbert Brown, whose schooling in natural history proves crucial to the group's early survival; two others, and a dog. A phenomenal storm carries them across America and the Pacific to an island off New Zealand, where they are marooned with nothing other than their clothes and a single match. 'The imaginary heroes of Daniel De Foe or of Wyss . . . were never in such absolute destitution', notes Verne.[27] Nevertheless Harding's practical knowledge enables the group not only to survive but to create a scientific utopia. They start with the skills of Defoe's Crusoe – cultivation and pottery – rapidly working through such inventions as iron smelting, gunpowder, hydraulic power, glycerine, soap, beer and tobacco, to electricity and radio. Their success is watched and occasionally aided by Captain Nemo, not destroyed in the maelstrom at the end of *Twenty Thousand Leagues under the Sea*, but living in the Nautilus within a subterranean cavern. He gives them his dying blessing before the volcano under the island erupts, destroying the island and leaving them to be rescued from a tiny plateau of rock conveniently remaining amid the Atlantic. Verne wrote two other Robinsonnaden, the satirical *School for Robinsons* (1882), where a millionaire buys a desert island for his son, and *Adrift in the Pacific* (1888), a parallel to *Lord of the Flies*, where a party of schoolboys are wrecked and survive on an island off South America.

Adrift in the Pacific was written for children, as were the majority of nineteenth-century Crusoe tales. This juvenile subgenre is huge. In

Britain alone Kevin Carpenter has listed over five hundred 'island stories' printed between 1788 and 1910, and many of these went through successive editions. This does not include the many dramatic versions, such as Isaac Pocock's *Robinson Crusoe: or, the Bold Buccaneers* (1817). Robinsonnaden also flourished in the United States and across Europe, including Scandinavia and Russia. In Germany, France and England, Defoe's version was sometimes replaced by Johann Heinrich Campe's *Robinson die Jungere* (1779), translated into English as *The New Robinson Crusoe: an Instructive and Entertaining History, for the Use of Children of Both Sexes* (1788 and frequently reprinted). It was however not Campe or Schnabel but Rousseau, writing some years earlier in *Emile* (1762), who gave *Robinson Crusoe* its central importance as a children's book.[28]

He effected this through the immensely influential Chapter Three, in which Rousseau describes how his pupil, at the age of twelve, begins to learn to relate to the world, developing the manual and mechanical skills that will in turn integrate him into society – for 'the exercise of the natural arts, which may be carried on by one man alone, leads on to the industrial arts which call for the cooperation of many hands.' He continues:

Since we must have books, there is one book, which, to my thinking, supplies the best treatise on education according to nature. This is the first book that Emile will read; for a long time it will form his whole library, and it will always retain an honoured place. It will be the text to which all our talks about natural science are but the commentary. It will serve to test our progress towards a right judgement, and it will always be read with delight, so long as our taste is unspoilt. What is this wonderful book? Is it Aristotle? Pliny? Buffon? No; it is *Robinson Crusoe*.[29]

Rousseau's choice was more provocative in 1762 than it would be today. *Robinson Crusoe* was at that time taken as a popular adventure story below critical notice. As Martin Green has pointed out, Rousseau treated *Crusoe* as an anonymous work, and neither he nor others who followed him in his elevation of *Crusoe* made any attempt to enquire after the author. Yet after *Emile*, *Robinson Crusoe* was established as a major European text.

Rousseau's reading was a heavily edited version which ignored the picaresque form of the novel as a whole, and in effect left out both the religious and moral issues, and Crusoe's relationship with Friday:

The novel, stripped of irrelevant matter, begins with Robinson's shipwreck on his island, and ends with the coming of the ship which bears him from it . . .[30]

The island was to become the context in which Emile played out his involvement with the world outside him.

We shall therefore make a reality of the island which formerly served as an illustration. The condition, I confess, is not that of a social being, nor is it in all probability Emile's own condition, but we should use it as a standard of comparison with all other conditions . . . Let [Emile] think he is Robinson himself; let him see himself clad in skins, wearing a tall cap, a great cutlass, all the grotesque get-up of Robinson Crusoe, even the umbrella which he will scarcely need.[31]

By taking the island as a 'real' place, Rousseau paradoxically makes it utopian. For it envisions an environment without complex social relationships, free from the complications of sex and of the need to earn money. When Rousseau himself played Crusoe later in life, it was not to face 'reality', but to hide in a secluded island on Lake Brienne away from 'the memory of the calamities of every sort which they have been pleased to heap upon me for so many years!'[32] Rousseau aligns Crusoe with the Romantic idyll, the natural state, an Eden that was to be envisaged in the *Paul et Virginie* (1788) of Rousseau's friend and translator, Bernadin de St. Pierre, which is set on the island of Martinique.

You Europeans, whose minds are imbued from infancy with prejudices at variance with happiness, cannot imagine all the instruction and pleasure to be derived from nature. Your souls, confined to a small sphere of intelligence, soon reach the limit of its artificial enjoyments; but nature and the heart are inexhaustible. Paul and Virginia had neither clock, not almanack, nor books of chronology, history or philosophy.[33]

Rousseau interpreted *Crusoe*, therefore, as a way of teaching Emile self-reliance among the hardships of life, but at the same time he set this experience as an *escape* from the harsh world into 'nature' on a utopian island. How were the two perspectives reconciled? The answer lay, for Rousseau, in the consciousness of late childhood. 'Make haste, then', he urged, to establish [Emile] on his island while this is all he needs to make him happy . . .'[34] In Bernadin de St. Pierre's story, Virginia's innocence is preserved, not by the island place, but by her premature death by shipwreck. After Rousseau, for many, *Robinson Crusoe* became seen as the utopia of perpetual childhood. Indeed, in Germany, the transitional period between childhood and the adult was designated, with varying interpretation as to the actual age, the 'Robinsonalter'.

Young Robinsons

Rousseau's *Emile* decisively directed readings of Defoe's novel towards children's literature. As was noted above, in Germany, and to a lesser extent in France and England, Defoe's work was sometimes replaced by J. Johann Heinrich Campe's *Robinson die Jungere* (1779), translated into English as *The New Robinson Crusoe*. Campe's young Robinson, at the age of eighteen, is cast away on the coast of America. With nothing but his resourcefulness – he gets his first tool by digging a large shell from the sand with his bare hands – young Robinson is able to build his own shelter, and make clothes, weapons and other needs. After he has rescued Friday from the Cannibals, he etches the words 'Industry' and 'Frugality' on the rocks outside his cave to remind himself there is to be no remission from self-discipline. He finally returns to Hamburg a celebrity – a model of industry rewarded. The book presents an island utopia where anything can be achieved through ingenuity and hard physical labour, a pastoral increasingly attractive amid the urbanization of nineteenth-century life.

Young Robinson also showed an unlikely development of Defoe's obsessively individualist story: retold for bourgeois readers of the early nineteenth century, it reflected the ideal of the family. Campe's tale is narrated by a Hamburg businessman to his children and their friends in daily instalments. The story is interspersed with the listener's reactions, and supplementary lessons on botany and geography, incorporating Crusoe's experience into the learning process of the family circle. This was taken further by one of the most popular Robinsonnaden of the early nineteenth century, Johann David Wyss's *Der Schwizerische Robinson* (1812–13), known in Britain after the title of the second edition of the English translation as *The Swiss Family Robinson* (1818). Wyss shows a father, mother and four boys wrecked on an impossibly prolific island (ostriches, for example mingle with kangaroos and penguins). This gives the autocratic father endless opportunities for instruction about nature, and moralizing on the benevolence of God's providence. It set a pattern for island stories where the island serves as museum and zoo for the education of the young 'Crusoes' and their readers.

The island experience also taught morality and good behaviour. One of the first English Robinsonnaden was Agnes Strickland's *Rival Crusoes* (1826), which was popular enough to merit six re-issues. Strickland introduced the device, taken from Thomas Day's *Sandford and Merton* (1783–9), of using two contrasting young heroes to highlight the moral theme. The haughty, noble-born Robert is shipwrecked with the insolent, tough, working-class Philip: with the aid of religious instruction from their Bible they reconcile their differences and come to educate each other, so that Philip learns about the arts, and Robert gains practical skills such as carpentry. The idea of using the island as a social microcosm in which children create a harmonious cooperative was to continue through Ballantine's *The Coral Island* (1857) to the later subversion of the theme in Golding's *Lord of the Flies* (1954).

These islands were utopias free from sexuality. Although Bougainville's discovery of Tahiti in 1768 had offered an island vision of unlimited sexual licence, the British Robinsonnade, like Defoe's original, was a rigidly male-dominated world, where any sexuality was sublimated into vigorous action. Even where women intruded, they were excluded from romance. Thus in Elizabeth Whittacker's *Robina Crusoe, and her Lonely Island*, published in the *Girl's Own Paper*, 1882–3, Robina is cast away on an island where she proves as tough as any male Crusoe. She rescues a wounded native woman from hostile savages, and, when she dies, Robina fosters her child, whom she calls Undine. Later Robina single-handedly tackles a band of pirates, on this occasion saving an English boy, Henry. When they are rescued they return to England. Henry marries Undine, and all three retire finally to their island. Robina, however, remains a spinster. The serial was accompanied by articles describing the brave exploits of other female castaways.[35]

By the 1850s, the English Robinnaden were turning from education to imperialism. At the end of the century, Leslie Stephen could hail Crusoe as the 'representative' of:

. . . the men who were building up vast systems of commerce and manufacture; shoving their intrusive persons into every quarter of the globe; evolving a great empire out of a few factories in the East; winning the American continent for the dominant English race; sweeping up Australia by the way as a convenient settlement for convicts; stamping firmly and decisively on all toes that got in their way; blundering enormously and preposterously, and yet always coming out steadily planted on their feet . . .[36]

Some later Robinsonnaden were written by authors who had lived the lives of 'boy Crusoes' themselves. Captain Marryat, who wrote *Masterman Ready* (1841) in reaction against the inaccuracies of Wyss's *The Swiss Family Robinson*, had joined the navy at the age of fourteen, and sailed the world. Ballantine, whose *The Coral Island* (1858) proved the most popular of all these adventure tales, went to Canada aged sixteen to join the Hudson's Bay Fur Company, and in later life gave lectures dressed in full frontier costume. Later 'boy Crusoes' are no longer constrained to a tropical island. They are marooned in the middle of America, Africa, the Arctic. They subdue Africans, Amazons and Indians. They reflected the age of colonial expansion and, as staple reading for the young Victorian male, they formed the attitudes of administrators, soldiers, missionaries and settlers, who in turn shaped the British empire. In name, they are no longer 'Robinson', but proletarian 'Jack' (one is even called 'Union Jack').

They became the staple of the boy's periodicals that burgeoned in later Victorian England following the launch in 1860 of Edwin J. Brett's *Boys of England*. This opened with 'Alone in the Pirate's Lair', the account of one young Jack successfully defending himself on a desert island against a multi-national horde of pirates. In a more sadistic island adventure Jack Harkaway – one of the most popular of these Jacks – watches a cannibal feast in which the victim is eaten alive; Jack is buried up to the neck in hot sand by the school bully, escapes, and in revenge has his enemy agonizingly tattooed from head to foot by the savages. He acquires and bullies a black servant called Monday.[37]

In 1879 the Religious Tract Society tried to tempt young readers to a more healthful diet of adventure stories with *The Boy's Own Magazine*. But the island story was to be killed as much by sophistication as by degeneration. Robert Louis Stevenson's *Treasure Island* (1883) made a parody of the island adventure, self-consciously manipulating plot and place. Twenty-one years later Barrie was to call the bluff of the Robinsonnaden in the sub-title to *Peter Pan* – 'the boy who wouldn't grow up'.

The Anti-Crusoes

By the twentieth century, changing views were transforming Crusoe's island from a utopia to a dystopia. The reaction set in as early as 1857, with Karl Marx's comments on *Crusoe* in the *Grundrisse*.[38] Writing on eighteenth-century ideas of production, Marx noted that *Robinson Crusoe* and the Robinsonnaden 'in no way express merely a reaction against over-sophistication and a return to a misunderstood natural life, as cultural historians imagine'. *Crusoe* in fact showed the progress *away* from natural man to free competition, which dissolves the bonds of communal living. Feminist and post-Freudian consciousness also changed the way *Crusoe* was read. Jean Giraudoux's light-hearted *Susanne and the Pacific* (1921) portrays Crusoe as a woman.[39] William Golding's *Lord of the Flies* (1954) dismisses the Adamic innocence of *The Coral Island*; Ballantine's brave leader Jack becomes a sadistic fascist, Ralph an ineffective liberal, and the boys' instinct for warfare destroys the natural habitat of the island by fire.

In some modern versions, Friday moves centre stage, while Crusoe is comparatively marginalized. Michael Tournier's complex *Friday: or the Other Island* (1967) on one level exposes Crusoe's pretensions to being a controlling, dominant figure. When first arriving on the island, he wallows in filth with a herd of peccaries, and copulates with the island vegetation. Later he is saved from a joyless obsession with possessions and order by the black boy Friday, who represents the fantasy and sensuous pleasure denied by European culture. Friday inadvertently blows up Crusoe's cave when secretly smoking his pipe, and helps Crusoe to his psychological release.

In British literature, Adrian Mitchell's play *Man Friday* (1972), which was filmed with Peter O'Toole as Crusoe in 1974, opens with the utopian community of noble savages from which Friday has come. They tell the story of Friday meeting Crusoe, 'a red-faced monster with a man inside its belly . . . The man who walks outside'.[40] Crusoe is portrayed as an eccentric, obsessed with the rituals of white 'civilization'; nevertheless, by the end he senses Friday's superiority and asks to join Friday's tribe. Friday objects that Crusoe will inevitably corrupt their innocence, and the audience is invited to vote on the right outcome to end the play.

Derek Walcott from St Lucia has explored the Crusoe myth from the point of view of one who is himself a black inhabitant of the Caribbean. In his poem 'Crusoe's Island', he contemplates Crusoe as the artist, having to create his poetry on an alien island, and unable to bridge the gap between language and action.[41] His play *Pantomime* (1978) is set on Tobago, one of the reputed originals for Crusoe's island. Harry Trewe, white, the proprietor of a run-down hotel and an ex-actor, uses his spare time to rehearse a pantomime version of Defoe's story, playing Crusoe to the Friday of his black servant, Jackson. As he enacts the roles, Harry becomes enmeshed in Defoe's racial stereotypes and tries to back off – Jackson however refuses to let him escape. In their pantomime, Crusoe and Friday play out their roles as complementary aspects of a potentially violent world set against itself.[42]

J. M. Coetzee's *Foe* (1986) subverts the very nature of Defoe's narrative. Crusoe can give little coherent information about his own life; his story is surmised after his death by a character called Susan Barton, who is also shipwrecked on his island. Her version is then rewritten by Foe. As in the versions of Tournier and Adrian Mitchell, the clue to the 'reality' is held by Friday, who however has been rendered dumb and castrated, presumably by the slavers, and is able to express himself only in music and dancing. The contrast between Friday's simple awareness of life, and Susan and Foe's struggle to understand and express this reality, is indicated in Foe's account of Friday making a libation over the sunken ship from which he was rescued:

Friday rows his log of wood across the dark pupil – or the dead socket – of an eye staring up at him from the floor of the sea. He rows across it and is safe. To us he leaves the task of descending into the eye.[43]

Like Walcott's Crusoe, wrestling to reach the identity of his island through language, Susan attempts to teach Friday to write, and at the end Friday is found dressed in Foe's decrepit wig and robes, scribbling across Foe's story. He has only mastered the letter 'O', tomorrow Susan will teach him 'A'. Friday's struggle to objectify experience through words will continue.

A Conclusion in Which Little is Concluded

This essay began by considering ways of interpreting Defoe's *Crusoe*, and has ended by considering versions that question whether any stable reading of the work is possible. Yet through all the many re-tellings of the story, certain constants persist. The very inconsistencies in Defoe's original have given the underlying structure the flexibility to adapt to the issues that it explores. The island, Crusoe and Friday form a framework through which each successive period can express contemporary attitudes to human aspiration and limitation. Since these issues are basic to the concerns of utopias and dystopias, if *Robinson Crusoe* is not a utopian novel, it has a central place in the history of the genre.

Nor is the end of the *Crusoe* saga in sight. Martin Green and Patrick Parrinder both note the natural affinities of the book with science fiction, where new 'Crusoes' explore galactic islands, or find themselves marooned on an Earth devastated by an atomic cataclysm.[44] Film versions of *Robinson Crusoe* include *Robinson Crusoe on Mars* (1964), shot in Death Valley, which describes how a Crusoe character rescues a humanoid slave from an intergalactic war. The story of Crusoe may have only just begun.

4
Utopianism, Property, and the French Revolution Debate in Britain

GREGORY CLAEYS

Utopianism, it is usually contended, was 'emphatically not to the fore of eighteenth century thought' in Britain.[1] Much of what we associate with the age of Enlightenment was largely French in character. In England – for Scotland is a different story – some, inspired by Protestant Dissent in particular, envisioned the steady march of society towards considerably greater knowledge and virtue, sometimes combining this with antici- pations of the millennium. A few deists foresaw at least a measured retreat by the proponents of Divine revelation in face of the convincing truths of natural religion. But for the most part, the Augustan age wit- nessed an essentially conservative, unspeculative and anti-perfectionist Enlightenment which to some scarcely merits the name.

The eighteenth century in Britain was a complacent and sumptuous age, and not one, despite its admiration for many things French, given to philosophical extremes. Its 'rights', as Burke was to emphasize in his *Reflections on the Revolution in France* (1790), were those inscribed in law and rooted in experience and hard-won compromise. They were not drawn from abstract concepts, and though they owed some debt (at least in the case of Whigs) to an imaginary state of nature, they did not hearken back to its pleasures. The concept of perfectibility was darkened by too- recent memories of the Puritan excesses of the English revolution, and a sense that the claims of reason had to be tempered by the record of history. The era enjoyed no love affair with the noble savage, though Rousseau left a lasting mark on the epoch's ideas of education. Instead, the age was more indulgent towards the luxurious and the modern than it was towards the visionary. Nor were its established clergy, often sufficiently broad-minded and progressive in their theology and social theory to avoid the scathing contempt of the nascent intelligentsia, despised to the degree that they were in France. Thus, fewer of the people desired that the Christian heaven be supplanted by a secular paradise. A lesser but achievable good, if it had not yet arrived, was believed to be emerging slowly from present circumstances, especially the steady march of what the Scots, more active intellectually than the English, called 'commercial society'. Its inauguration required no revolution or swift illumination of the popular imagination. The ideal society lay neither in the past or the future, but the present.[2]

If this portrait remains largely accurate, especially compared to France, many interesting utopias were nonetheless written in eighteenth-century Britain, such as Robert Paltock's *The Life and Adventures of Peter Wilkins* (1751), Sarah Scott's *Millennium Hall* (1762), and Simon Berington's *The Adventure of Sig. Gaudentia di Lucca* (1776). At the same time, as we might expect, there was a concentration of such works, infused with a sense of immediacy and relevance that they had earlier lacked, during the revolutionary era at the end of the century. Here I want to address the question of the role played by utopian thought, or the description of imaginary ideal societies, during the heated and prolonged debate in Britain about the meaning and implications of the French revolution. That the revolution itself in France was regarded by its detractors as impossibly utopian (in the negative sense) is undoubted. The scope of its ambitions was immense: the overturning of political institutions, the secularization of religion, the introduction of a radically new calendar and of hundreds of new words to the French language. Perhaps most importantly, the revolution seemingly assumed an astonishingly great faith in the progressive rationality of humanity. Some have found such attributes, when enforced by the Terror, to reveal the roots of modern totalitarianism. Others, less sceptically, believed at the time that they represented the culmination of a lengthy process of enlightenment which, even if it fell short at present, foretold a brilliant future for mankind. For at least in France, the combination of the American revolution, scientific and commercial progress, and the extension of Enlightenment ideals had predisposed many writers of the late eighteenth century to presume that a more perfect polity and society could be created. Condorcet, Mercier and others thus cultivated an ideal of scientific and technical progress which built upon Baconian foundations.[3]. Its highest point of optimism was probably Condorcet's *Sketch for an Historical Picture of the Progress of the Human Mind* (1795), aspects of which were extended in France by social theorists of the early nineteenth century such as Fourier, Saint-Simon and Comte.

In Britain some observers were, at least initially, similarly optimistic about the implications of the revolution. It is commonly asserted that during the 1790s and the early years of the nineteenth century, utopian-

ism, political thought and practical politics merged in Britain to a degree
unparalleled since the mid-seventeenth century, if to a lesser extent than
in France. Britons, too, contemplated for a time the modern conception
of revolution. Society, some thought, might be transformed dramatically
for the better by creating startlingly new institutions instead of, as
reformers had so often thought, returning to a rosier past. Probably
Britain was closer to revolution during the 1790s – if still a good distance
away – than at any time since, and this climate of revolution was aided by
the growing confidence of the religious dissenters and the inspiration of
American and French experiments. Certainly the great radical texts of the
age, Thomas Paine's *Rights of Man* (1791–2) and William Godwin's
Enquiry Concerning Political Justice (1793), sought a greatly altered
society, though Paine chiefly aimed at political reform modelled on the
United States, and sought to combine republicanism and commerce;
while Godwin, insisting on moral improvement which would give
primacy to reinforced notions of Protestant conscience, on the whole
rejected commercial society.

   While the great works of the decade are well known, most of the
'utopian' texts (in the sense of fictional representations of ideal societies)
published in Britain during this period have not been examined carefully.[4] Here my aim is to explore several of these in light of the political
controversy of the 1790s, which reveals the main context for understanding contemporary utopianism as well.[5] During this decade, an intense
debate took place (it was indeed one of the great paper wars of British
history) between reformers and their opponents in Britain. While it
ranged over a wide variety of constitutional, legal, social and religious
issues, this controversy focused to an important degree on the relationship between commerce and equality. In so doing, I will argue here, it
revived and intensified, in a fashion unknown since the 1650s, the
question of the degree to which more egalitarian societies – such as those
associated with the Spartan and Classical utopian traditions, as well as
the monastic ideal – were practicable on a large scale. Political commentators such as Rousseau had suggested that they were not, and much of
the practical wisdom of the age concurred.[6] Similarly at issue was the
problem of whether the manifestly greater need for increased public
virtue in such communities could be elicited from existing unequal,
refined and selfish societies dominated by the pursuit of wealth. Public
virtue might thrive in the new, distant and more primitive colonies, where
fictional utopias were often situated. Britain and France were a vastly
different matter. Put bluntly, the French revolution asked, among other

things, whether utopia was compatible with the modern, commercial nation-state. Moreover, this debate heralded many of the greatest controversies of the subsequent two centuries. For the possibility of extending the more pristine virtues of small-scale communities, even of the monastery, to a mass-based political party originating within the boundaries of the nation-state, even to an association of nations, became, in the modern era, *the* utopian question *par excellence* – and this was largely because of the influence of the modern communist movement.

Several different kinds of answers were given to these questions in Britain during the last decade of the eighteenth century. Following the example of the American revolution, and particularly the restatement of its principles in Paine's *Rights of Man*, most parliamentary reformers in the 1790s aimed at political rather than any more explicitly social equality. Their concerns focused primarily on extending the franchise at least to sections of the middle classes, reducing the expenses of a corrupt, patronage-ridden Parliament, and curtailing the government's manipulation of the electoral process. In addition, most reformers in this period were, unlike many of the preceding republicans of the Machiavellian tradition to whom they were much indebted, explicitly 'modern'. That is, they were on the whole optimistic about the progress of commercial society and freedom of trade, and little concerned about any ensuing increase of national debt and the growth of luxury. At the same time, however, there also remained a strongly anti-commercial, stoical, even primitivist strain in republicanism, which had been markedly present in a variety of eighteenth-century utopias, such as the renowned Dissenting teacher and political writer James Burgh's *An Account of the First Settlement, Laws, Form of Government, and Police, of the Cessares, A People of South America* (1764).[7] It is this latter trend, much indebted from the 1790s to Godwin's *Political Justice*, which tends to be most prominently represented in the literary utopias of the period, such as Thomas Northmore's *Memoirs of Planetes; or a Sketch of the Laws and Manners of Makar* (1795).

Because of the modernity of mainstream republicanism, however, anti-commercial works of this type became in the 1790s even more 'utopian' than similar works of the early or mid-eighteenth century. For they were now less likely to be implemented by most reformers, given the progress of trade and urbanization and the acceptance of this progress by most of the population. The contrasting appeals of austere virtue and comfortable opulence were increasingly replaced by a more monolithic commercial idea. Just when radical mass movements seemingly made possible the founding of more perfect, essentially closed and economically restrictive societies of the utopian type, therefore, commercial developments, greater freedom of trade and social fluidity seemed to render such models less acceptable, even to radical critics of government. Appeals for the restoration or creation of a simpler and more virtuous society became even more unlikely, moreover, in light of the counter-attack launched on republicanism by 'loyalist' opponents of reform and the French revolution, who heralded much of Malthus's better-known onslaught on all grand-scale rationalistic reform in the *Essay on Population* (1798). Utopian thinking thus became outdated for many just at the moment when others thought its realization most likely. (Their descendants would again raise the banner of utopian reform with the foundation of socialism after 1815.) Nonetheless, some of the more interesting anti-commercial republican arguments of this period were stated in utopian form, and dismissed the alluring baubles of modernity, as More's Utopians had done, for something more nearly approaching an austere, stoic and Christian commonwealth of virtue. To see how these disagreements unfolded, we will review the relations between the revolution debate, republicanism and utopianism in eighteenth-century Britain, and then examine the character of utopian writing in Britain in the 1790s.

The French Revolution Debate in Britain

As elsewhere, the debate instigated by the French revolution focused in Britain on the issues of liberty, equality, and popular sovereignty. Many of the prerequisities for rebellion were lacking in Britain however. In particular, the chief reason Britain had no revolution at the end of the eighteenth century was that she was the wealthiest nation in Europe, and considered her own commercial opulence and constitutional monarchy as the only model worth displaying to the rest of suffering humanity. These achievements were rooted in the rule of law and a modicum of civil equality, but rested as well on Britain's social inequality. The progress of modernity was thus not necessarily towards democracy. In Scotland, writers like Smith, Hume and Robertson plotted the gradual passage of mankind from primitive to polished society, and defended the opulence and manners of commercial society as superior to the slave-based, unproductive economies and war-like demeanour of the ancients, even of the Greeks and the Roman republic. But most of the Scottish philosophical historians were cautious Whigs. Few were prepared to believe that popular political participation, and the much greater development of the working classes in intelligence and administrative capacity, were a likely outcome of this process, at least in the near future. Society would gradually expand its opulence by increasing the division of labour and trade. But while these would promote greater social harmony and international peace, most did not believe that they either required or necessarily produced greater education or rationality among the lower orders. (Some Dissenters, however, such as Joseph Priestley, were both more democratic and envisioned greater public enlightenment in general.)

The most important strand of republicanism in the 1790s shared much of this confidence about commercial opulence without being sceptical of the benefits of popular political participation. One of the best-selling political tracts ever written, Thomas Paine's *Rights of Man* (1791–2), proposed a representative, democratic republic which also curtailed the powers of the landed aristocracy and established Church. Paine had few traditional republican fears of the corrosive effects of commerce upon public virtue. Instead, commerce might be the means of peaceably linking all nations in the desire to fulfil mutual needs, once warfare based upon monarchic rivalry had ceased.[8] This commercial humanism was crucial to Paine's vision of the future development of European relations. Within any nation, similarly, commerce might distribute the benefits of production when heavy taxation to support a corrupt monarchy and aristocracy had been lifted. Such arguments derived much sustenance from the assumed achievements of the new American republic. The United States by 1789 seemed to have successfully wedded a modern, extensive form of representative republicanism to many of the virtues associated with the earliest stages of human society; in particular the United States seemed exceptionally resistant, among advanced commercial societies, to the debilitating effects of luxury. France, many hoped, might well replicate such virtues, even though she had to commence from a starting-point that was made problematic by her ancient and long-corrupted monarchy and much social inequality. Judging by the reception of the *Rights of Man*, it seems probable that most radicals were pro-commercial. Even Thomas Spence, whose schemes for land nationalization and parish management of the resulting collective property were influential through the 1840s, nonetheless assumed a relatively high level of commercial activity.[9]

Such optimism about commercial republicanism was by no means shared by all of the radical critics of the existing system of government, however. Writers such as the Dissenting minister Richard Price, whose sermon provoked Burke's caustic dismissal of the French revolution,

thought that much that was called progress, especially in politics, could
be attained only by returning to a more virtuous past. The 'balanced'
tripartite British constitution had become corrupted by aristocratic
influence, an overweening monarchy, and the interference of the government in the House of Commons. Price also clearly assumed that it was
America's more limited commerce which permitted her patriotism to
flourish.[10] Other radical reformers sought similarly to return to a more
virtuous polity, be it an Anglo-Saxon 'ancient constitution' or a republic
of the Greek or Roman ilk with Christian embellishments. Correspondingly, much British utopian writing of the eighteenth century upheld a
fairly primitivist republican ideal which was scathing in its rejection of
luxury, and envisioned a fairly regulated society, sumptuary restrictions
and even the curtailing of commerce generally.

Such hostility to commerce, and particularly the luxury trade, as an
essential threat to virtue, remained a significant concern for some
prominent radicals in the 1790s. The former Dissenting minister William
Godwin, in particular, sought to combine an austere moral and political
ethic with an image of the increasing rationality and perfectibility of the
human species. Godwin stressed both the natural growth of society
through stages of knowledge, and the human capacity for nearly
complete self-control, with illness, sexual desire and even old age being
gradually conquered by human ingenuity. But this would be possible only
through a return to a much simpler society. Here luxury would be
abolished, necessary labour reduced to a minimum, most forms of cooperative endeavour eliminated in order to ensure individual independence, and property would be defined by a social obligation to support
the needy.[11] Godwin's famous *Enquiry Concerning Political Justice*
(1793), whose readership was composed mainly of the young, often
Dissenting, middle classes, extended a number of important republican
themes in various directions; these themes included the centrality of
virtue to the good polity, the need for rotation to inhibit political
corruption, and a hostility to a narrow division of labour and to the
establishment of standing armies. In addition, Godwin combined
republican concerns with a militant Dissenting, even 'puritan' perspective, and a rigorous determination to pursue first principles rigorously to
their logical extremes. This led him to positions foreign to most
mainstream republican thinking, including what is now usually termed
philosophical anarchism.[12] Another variety of anti-commercial republicanism in this period was expressed in the London doctor Charles Hall's
The Civilization of the People in European States (1805), which urged an

agrarian law to limit landed property to 36 acres per family, and the curtailing of heavy manufactures and luxury goods. Both Hall's and Godwin's views were of some influence on early British socialism.

Hall wrote early in the new century (and met with little immediate response). In fact, support for primitivist proposals probably declined during the 1790s, principally because fervent attacks on republicanism, from 1792–5 in particular, dented enthusiasm for dramatic social experiments that involved much greater equality of property. This loyalist reaction occurred after the republication of the *Rights of Man* had helped to swell an already burgeoning popular radical reform movement into what appeared to be a genuine revolutionary threat, with a constitutional convention of reformers even calling for a new Parliament elected by universal suffrage. Few of the radicals were the 'levellers' denounced by their opponents, however. Paine's scheme for taxing landed property to aid the poor included permitting an absolute maximum on the annual value of landed property of £23,000 (a sum worth perhaps five hundred times as much in current values). But it allowed estates that were worth up to £13–14,000 annually to remain profitable, and so would have affected only the two hundred wealthiest families in Britain. It was thus hardly a stringent egalitarian proposal. Nonetheless, this taxation plan, and the appeal of the language of the rights of man, disseminated on a previously unknown scale, led at least some of Paine's less educated readers to presume that he proposed a much more considerable and immediate distribution of landed property. Correspondingly, his 'anti-Jacobin' critics charged in turn that he sought to dismiss the economic achievements of Britain's existing society, which was unequal but highly productive, and instead to commend a considerably more primitive society guided by republican political institutions (such as Godwin indeed recommended). Paine's followers tried to refute this charge, but to little avail.

During its peak this debate produced some hundreds of pamphlets, articles, books, and broadsides on the questions of liberty, rights, property and revolution. Most of these emanated from the loyalist side, and were often directed specifically at the *Rights of Man*. From about 1792 onwards, the accusation of 'levelling' became central to this dispute about the meaning of the French revolution and the claims of its proponents; the charge was made most vociferously by an organization led by a former Newfoundland justice, John Reeves, called the Association for preserving Liberty and Property against Republicans and Levellers. As I have shown elsewhere, one of the main issues here concerned the compatibility of a republican political form, such as America possessed, with a modern commercial society such as Britain's (American commerce was at that time by no means fully developed).[13] We still tend to read this discussion as if it chiefly concerned only whether men possessed natural rights (often assumed to be Paine's view) or only civil rights (the conception usually associated with Edmund Burke's *Reflections on the Revolution in France*, 1790). In fact Paine's appeal to natural rights was often taken by his opponents to mask a desire to return to the social equality usually associated with the state of nature, where such rights originated. Merely claiming such rights, they argued, thus implied a demand for equality of property and a much simpler society. This was a patently false, deeply politicized reading of Paine's views. But the charge was so widely and persistently publicized that it probably helped convince at least some of the wavering middle ground of reformers that such an appeal, if successful, would terminate Britain's current status as the premier merchant of the world, because this achievement was assumed to rest on her existing social inequality and the complex demand for produce that this inequality generated.

To the loyalists, Painite republicanism meant a return to nothing short of 'ancient rusticity', and they were thus able to argue that the poor man in Britain enjoyed 'comparative riches', even in his present 'state of subordination', compared to what he would receive 'in such an equality as is recommended to him'.[14] Satires such as *A Trip to the Island of Equality* (1792) portrayed republicans as wearing fox-skins and living in caves in consequence of their egalitarian political ideals. Central to this debate was the allegation that political equality was incompatible with commercial society, and that social equality could not lurk far behind the granting of manhood suffrage. For Paine's opponents, too, the American model thus lacked any positive relevance for Britain. Some conceded that representative republicanism suited countries where there was much free land, a relative social equality, and little luxury or developed commerce, with its accompanying corruption and vice. But both republicans and loyalists could agree that Britain in the last decades of the eighteenth century fell into the opposing economic category. For the loyalists, applying the American model to Britain was clearly impossible.

The Utopian Genre in the Revolutionary Period

These disagreements about the relationship between commerce and republicanism are the main context for understanding British utopian writing in the 1790s. Paine himself had clearly upheld civilization and commerce, and had stated unequivocally that no return to the state of nature was possible or desirable. But while his followers found it difficult to refute the charge that his writings had levelling implications, other radicals, especially the more 'philosophical' reformers, had little desire to do so. Both the pro- and anti-commercial forms of republicanism found expression in the seven or so positive British utopian tracts known from the literature of the 1790s.[15]

We have already noted that one of the most important anti-modernist texts of this period was Godwin's *Enquiry Concerning Political Justice* (1793). This helped to inspire two of the more important British utopias of the 1790s. The first of these was the landowner, geologist, and inventor Thomas Northmore's *Memoirs of Planetes; or, a Sketch of the Laws and Manners of Makar* (1795). In this work, which cited Godwin ten times, the stiff formality of European civilization is contrasted with the ease and freedom which results from innocence and contentment. The distant land of Makar, reached only after a lengthy voyage, is a hundred years ahead of Britain in its level of civilization. Here there is little beggary or vice, great leniency in punishments, easy access to education, and cheap clothing and provisions. Public virtue is rewarded by general approval, rather than by financial incentives. Hereditary distinctions and primogeniture have been abolished after a revolution and the creation of a new republican constitution, though Northmore emphasizes that lower-class vice and misery had to be diminished before great changes in government were possible. Government is treated as a manifest evil, even if a necessary one, but republican rotation (one-third of a unicameral legislature annually) is practised to limit political corruption. Oaths, capital punishment, and entail have been abolished, and marriage made a civil contract alone. Property is held only on trust, and is disposed of according to the principle of universal benevolence or philanthropy, while social relations are governed by truth and sincerity. Although the great advantages of commerce in providing a surplus of produce to mankind are stressed – which was more than Godwin conceded, at least in 1793 – emphasis is also laid on the fact that the frugal Macarians are 'almost total strangers to luxury', for example in their diet, and are deeply hostile to vice (abjuring, for example, from card-playing). This is clearly the product of a republican and Dissenting marriage of political and moral ideals.[16]

A second text clearly indebted to Godwin, though departing from him in several crucial respects, is the curious *An Essay on Civil Government, or Society Restored*, published in 1793 but apparently written in the previous year, and hitherto wholly neglected by historians. Supposedly written by an Italian, identified only as 'A.D.R.S.', the book in fact seems to have been composed by someone (or several persons, given the extensive commentary in notes on the main text) fairly close to Godwin. (It notes of *Political Justice*, probably very soon after its publication or even beforehand, that it might well be 'worth 10 of Paley's' – a reference to Paley's *Principles of Moral and Political Philosophy*, 1786). *An Essay on Civil Government* then goes on to propose a limitation of cities to a population of 20,000, with only two main classes, the liberal arts and traders (whom Godwin, in search of the greatest personal independence, would just as soon have dispensed with entirely). Basic wants are to be supplied by society (which was again anathema to Godwin's individualist perspective). Crucially, the effects of individual property are deemed so pernicious that the editors agree that the 'next step seems clearly to be that of *community of property*, or some approach to it, as a proper remedy to the vices and evils of the present.' This is to be achieved by first equalizing inheritances, then extending land leases for life, and finally putting 'all in common' (with Plato cited as a major authority for this aim). With reference to the debates surrounding the *Rights of Man*, the editors insist that 'the principle of the original and political equality of men, now so much insisted upon, is inapplicable and impossible, without a community of property'. Like Godwin, the *Essay* argues that 'small manageable societies, and federations of these, constitute the best form of associating human beings, and are capable of any extent, even round the globe', which was of course to be the principle of the later communitarian socialism of Owen, Fourier and others. Here there were to be few laws and no lawyers. Like Godwin, too, the *Essay* is greatly concerned to insist that, 'In man, as the *social* gains upon the anti-social and selfish affections and habits, every other improvement must probably follow:– reflection or reason must assume her place of guide or ruler: the moral gain upon the physical causes; justice over injustice; reason over passion, in the minds and perhaps the voluntary over the involuntary motions of the body, – the moving power, the energy of the brain, being as yet almost unknown, may all then be understood and properly directed.' Echoing Godwin's cautious approach to reform, too, is the recommendation that the new world be ushered in by 'a small number of wise and just men', such as Godwin himself, who would 'gradually inform, reform, and lead the world, by means of truth', in particular exercising 'frankness and sincerity'. Also notably Godwinian and Wollstonecraftian was the observation that 'Perhaps nothing else shews clearer the infancy of the human race, than the yet domineering spirit of the male over the female sex.'[17]

Similar in its approach to property was a remarkable tract that is often ascribed to a radical Irish physician, James Reynolds, after his exile to the United States in the mid-1790s, though in fact the piece was written by a Scottish emigrant, John Lithgow.[18] Often described as the first American utopia, though it is certainly more indebted to contemporary Anglo-Scottish than American debates, *Equality – A Political Romance* (1802) concerns the island of Lithconia, where money is not useful, all lands are held in common, and four hours' daily labour are required of all aged 18–50. No great cities or markets exist, but farmers and manufacturers deliver their products to public stores, of which there are three in every district to supply all necessities; no person is permitted to labour for another. Sexual freedom exists and, marriage having fallen into disuse, only women seduce now, with most of the population living together in groups of nine or ten 'friends'. But in some respects *Equality* is much less daring and libertarian, and in fact demands a quite regulated society. (Permission to travel is required, for example.) There are no lawyers, priests, physicians or soldiers (probably echoing Godwin). Government is performed by all 'superintendents' aged 50 years and over, and since all succeed to such governing positions, elections are rendered unnecessary. In an extraordinary departure from the republican principles which dominated most utopias of the period, the principle of election itself was thus replaced by that of 'seniority'. (This is also a remarkable anticipation of Robert Owen's later gerontocratic socialist politics.)[19] Given the simplicity of this system of government, one grand assembly, assisted by occasional district meetings, decides questions of production and distribution. In a curious mixture of modern technological development and austere sumptuary regulations, cotton, woollen and linen are spun by machinery, inventors are excepted from work, and passenger-propelled vehicles run on tracks, but no variation of dress or 'equipage' is permitted. This scheme of society and government is described, in a narrative relating how Lithconia achieved such delights, as a Rousseauist restoration of the advantages of the earliest state of innocence and common goods, before the stages of hunting, herding, agriculture and barter emerged. Indeed, the Lithconians are described specifically – here perhaps to spite Paine – as progressing from a state of civil society to the state of nature.[20]

Northmore's *Memoirs of Planetes, An Essay on Civil Government*, and Lithgow's *Equality* were all crucially innovative in their views of property, and are for this reason also important as foreshadowing early nineteenth-century socialism. All are indebted to a specifically Christian republican tradition of utopian writing which took Thomas More's injunction in *Utopia* (1516) to hold goods in common to reflect both the essence of Christian teaching and the culmination of Machiavellian and Harringtonian republican efforts to restrict social and political corruption.[21] A similar combination of aims is evident in various of the works of the Newcastle printer and radical shoemaker Thomas Spence. Several of Spence's works published in this period, notably *The Constitution of Spensonia* (1803), use the loose device of a fictional country to publicize the land nationalization programme that Spence had first revealed as early as 1775. *The Constitution of Spensonia* is even less fictional than Spence's earlier *A Supplement to the History of Robinson Crusoe* (1782), and was preceded in addition by a similar pamphlet, *A Description of Spensonia* (1795). As in his other works, Spence here proposes the ownership of land in common and its management by local parishes, who would rent out plots to the highest bidder. Otherwise 'the right of property' is described as belonging 'to every citizen to enjoy and dispose of according to his pleasure, his property, revenues, labour, and industry', property in land alone excepted. No other kind of 'labour, culture, or commerce' is forbidden. Education is to be provided for all, and public functions are to be considered as duties rather than as privileges to be awarded; the trade in grain was to be regulated, and an elaborate democratic electoral system put in place which would include annual elections – a frequent radical demand earlier in the century.[22]

Unlike the preceding group of texts, one other major utopian tract of this period embraced modern republicanism, and remained closer to Paine in its views of property. However, it went well beyond him in its efforts to abolish poverty, while not approaching as closely to socialism as *Equality* or *An Essay on Civil Government*. Like the other utopias of this period, the London hatter William Hodgson's *The Commonwealth of Reason* (1795) aimed to eliminate political corruption, 'the most dreadful evil that can possibly affect either public or private life'.[23] But Hodgson's scheme is more narrowly political than, for example, Lithgow's *Equality*, partly because corruption is seen in more traditionally republican terms, as emanating from power too long concentrated in the hands of a few individuals. In *The Commonwealth of Reason*, accordingly, all are treated as equal by nature, though unequal in virtue. But there are neither titles nor separate and opposing interests. The great political error is conceived to be delegating power without control, and hence all positions of influence, following an essentially Harringtonian plan, have been made 'REVOLUTIONARY OR ROTATIVE'. The key cause of corruption for Hodgson, however, is declared to be the accumulation of immense wealth by a few, and primogeniture, entails, sinecures and enormous salaries have accordingly been abolished. An elaborate constitutional system and a declaration of rights ensure rule by free consent. Following the practice of some American states, judges are elected. A committee of agriculture, trades and provisions is empowered to inspect food production and guarantee that all possess a sufficiency, with granaries ensuring supplies are maintained (which is certainly more regulation than Paine envisioned). A minimum price for labour of a bushel of wheat daily is established. Waste lands have been cultivated, and roads and canals are built at public expense. There is a national educational establishment, marriage is merely a civil contract, capital punishment has ended, the state Anglican church is disestablished, and a citizens' militia has replaced a standing army. Inheritance has also been equalized, while national manufactories in every district offer employment to all who require it (this is also an extension of one of Paine's proposals, which he had applied to London alone). All over the age of fifty receive a pension (another Painite idea).[24] Despite these welfare provisions, however, there is a notable lack here of an agrarian law, sumptuary regulations, or other limits upon property-holding or commerce. Essentially this is a modern, if considerably more interventionist, Painite republican political régime in which liberty of trade is pursued unhampered by class inequalities – inequalities which, the radicals believed, denied the benefits of trade to the majority.

Three other utopian tracts of this period also merit a brief mention. *A Voyage to the Moon Strongly Recommended to All Lovers of Real Freedom* (1793) is a short satire on Reeve's Association for Preserving Liberty and Property and Edmund Burke ('Edmuldus Barkwell'). The piece depicts a happy island without oppressors, where the rich are kind and the poor happy; it attacks hereditary rights and parliamentary corruption while praising the American republic.[25] *Modern Gulliver's Travels*, published in 1796, is a late contribution to the genre of Swift imitations. Set in a contemporary context in which 'cursed democracy' has taken over Blefescu (France), its purpose is much more satirical than the works discussed above. The text takes aim especially at the corruptions of courtly life, the effects of heavy taxation on the poor, the tendency of the monarchy to foreign conquests and adventurism, the abuses practised by the legal system, and the efforts of a loosely-disguised Burke to secure a pension by writing a work entitled 'Beauties of Aristocracy' (intended to parody Burke's famous *Reflections on the Revolution in France*).[26]

Thus, in all of the major utopian works of the 1790s we see mirrored the same central disagreements which divided the more straightforward political literature of the period. Of particular importance in this regard was the question of commerce. Northmore's *Memoirs of Planetes, An Essay on Civil Government*, and Lithgow's *Equality* describe a more primitive, neo-classical, stoical and puritan republican society that seems quite divergent from the more modernist emphases of the mainstream reform movement, and which is reminiscent instead of works such as the republican James Burgh's *An Account of the First Settlement, Laws, Form of Government, and Police, of the Cessares, A People of South America* (1764). In this sense the issue of luxury, the restraint of needs, and the attitude taken towards commerce were central in dividing both utopianism and the wider radical and republican movements in this period. And once again, as so often, the utopian form masks far more extreme proposals for social and political change than most of those espoused in the mainstream literature.

A comparison of utopian tracts and radical pamphlets of the 1790s reveals that many reformers were attempting to grope towards some form of compromise between the continuing appeal of the imagery of the state of nature, republican independence and primitive virtue, and the need to provide for citizens already depraved by the consumer revolution, whose needs far outstripped anything natural society had been able to provide. In this sense, what continued to prove attractive about a more primitive, primarily agricultural society was its equality and virtue, rather than the restrictions it placed upon trade and the expansion of consumer needs. The increasing centrality of commerce and luxury to republican thought in this period is revealed in the fact that the two leading republicans in Britain in the 1790s, Paine (in exile in Paris after 1792), and his most important radical successor, the popular lecturer and London Corresponding Society leader John Thelwall, both wrote tracts published in 1796 attempting to outline a new strategy for reconciling trade, commerce and republican political institutions with egalitarian demands and the growing issue of poverty.[27] After 1800 the need to 'modernize' republicanism became clearer still with the severe setback dealt to Godwin and other reformers by Thomas Robert Malthus's *Essay on Population* (1798), which for many refuted the view that any substantial social reforms were possible as long as the sexual passions of the poor remained unrestrained.

Equally indicative of some reformers' efforts to rethink the virtues of commercial society was the attempt by Godwin to redefine luxury. He sought in the later 1790s to avoid seeing luxury merely as the possession of certain types of refined goods that could not be classed as necessities, declaring after 1796 that these items were relatively harmless. Instead he now tried to concentrate upon the vicious effects of luxury as a source of the oppression of others, by adding a greater burden of labour to the poor. This sort of shift in emphasis resulted to a large degree from debates about the nature of the French revolution, its principles and implications. It indicated, moreover, a fundamental transformation in utopian think-ing. To an important degree, utopianism no longer implied the juxta-position of natural or primitive society to commercial society, or at least this was no longer its sole concern. Instead the question of unequal versus more egalitarian commercial societies, and of the just distribution of wealth to the producer as it was earned, in the form of wages, now became increasingly important. Thus both the utopian ideal of a community of goods, and the republican conception of an agrarian law that would limit landed property, were increasingly adapted to meet widespread demands for the maintenance of the advantages of commer-cial society.

This was to become the point of departure for early British socialism, which as espoused by Robert Owen – and, even more, John Gray – acknowledged the probability of expanding needs, and of the subsequent value of a more equitable form of commerce and a less destructive use of machinery.[28] The main expression of early British socialism after 1815 was in practical community planning. But there were also many Owe-nites to whom 'community' still evoked an essentially rural, arcadian image that seemed ill at ease with commercial society; such themes are common in the Owenite-inspired John Minter Morgan's *Hampden in the Nineteenth Century*, 1834, for example. Thereafter, and well into the twentieth century, socialists continued to be attracted by the vision of an essentially pastoral, harmonious past. (Otherwise we would have diffi-culty explaining the later popularity of, for example, William Morris's *News From Nowhere*, 1890.) Marx and Engels, throughout the 1848 revolutions and in the *Communist Manifesto*, continued to pay at least lip-service to the notion of transplanting the unemployed to the countryside in an attempt to combine the advantages of rural and urban life.[29]

A century later, what remains of socialism is returning to a much 'greener' emphasis, and again occasionally trumpets the virtues of a simpler society. But it is certainly true that the socialist movement has often been deeply divided over the price to be paid for either returning to a pre-commercial past, or embracing the greatly unequal, deeply corrupted commercial present and somehow creating a more just regime from such wretched materials. Nonetheless, the notion of socialism as a just commercial society, expanding production in response to human needs, was to a large extent created out of the interaction in the 1790s between republican and utopian images of the ideal past and the ideal of commercial progress towards a more perfect society. From this juxtaposition, to an important degree, came a new utopian vision in which the future ideal society was not to be found in a return to the past, but in a creative redevelopment of the present out of materials created by commerce and industry. Until our own times, this has been the modern utopia.

5

The End of Socialism? The End of Utopia? The End of History?

KRISHAN KUMAR

Our country has not been lucky. Indeed, it was decided to carry out this Marxist experiment on us – fate pushed us in precisely this direction. Instead of some country in Africa, they began this experiment with us. In the end we proved that there is no place for this idea. It has simply pushed us off the path the world's civilized countries have taken. BORIS YELTSIN[1]

Two years of unbelievable political change in Europe have been sufficient to proscribe the use of the word 'utopia'. No one talks about utopia any more. WOLF LEPENIES[2]

I do not believe . . . that utopianism is at an end. Quite the contrary. Perhaps it is only now that we can invent utopian utopias. IMMANUEL WALLERSTEIN[3]

'Endism' is rampant, and likely to become even more so as we get closer to the end of the second millennium. Millennial endings, even more than centurial ones, give rise to millennial imaginings.[4] But there is a profound difference between the millennial thoughts of our time and those of earlier ages. For thinkers such as Joachim of Fiore, the 'Last Days' marked a radically new beginning. They portended a new age of the Holy Spirit, a millennial age of love, freedom and joy. What was contemplated was not simply an end but a renewal, a new dispensation based on radically different principles.

For our thinkers, on the contrary, the 'end of history' brings nothing new. Quite the opposite. It announces the final victory of the old. What was thought to be new has failed. It was, in any case, a bundle of delusions, unnecessary and destructive deviations. There is no need to imagine anything new. We already live in the millennial new age, the last age. The Messiah has already come, and fulfilled his mission; the Everlasting Gospel is with us; all we can do now is wait wearily, like St Augustine, for the sands of earthly time to run out. No wonder that even the most confident pronouncements of the end of history in our time are tinged with melancholy at the predicament of the 'last man'.[5]

It is not, of course, simply the end of a century and a millennium that inspires these oracular utterances. The idea that we may have reached some final point of historical development is linked to other, more familiar notions. There is the announcement of the death of the socialist ideal, an idea already prominent in the writings of many East European dissidents in the 1960s and 1970s, which reached a crescendo in both East and West following the revolutions of 1989 in Central Europe and the collapse of the Soviet Union in 1991.[6] The view that utopian thought, which for nearly five hundred years had fired the European imagination with dreams of a better future, was now bankrupt, can be seen to have been widely held even further back in the century.[7] Since socialism of one kind or another had become the central component of the modern utopia, the fate of socialism in the last part of our century might seem to bury utopia comprehensively. In 1919, two years after the Russian Revolution, the American writer Lincoln Steffens returned from a visit to Russia and made the famous remark, 'I have been over into the future, and it works.' Now not only the Soviet Union but all the other putative models of utopia appear defunct. 'The Soviet Union', says Anthony Sampson, 'has finally gone the way of all Utopias; along with China, Cuba, Sweden and Tanzania, denounced and discredited by its own inhabitants.'[8]

This collapse of socialism contrasts with the perception that the capitalist democracies of the West have, for all their faults, survived and prospered, so that they alone appear to have a continued appeal for the rest of the world; it is not difficult to see why a general sense of self-congratulation, not to say complacency, should have overtaken the western world. The West has won; its system, evolving steadily since the sixteenth century, has now triumphed over all rivals and competitors. There can be no further meaning to history than the elaboration and firmer implementation of western principles throughout the globe.

I shall return to this topic later in this essay. Here I am mainly concerned with the effect of the 1989 revolutions on the idea of utopia. Have they, as many claim, put the final nail in the coffin of utopia? Is the story of utopia therefore one of unremitting decline in this century? What further function might there be for utopia, in a world where there no longer seems to be any place for radical alternatives to the present order?

The Assault on Utopia

Utopia, in the twentieth century, has not had many friends. For left-wing thinkers, who might have been expected to be sympathetic, it was a standing reminder of the origin of their own ideas in a form that they were anxious to distance themselves from. In any case, had utopia not been sufficiently realized in the Soviet Union? What need was there now for utopias? Was not the main task now the support, through propaganda and action (e.g. spying), of the country that was the spearhead of the Third International?[9] For those socialists who were less convinced that the Soviet Union was utopia made real, utopia was still unwelcome. It distracted from the main task of organization. Whether parliamentary or revolutionary, socialists in the twentieth century have been less interested in elaborating their view of the future society than in planning, like a General Staff, the tactics of gaining and maintaining power.

The Right and the Centre have, not surprisingly, been even more virulent in their attack on utopia. For them utopia is, by definition, an affront. Even if they accept that utopias are not to be taken literally, that their authors are not in most cases writing blueprints for the perfect society, the whole enterprise is to liberals and conservatives deeply suspect. It is an act of hubris. It makes claims for human reason that are unreal and liable to encourage dangerous ventures in practice. History is littered with failed utopian experiments, many of them unappealing in their lifetime and bloody in their end.

This kind of response to utopia has been familiar from the earliest times, for instance in Aristophanes's mocking of Plato's *Republic*, and Swift's satire on Francis Bacon's scientific utopia. But the attack has taken on a heightened urgency in the twentieth century, largely because of a presumed connection between utopian thought and the totalitarian regimes of this century. Fascism is a utopia; so too is Communism in its Soviet form.[10] They are utopian, it is argued, precisely in their worst aspects, in their belief that they have discovered the secret of history and that, armed with this discovery, they are in a position to rule and regulate society totally, in all its aspects.

The most celebrated rendering of this view was George Orwell's anti-utopia, *Nineteen Eighty-Four* (1949). Despite Orwell's protestation that the book was not meant to be anti-socialist, his portrait of totalitarianism – often identified by careless readers with Stalin's Russia – was grist to the mill of anti-utopian liberals and conservatives (and certainly upset many socialists, such as Isaac Deutscher).[11] It chimed in particularly well with the wide-ranging critique of radical politics that was conducted by a group of brilliant and highly influential European emigré intellectuals who felt themselves the victims of the utopian politics of their native countries. In exile in France, Britain, America, Canada, Israel, they launched a vigorous and often bitter and passionate polemic against the whole utopian tradition, seen as a pestilential inheritance.

One could say that this wave of protest began with Yevgeny Zamyatin's *We* (1924), a piercing satire on the new Soviet state, for which Zamyatin was lucky to receive no worse punishment than exile to Paris. However, due largely to the exigencies of publishing, this novel did not become widely known until the 1950s, when it was taken up partly as the result of the success of *Nineteen Eighty-Four*.[12] A much greater impact was created by Arthur Koestler's *Darkness at Noon* (1940), another anti-utopian novel that reflected bitterly on the author's experience of the communist mentality as an erstwhile member of the German Communist Party and as a journalist during the Spanish Civil War.[13]

These were novels, fictional treatments of totalitarianism.[14] Matching them, and indeed making very much the same kind of points, were a series of works in social and political theory that were written by the emigrés (there is a strong parallel here, not to say thematic continuity, with the conservative response to the French Revolution, in the writings of Burke, Bonald, de Maistre and others). From a haven in Christchurch, New Zealand, Karl Popper wrote *The Open Society and Its Enemies* (1945) – 'the final decision to write [which] was made in March 1938, on the day I received the news of the invasion of Austria' by the Nazis.[15] Not just fascism but, even more, Marxism were denounced for their historicism – their belief in general laws of history which pushed societies inexorably along a predetermined path.

But Popper also reserved some of his fire for 'Utopianism', which he saw as 'a necessary complement to a less radical historicism' deriving from Plato and the utopian tradition. This Utopianism was pernicious for holding that it was possible to devise a 'blueprint' of the Ideal State, to which all political activity should be subordinated. It was not, as in the common criticism, the 'idealism' or unrealizability of utopia that Popper saw as its main weakness; it was its recommendation of 'the reconstruction of society as a whole', in accordance with some supposedly absolute and rational idea. It was this that must lead to violence and tyranny. Utopianism 'with the best intentions of making heaven on earth . . . only succeeds in making it a hell – that hell which man alone prepares for his fellow-men.'[16]

The Open Society and Its Enemies has remained the most thorough-going and influential critique of utopianism from the pen of a modern social theorist – it is, we might say, the non-fictional equivalent of *Nineteen Eighty-Four*.[17] But other emigré intellectuals have also made famous contributions to the same basic enterprise. Removed, like Popper, from his native Austria, Friedrich von Hayek sought to arouse controversy with the London publication of *The Road to Serfdom* (1944), a stinging attack on 'the great utopia' of collectivism which he saw exemplified equally in German Fascism and Russian Communism. Like Popper too, Hayek identified the enemy as the hubris of reason and the idea of a total reconstruction of society by political means. Jacob Talmon escaped the Central European Holocaust via London and Jerusalem; in *The Origins of Totalitarian Democracy* (1952) he traced the roots of modern totalitarianism back to the utopian ideas of Rousseau and other French thinkers of the eighteenth century.[18] Going further back, Norman Cohn, resuming an inquiry 'first begun in the ruins of Central Europe fifteen years ago',[19] sought the seeds of totalitarian Communism and Nazism in a different variety of utopianism: the millenarian beliefs and movements of the European Middle Ages.

The inquiries of Popper, Hayek, Talmon and Cohn were predominantly historical. They wished to show that the catastrophe of Europe in the twentieth century could be traced back to a set of thinkers and ideas deep in the European past. These ideas they equated with a long-standing utopian strand in European thought. Against this they set, with a reasonable degree of optimism, a tradition of thought that originated with classic liberal thinkers such as Alexis de Tocqueville and John Stuart Mill. To Isaiah Berlin and Leszek Kolakowski – perhaps because of their provenance from a more easterly direction than most of these others? – the problem of utopianism appears more intractable. It is seen as an almost natural distemper of the human mind whose cure probably lies well beyond the realm of the usual liberal remedies. Berlin, forcibly displaced by revolution from Riga and Petrograd to an English public school and Oxford, meditates on Kant's dictum that 'out of the crooked timber of humanity no straight thing was ever made.' The utopians, from More to Marx, flatten out human nature, 'downgrade man's role as creator and destroyer of values . . . as a subject, a creature with an inner life denied to other inhabitants of the universe.'[20] Utopia has declined in the twentieth century, but Berlin acknowledges its perennial appeal and the possibility that it may resurface in such forms as militant nationalism – and, he might now add, religious fundamentalism. Moreover he admits the limited attractions of the liberal model that he offers as an alternative.[21]

Kolakowski – Polish dissident and Oxford don – is so struck by the recurrence of 'the utopian mentality' that he wonders whether we may not have to do 'with an everlasting form of human sensitivity, with a permanent anthropological datum for which an English thinker in the sixteenth century simply invented an apt name.' He rejects this notion as supplying an unhelpfully wide definition of utopia. In any case, like Berlin, he thinks utopia is in decline, that 'utopian dreams have virtually lost both their intellectual support and their previous self-confidence and vigor.' Utopia has been discredited by the realization that its attainment would bring 'a perpetual deadly stagnation' and death of human creativity and striving. All change is a response 'to dissatisfaction, to suffering, to a challenge' – precisely those aspects of human life which utopia seeks to expunge. Utopias were harmless so long as they remained 'literary exercises'. In our century what has made them 'ideologically pernicious' is the conviction of their advocates that they have discovered 'a genuine technology of apocalypse, a technical device to force the door of paradise.' Worst of all in this respect has been the Marxist utopia, which became 'the main ideological self-justifying and self-glorifying support of the totalitarian cancer devouring the social fabric of our world.'[22] No doubt Kolakowski rejoices at the downfall of this utopia in his native Poland and the rest of Eastern Europe.

Kolakowski has observed, *a propos* the popularity of utopia, that 'it is an interesting cultural process whereby a word of which the history is well known and which emerged as an artificially concocted proper name has acquired, in the last two centuries, a sense so extended that it refers not only to a literary genre but to a way of thinking, to a mentality, to a philosophical attitude . . .'[23] It is equally interesting that Kolakowski does not appear to see the relevance of this observation to himself, nor to most of the other twentieth-century critics of utopia. For what is striking about their treatment of utopia is precisely the tendency to turn it into an abstract current of thought, or a psychological or temperamental propensity. Utopia becomes utopianism, the utopian mentality, the utopian impulse. Or it is equated with a particular style of thought that thinks in terms of wholes and systems – so Popper can talk of 'the Utopian planners', 'the Utopian engineers', 'the Utopian blueprint'.[24] This does not necessarily lead to the view that utopianism is some universal, transhistorical human propensity – indeed most of the critics are concerned to stress its historical origins. But it does make it easier to see utopianism at work in a host of modern ideologies, many of which have never been the subject of a formal utopia.

This is the important point. There is no harm in talking about certain forms of thinking, and certain thinkers, as utopian. It is almost impossible not to do so in the case of thinkers such as Rousseau or Owen, perhaps even Plato and Marx. But it becomes dangerous when all forms of thinking about 'the good' or 'the best' society are labelled utopian, and given a systematic description such that they can hardly avoid being characterized as 'totalitarian'. Utopia has performed many functions in its long history, and systematic thinking about the future of society is only one of them. The same is true of 'the design of the perfect society'. The different forms of utopia – from Socratic dialogues and Biblical prophecies to ideal cities and ideal societies, from social and political speculation to satires and science-fiction, from the realist novel to the popular culture of films and television – need to be treated with respect for those differences, and the different aims and meanings that they carry.[25] The fact that none of Plato, Rousseau, Owen or Marx (not to mention Hitler) ever wrote a formal literary utopia should be as important in assessing their utopianism as in the assessment of those of their disciples who did write such utopias. It may be useful for certain purposes to treat the *1844 Manuscripts* or the *Communist Manifesto* as utopian; but a comparison with, say, Edward Bellamy's *Looking Backward* or, again, William Morris's *News from Nowhere*, should make us aware of the differences as well as the similarities.

One other confusion is particularly important for present purposes. It is one thing to conflate, as we have just noted, the fictional utopia with various forms of 'utopian' social theory. It is even more dubious to treat as a unified entity utopian speculation and various forms of social experimentation which dub themselves or are dubbed utopian. This too is a common procedure of the anti-utopian critique. The refusal to distinguish between these spheres, each of which has its own forms and logic, is one major reason why utopia can be made to seem dangerous. 'Utopian' communities, such as Robert Owen's New Harmony in nineteenth-century Indiana, or many of the 'counter-cultural' communes of the 1960s, often end in disillusion or débacle. Their repeated failure can then be used to discredit the utopian enterprise as a whole.[26]

The fate of both socialism and utopia has been partly determined by this kind of argument. Utopia in the last two centuries has come to be closely connected to the socialist project, even to an extent identified with it. Socialism in its turn has been judged by the success or failure of certain kinds of social experiment, notably that carried out in the Soviet Union. The decisive failure, as it appears, of socialism in the closing years of this century has therefore brought with it the refrain that utopia, too, has died.

We shall turn to this in a moment. But as a footnote to the twentieth-century assault on utopia we should note the unexpected career of Aldous Huxley's *Brave New World* (1932). Huxley's anti-utopia is matched only by Orwell's for its fame. Here too there were important Continental precursors and influences, an important one being the thought of the Russian emigré Nicholas Berdyaev. *Brave New World* indeed carried as an epigraph an observation of Berdyaev's that summed up its central message: the tragedy of the modern world was not, as was often claimed, that the modern utopia – the utopia of science and socialism – was too idealistic to be realizable, but, on the contrary, that it had been realized, with disastrous consequences to the individual and society.[27] *Brave New World* portrayed a hedonistic paradise in which all needs and desires were painlessly satisfied – but also rigidly shaped – by the ruling elite of scientific controllers in the interests of social stability. The casualties, Huxley suggested, were freedom, love and creativity, indeed all that made human life truly worthwhile.

It seems clear that Huxley's anti-utopia has not seemed as threatening to the generations of the second half of the twentieth century as Orwell's creation. Perhaps this has something to do with Huxley's own recantation in *Island* (1962), where something in many respects quite close to the Brave New World was presented in a utopian rather than anti-utopian light. It is in any case an irony that, as reported by several American college professors, many young people read *Brave New World* as a utopia rather than as an anti-utopia. Huxley's attack on hedonism appears to them rather a celebration of sex, drugs, and effortless living – the very things that they crave.[28]

And are they not in a sense right? Has not the society of *Brave New World* become the Western utopia in the second half of our century? Economic abundance and uninterrupted increases in one's personal standard of living – are not these the highest goals put before the populations of western industrial nations? It is indeed precisely this consumerist utopia, in the opinion of observers such as Ernest Gellner, that has been the principle dissolving force of the regimes of Eastern Europe.[29] Consumerism has killed Communism; East as well as West now inscribe on their banners, 'live now, pay later'.

Utopia, Socialism and the 1989 Revolutions

The break-up of communism in Eastern Europe was bound to bring with it fresh denunciations of utopia. Dissident thought in the area had for long identified the ruling systems with a misbegotten and disastrous utopian experiment. Solzhenitsyn in Russia – and even more out of it – Havel and Kundera in Czechoslovakia, Michnik and Geremek in Poland, all inveighed against the utopianism that had infected the politics of the region. The Soviet Union was the exemplary case of what Solzhenitsyn called 'the Marxist-Leninist utopia, which was blind and evil at birth.'[30] For the Czech philosopher Milan Simecka, 'in the course of some sixty years, the hitherto greatest utopia of all has been turned into a social order whose immobility and intellectual sterility is reminiscent of the nightmares of the ancient utopias.' The 'real socialism' of Eastern Europe was for Simecka a standing reminder of the truth that all utopias must betray their ideals when put into practice:

'All the indications are that utopias are nothing but the instrument of a historical deception, the bait set out for the desperate, a false rainbow beneath which the people is easily to be led into a new slavery.'[31]

Simecka refers to Karl Popper as having powerfully put this view of utopia; at the same time he invokes *Nineteen Eighty-Four* – 'surely one of the most exciting books in world literature' – for its prophetic under-standing of the nature of the Communist utopia.[32] There is a clear indication here of the link between the earlier anti-utopian critique and the present recoil from utopia. The current anti-utopians also see utopia as a poisonous inheritance. Its burial by the revolutions of 1989 in Central and Eastern Europe is an event to be celebrated, not mourned, according to Hans Magnus Enzensberger. We should not fear that by bidding 'farewell to utopia' we would be losing the element of dream or desire in society. These are, unlike utopia, anthropological constants. What we would have discarded 'would above all be the most fatal elements of utopian thinking: the projective megalomania, the claim to totality, finality and originality.'[33]

Yes indeed. But is that the main legacy of utopia – a totalitarian aim and ambition? It might seem so, if utopia is equated with specific experiments, in this case the state socialism of Eastern Europe. Scarcely less damaging is the claim, made by Jürgen Habermas, that 'the exhaustion of utopian energies' is bound up with the perceived failure of modern social democracy and the welfare state – the more general expression of 'the utopian idea of a labouring society' that included not just Marxism but all hopes based on transforming the sphere of work and production.[34]

In both these cases the fate of utopia is tied to particular social philosophies and to particular social practices. While it is important to see that utopia does receive specific embodiments at different periods of its history, that is quite a different matter from identifying it with any of those embodiments, however comprehensive. Since the eighteenth century, utopia has certainly found its principal expression in socialism. But socialism is not one thing but many things; moreover, even if socialism has lost its capacity to inspire utopian visions, that does not exhaust utopia. There is still much for it to do.

Even in the nineteenth century socialism was a multifarious project. It included – to name only the principal forms – Owenism, Saint-Simonism, Fourierism and Fabianism in addition to Marxism, not to mention the anarchist and syndicalist varieties of socialism among the followers of Proudhon and Bakunin, or the decentralized socialism of John Stuart Mill. All these pointed in very different directions, as is well illustrated both by the socialist communities of nineteenth-century America and by the different kinds of socialist movements and parties that emerged in nineteenth-century Europe.[35] The different forms of the good life to which competing conceptions of socialism could lead were also vividly portrayed by two famous utopias of the late nineteenth century, Edward Bellamy's state-socialist *Looking Backward* (1888) and William Morris's eco-socialist *News from Nowhere* (1890).

In our century the Russian Revolution of 1917 and the Chinese Revolution of 1948 added yet other varieties to the mixture. And there have also been 'African socialism' and the socialism of the Israeli kibbutzim. No doubt the Soviet Union – like America in the parallel case of liberal democracy – came to be seen as the exemplary expression of the socialist utopia. Its downfall equally poses the greatest challenge yet to the whole socialist enterprise. There is no telling now whether socialism can survive the challenge. Nor do its devotees take much comfort from the fact that the socialism of Eastern Europe can justly be held not to have been very socialist at all, not, at any rate, as its putative progenitor Marx envisaged it. Andre Gunder Frank says that 'the real practicality' of this 'well-meaning' argument 'clashes with all world social-political-economic reality . . . It is wholly unrealistic to think that the damage of the whole experience to the idea of socialism . . . can simply be wished away by latter-day professions of one's own purity against others' former sins.'[36]

Is this being too pessimistic? Already there are commentators who have sought to rescue socialism from its productivist, factory-based orientation, as a 'utopia of work', and to see its relevance to the organization of life beyond the world of work. Drawing upon Marx's well-known observation in the third volume of *Capital* that the 'realm of freedom' lies beyond 'the realm of necessity', beyond, that is, economic life *per se*, thinkers such as André Gorz have elaborated a utopian vision of socialism that encompasses family, community and 'own work' in the social space and free time that could be released by the prodigious capacities of modern industrial technology. 'What is involved is the transition from a productivist work-based society to a society of liberated time in which the cultural and the societal are accorded greater importance than the economic . . .'[37]

The issue here is not so much the immediate (or even ultimate) practicability of this vision, as that it shows socialism's great capacity for renewal as an alternative to existing forms of society. And there are other current varieties, such as the 'eco-socialism' of many contemporary Green thinkers, or the 'market socialism' of many Social Democrats.[38] Indeed one might go so far as to say that as long as there is industrial civilization there will always be socialism. Socialism was born in the eighteenth century at the same time as industrial capitalism. It has always accompanied its evolution, as critic and 'counter-culture' to the values and practices of capitalism. It is even possible to argue that had it not been for socialism as its *alter ego* capitalism would have succumbed, as Marx predicted, to the contradictions of its development (though socialism would not necessarily have been its successor). Socialism has kept capitalism on its toes, has reminded it of its promises, has forced it to tone down its harshness and regulate its operation out of consideration for the social consequences that, disregarded, might have undermined its stability. Capitalism needs socialism; if it did not exist it would have to invent it.[39]

Nowhere is this more relevant now, perhaps, than in the post-communist societies of Central and Eastern Europe. In this region a veritable frenzy of pro-capitalist, pro-market enthusiasm, urged on by the IMF and sundry western economists, has seized intellectuals and politicians. East-Central Europe may think it has turned its back on utopia, but it has only too evidently exchanged one utopia for another, the capitalist and consumerist utopia. And America, still the world symbol of capitalism/consumerism, has somewhat to its surprise recovered something of its former utopian appeal, at least to non-Americans. Writing in the year of revolution, 1989, George Steiner observed:

It is a TV-revolution we are witnessing, a rush towards the 'California-promise' that America has offered to the common man on this tired earth. American standards of dress, nourishment, locomotion, entertainment, housing are today the concrete utopia in revolutions.[40]

But it is precisely in this sphere that socialism, not necessarily so-named, is likely to see its resurgence. The capitalist cornucopia, even if it fills within reasonable time in this economically shattered region, will not distribute its fruits at all equitably without active intervention by the state. That, after all, has long been the situation in Western capitalist societies, as John Kenneth Galbraith is fond of pointing out to East European free marketeers.[41] The populations of East-Central Europe seem already to be realizing this. They are reacting with growing disillusionment and apathy to the power struggles taking place in the political arena, where social policies are looked upon with suspicion as smacking of the old discredited communist system. In Poland and Hungary participation in parliamentary elections has dropped to 40 per cent. The massive group of non-voters provides, it has been plausibly argued, a natural constituency for a renewed social democratic alternative.[42] The demand for economic security and social justice is also showing a more active, and in some ways a more disturbing, side. In the Polish elections of October 1991, the socialists (ex-communists) gained 12 per cent of the vote; in the Bulgarian presidential election of January 1992, the socialist-backed candidate received 47 per cent of the vote; and in Russia Boris Yeltsin's vice-president, Alexander Rutskoi, found a heartfelt popular response to his fierce public criticism of the liberal free market policies of the government.[43]

If Eastern Europe may once more rediscover socialism, one might say that, whatever the fate of this or that socialist or labour party, socialism has never really left Western Europe. Communist parties may dissolve, but the social democratic presence remains strong in many Western European countries – France, Germany, Spain, Italy, Austria and the Scandinavian countries especially. The accelerating changes in work and employment that are being brought about by the micro-electronic revolution and the intensified globalization of capitalism are likely to produce sizeable constituencies for a serious challenge to unmodified free market philosophies. As André Gorz shows, the 'post-industrial pro-letariat' of the unemployed and the casually or insecurely employed is already close to 40–50 per cent of workers in many Western countries. 'The two-thirds society has already been left behind' – and with it, perhaps, the automatic majority of right-wing parties.[44] Socialism will need to work energetically to be the beneficiary of the sea-change in economic life; there are many other contenders for the voices and votes of the disinherited and dispossessed. But the material for the recovery is there.

R. W. Johnson has pointed to the deep entrenchment of socialism in the values and practices of Western Europe. Socialism, as much as capitalism, has become part of the fabric of European society. With communism seen off, it becomes easier to see the natural and necessary function of socialism in an economy and society dominated by the institutions of private property. Socialism here returns, as it should, to the legacy of the great social democratic movements of the late nineteenth century:

The world's leading social democratic party in 1992 is the same as in 1892, the German SPD. The lasting monument of this movement is a successful European tradition of mixed economies and extensive welfare nets which give concrete expression to the notion of a comprehensive citizenship in communities which, for all their faults, are closer to the Rawlsian ideal than any others on earth. The preservation, advancement and integration of these communities is, perhaps, the true vocation of Western socialists. In this they have large consensual majorities on their side, despite their current ragged state as parties.[45]

Even if socialism as a movement does not, at least for some time, regain its vitality, must that also be true of socialism as a utopia? Even those, such as Frank Manuel, who are performing the obsequies over Marxism as a theory and a practice, are still aware of its power as the most compelling embodiment of the European Enlightenment. 'The ideal of physical and psychic actualization as an individual human right, embedded in the Marxist utopia and long repressed, may yet find a place as a moral statement acceptable to both a secular and a religious humanism.'[46] The downfall of Marxism as a system may paradoxically release suppressed elements in Marxism that could regenerate utopia – not least in that part of Europe that has been most vehement in its rejection of both Marxism and utopia (which have been seen as synonymous). Erazim Kohák has argued that 'the absence of a legitimating vision may ultimately prove the biggest obstacle to building viable societies in the lands of the erstwhile Soviet empire.'[47] Even Milan Simecka, one of the most passionate critics of utopias, arrived finally at the view that for all their dangers utopias are an indispensable component of a true politics:

A world without utopias would be a world without social hope, a world of resignation to the status quo and the devalued slogans of everyday political life . . . We would be left with hopeless submission to an order which is only too natural, because it can, as yet, modestly feed the people, give them employment and a secure daily round. It is unable to provide for the unnatural demands of man, for the utopian ideas of its beginnings such as justice, freedom and tolerance, and to carry them further. This order no longer understands such demands, considering them unnatural and utopian; a remarkable case of amnesia.[48]

With this we have of course moved a long way from the specifics of Marxism or socialism. But the house of utopia, like that of Marxism itself, contains many chambers. Even if the socialist utopia, in its many guises, proves unpalatable, that still leaves a myriad of possible forms for utopia to take. Ecologists, taking their cue from Morris's *News from Nowhere* and, more recently, Huxley's *Island* (1962) and Ernest Callenbach's *Ecotopia* (1975), have seized upon utopia as an admirable vehicle for the expression of their planetary concerns. Ursula Le Guin's *The Dispossessed* (1974) has rightly been hailed not just as one of the best ecotopias, but even more for its rehabilitation of utopia as a literary genre. Le Guin also provides a bridge to the feminist utopia: the most thriving of the current reworkings of utopia, and one that has importantly re-established the connection with science fiction that lies at the root of the genre.[49]

There has even been, in a fittingly playful fashion, the elaboration of a 'liberal utopia', post-modernist style, which proclaims the contingency of self, morality and community but which can imagine an ideal social order in which the recognition of this contingency – by 'liberal ironists' – is the ground of private and public life.[50] This is attractive, but at first sight surprising. Have not the post modernists generally been among the most scornful critics of utopia? Utopia for them is identified with the belief in Reason, Progress and History, with the 'metanarratives' encompassing all of these in some unified view of humanity and its destiny. As such, utopia belongs with all supposedly scientific theories of society – on the scrap heap.[51]

But of course there is a utopia, or utopias, in postmodernism. The announcement of 'the end of history' and the rejection of all future-oriented speculation merely displaces utopia from time to space. To this extent postmodernists are returning to the older, pre-18th century, spatial forms of utopia, the kind inaugurated by More. The postmodernist utopia has been described as 'a vision of a neo-tribal paradise in which a set of spatially set forms of life carry on experiments, each in their own culture.'[52] But there is also a certain spatial dynamism in the vision, commensurate with the global reach of postmodernism. One is free, indeed encouraged, to move between local cultures, like a tourist. Disneyland may not unkindly be taken as some sort of model of the postmodernist world: a range of cultural experiences drawn from different times and places which one can mix according to taste.

Indeed, the 'spatialization of the temporal' in postmodernism has been seen by Fredric Jameson as a powerful force in revitalizing the utopian impulse of our time. In spatial utopias 'the transformation of social relations and political institutions is projected onto the vision of place and landscape, including the human body. Spatialization, then, whatever it may take away in the capacity to think time and History, also opens a door onto a whole new domain for libidinal investment of the Utopian and even the protopolitical type.' Jameson professes to find today, especially among postmodernist artists and writers, 'an unacknowledged "party of Utopia" . . .'[53] If this is so, if the desire to restore 'the broken unity' reasserts itself against all the forces of fragmentation currently ranged against it, then not only is there no 'death of utopia', but on the contrary, we find an affirmation of the persisting vitality of a way of thinking that Isaiah Berlin has seen as 'a central strand in the whole of western thought.'[54]

The Future of History

Does the likely persistence of socialism as an oppositional force, even an ideal, contradict the view of Francis Fukuyama and others that we have reached 'the end of history' – the end, that is, of the competition between fundamentally different ideologies? Not necessarily, and not by itself. For Fukuyama's argument is that nowhere in the world is there now a realistic alternative to the idea of liberal democracy, still less to its economic counterpart, capitalism or the market. Socialism may continue to provide a critical counterpoint to capitalist development, but it cannot offer itself any longer as a systematic alternative to it. The collapse of communism since 1989 has, for Fukuyama, been the decisive thing. It has confirmed the worldwide movement towards democracy that in the last decade or so has toppled dictators on all continents.

As mankind approaches the end of the millennium, the twin crises of authoritarianism and socialist central planning have left only one competitor standing in the ring as an ideology of potentially universal validity: liberal democracy, the doctrine of individual freedom and popular sovereignty.[55]

Despite some rude noises and scornful denunciations of Fukuyama, it is striking how few of his critics have answered his repeated challenge to them to show what might upset the hegemony of liberal democracy as a worldwide aspiration. Piotr Sztompka, for instance, calls Fukuyama's concept of the 'universal homogeneous state', based on liberal principles, 'a perverse, counter-utopian utopia'. But he then goes on to admit that 'there is a worldwide ideological and political trend toward liberal democracy . . . growing in salience and acceptance' – thus conceding the main point.[56]

The critics are probably right to say that Fukuyama smooths over persisting differences between contemporary states and nations, that he too readily embraces them with the cover-all term 'liberal democracy'. Alan Ryan observes that 'it is only from an altitude so great that most of human life is invisible that Japan and the United States could be passed off as examples of the same socio-political system.'[57]

But the existence of authoritarian capitalist regimes in Asia and elsewhere – Lee Kuan Yew of Singapore calls his system 'East Asian Confucian capitalism' – does not appear to constitute a major contradiction to Fukuyama's thesis. Fukuyama is himself too anxious to distinguish the capitalist economy from the liberal polity, regarding their joint victory as the result of the triumph of fundamentally different principles.[58] Historically they have in fact been closely, if not indissolubly, connected.[59] One need not argue a full-blooded materialist position to say that it is capitalism that has given the general character to modern liberal societies. It is capitalist institutions and values – private property, profit-seeking, individualism, consumerism – that colour the attitudes and beliefs of the majority of the populations of modern societies.

Certainly these attitudes can partially be offset by the persistence of traditional cultural features – for instance, the often-remarked 'group' orientation of the Japanese, which mitigates the extreme individualism of capitalism. But this does not seriously qualify the fundamentally transformative effect – as Marx argued – of capitalist social relations across the whole society. One of these effects is a tendency towards individualism and political democracy, though sometimes of a somewhat illiberal kind. But this is, despite Fukuyama, perhaps not the most important thing – it is certainly the most fragile one. When Fukuyama talks about the worldwide spread of liberal democracy, he is really talking about the worldwide victory of capitalism. And there certainly seems, at the moment, no real rival in sight.

The real challenge that Fukuyama throws up is when he says that 'we cannot picture to ourselves a world that is *essentially* different from the present one, and at the same time better.'[60] This is, once more, a rejection of the classic utopian function, on the grounds of its obsoleteness. Enough has already been said to suggest that this rejection is misplaced, the result partly of a misunderstanding of utopia's traditional concerns. But there is a need, nevertheless, to state why one might think that the engine of history has not stalled, that history has not reached its *telos*.

Fukuyama is right, I think, to say that the recrudescence of ethnic and national passions is no contradiction of his claims. They are, after all, in however rough a form, no more than reassertions of principles that are linked ultimately to the American and French Revolutions, the joint ancestors of liberal democracy. He is also right to point out that resurgent Islamic fundamentalism, a possibly competing ideology to liberalism, has had 'no appeal in areas that were not culturally Islamic to begin with. Young people in Berlin, Tokyo, Rio or Moscow are not rushing to don *chadors*, as they were once tempted by Communism.'[61]

But there are far greater challenges to liberalism and capitalism than these. Fukuyama is fully aware of the subjective and expressive discontents of the 'last man' – Nietzsche's term for a humanity bereft of the supports of religion and philosophy. Liberal capitalism, he argues, undermines the sense of solidarity and community. It creates a culture of amoral hedonism and consumerism. It might bore us to death, in its lack of challenge to our more active faculties. This is the price we pay for the freedom and plenty of the 'universal homogeneous state' of capitalist liberal democracy.[62] If only this were all! For if so, most of us might settle for a quiet private life of comfort and consumption, and let those who want to worry about the higher things of the mind.

But capitalist industrialism does not only strip us of culture and community. More dangerously, in the immediate future, it is undermining the life-support systems of the planet itself. This is where history comes back in, with a vengeance. If the challenges to liberal capitalism were no more than those Fukuyama indicates, it might indeed be plausible to say that it can see them off without too much trouble. But what if capitalism, consistent with its world-transforming potency, in its restless and relentless expansiveness consumes the very seed-corn of its being and growth? What if it threatens the health and habitations of whole cultures across the globe? How can it possibly be held, not simply that there is no more for utopias to do, but that historical choices of the most fundamental kind do not face us more urgently than ever before? What could be more challenging than the fate of the planet?

In facing this challenge we will have to see that liberal capitalism may not after all be the final form of history. Its excessive individualism may need to be severely restrained by national and international bodies concerned with regulating the use and disposal of the earth's resources. The invisible hand of the market may need to be made more visible and given more guidance in the interests of social stability and social justice. 'Consumer choice', in so far as it is more than a myth of manufacturers

and advertisers, might have to be curtailed out of consideration for the
finitude or scarcity of particular materials (not to mention the battered
sensibilities of supermarket shoppers), or because of the ecological
damage inflicted in the making or consuming of particular products, for
instance hamburgers, on a world scale.[63] There may even be the need for
the promotion of some sort of new religion, stressing mutualism and
planetary solidarity, in the face of the impending catastrophe.[64] Not for
nothing does Durkheim seem increasingly to be the prophet of the 21st
century.[65]

In all these ways, liberal capitalism may have to undergo such
extensive modification that it might become impossible to use the term
with any real meaning in the not too distant future. Communitarianism
and authoritarianism, not necessarily opposed to each other, could as
much be our future as some variety of liberal individualism. Certainly
there still seem to be some strong contenders for the soul of modern man,
even if some of them appear in novel form. Our historical condition – one
in which life itself is threatened with insupportable damage, perhaps even
extinction – is unprecedented. There is nothing to guarantee that we will
find our way out of this mess. But at the very least we can think about, we
must think about, alternatives to the system that has got us into it.

East Europeans are very well aware of the poisoning of their land and
the pollution of their atmosphere by unchecked industrialism. In their
case it was called socialism, in ours capitalism. Some Eastern Europeans
also see that the solution to their problems cannot therefore be the
wholesale importation of market capitalism in all its unadorned glory.[66]
In that sense East Europeans cannot, as some of them hope, go back to
their past to 'restart' their history. That history has been indelibly marked
by the Communist episode, and they must interrogate and come to terms
with that experience.[67] Even more importantly, to go back would be to
do no more than imitate the pattern – probably as dependent or
peripheral elements – of Western development. This pattern is now, in
several essential respects, unviable. There is indeed an opportunity, as
well as a need, for the 'rebirth of history'. That is one of the great
consequences of the 1989 revolutions. But we must understand this not
as the resumption of the sway of the past, but as the invention of
something new, a rebirth that is also a renewal of history.

6

The Metamorphosis of the Apocalyptic Myth: From Utopia to Science Fiction

VITA FORTUNATI

As history has demonstrated, and scholars of prophetic-apocalyptic thought such as Frank Kermode and Jacques Le Goff continue to remind us, no end-of-the-century fails to assert itself as a time of crisis, as a moment of passage. That this should be so is hardly surprising, as the moment lends itself so naturally to the contemplation of both the 'end' and the 'beginning' – a brand new start to a brand new era. This fast-approaching end-of-the-century of ours is obviously no different. Already it is permeated with apocalyptic and eschatological sentiments, and these oblige scholars of utopia, although caught up in the living of this critical time themselves, to investigate the inextricable link between utopia and millenarianism; that is, the link between what emerges as a rational and secular type of future planning, and what is a purely religious belief in the supreme instant of mankind's redemption and rebirth.

In approaching this millennial change of ours as one that constructs an exceptional sort of bridge with the future, there is certainly no shortage of events and signs presaging its importance. To name but a few: the fact that in some part of the globe, at any given time, a state of what can only be defined as war exists; the fact that our physical environment is deteriorating at an ever-faster and more alarming rate; the phenomenon of overpopulation, and the corresponding inability of economic science to come up with even partially credible answers to the abject poverty and misery in which four-fifths of the world's inhabitants are forced to live; and the radical, even genetic, manipulation of living organisms, including human beings, that has been made possible by an overwhelming, exponential increase in scientific discoveries. Furthermore, in world politics the apparent failure of Communism as a viable alternative – a myth, it should be stressed, which fairly dominated our century – leaves us face to face with the terrifying vision of a single world power that is now free to operate unchecked, unopposed.

Clearly, such a scenario lacks none of the requisite characteristics of the apocalyptic paradigm, and it is hardly a coincidence that, as the American historian Paul Boyer warns in his *When Time Shall Be No More*, the United States is currently overrun with a rash of prophetic, irrational impulses.[1] The propaganda that was produced by the media in America during the recent Gulf War serves as one example, and the avalanche of religious paperbacks that at present feature Saddam Hussein as the new Antichrist who would rebuild 'the lost city of Babylon', heralding the coming of Armageddon, is an even better one.

It seems an appropriate time, then, to re-examine this myth of the Apocalypse within utopian studies, not least because such a re-examination will allow us to better see how at the base of the utopian proposal there is an odd, but undeniably intricate, mixture of both rational-secular and mythical-religious elements. As Manuel so aptly put it, utopia is 'a hybrid plant, born of the crossing of the paradisical belief of Judeo-Christian religion with the Hellenic myth of an ideal city on earth.'[2] Indeed, those who have gone in search of the archetypes of the utopian idea (e.g. C. Walsh, F. Polak, J. O. Herzler) have been obliged to admit that the Greek ideals of *The Republic* and Plato's Laws meet and intermingle with the Judeo-Christian Biblical tradition – especially its Messianic (*parousia*), millenarian (*chiliasmos*), and apocalyptic aspects – even in the earliest traces of the genre. And yet, I suggest, decidedly less attention has been paid to the influence of the Bible on the utopian tradition, than to the influence of Classical thought.

It is this dual origin which makes utopia the complex concept that it is, it being inevitable that the substantive differences in the two philosophical traditions should inform the utopian vision in markedly diverse ways. Boman, in his seminal comparative study of Greek and Hebrew philosophy, notes how the Greek conception of history is cyclical, without direction, and how the divinity in Plato is supreme, immutable. In the Hebrew vision, on the other hand, it is fluidity that prevails.[3] The Hebrew God is dynamic, an agent who intervenes directly in history – in the events which mark the existence of His chosen people. History is seen as working towards a goal, pre-destined by an omniscient Creator. Whereas Hebrew thought moves primarily in time, the realm of its Greek counterpart is more properly space (think for a moment of the characteristic spaces of mythical Hellas: the Elysian Fields or the 'Isles of the Blessed', Atlantis etc.). It is precisely this sense of historical becoming that Hebrew thought introduces into the utopian tradition: a teleologic time that progresses towards an end that is the Promised Land. The Apocalypse – a perfect illustration of the Biblical paradigm that sees the history of man as controlled by a well-defined and detailed design – reveals this same teleologic conception: salvation and the new world lie at the end of a purposeful path that began with the first breath of Creation and which eventually leads to the Apocalypse itself.

Before examining the metamorphosis of the Apocalyptic myth in the period between the English anti-utopian novels of the last *fin de siècle* and the anti-utopian science fiction of the 1970s, I will attempt to outline briefly some of the recurring characteristics of this Apocalyptic paradigm.

Firstly, precisely because the Apocalypse is such a brilliant metaphor for the human condition, it has proved to be an elastic, flexible myth with a significance that has been continually modified in successive periods of history. The Antichrist, for instance, has over time variously taken on the semblance of Mohammed, Hitler, Mussolini, and not a few disreputable Popes.

Secondly, the Apocalypse, as Abrams reminds us, is a dual-myth with a bipolar internal structure of positive and negative elements.[4] The apocalyptic paradigm is thus distinguished by a juxtaposition of Light vs Dark, Death vs Rebirth, Terror and Decadence vs Hope and Regeneration – a symbolically rich Manichaean vision in which Fire and Water become the principle signs of cosmic destruction.

Thirdly, the three basic elements of apocalyptic writing are: Destruction, Judgement and Regeneration. The rhetoric of this writing belongs to he who exudes awareness of his superiority, his worthiness to be spokesman for the elect, the chosen heir to the apocalyptic vision.

Fourthly, in the rewriting of the myth, the 'end' may take on various nuances. It can be total, where end-of-the-world also translates into an end-of-the-words with which the apocalyptic event can be portrayed. Or it may be an end that curves back upon itself, an eternal tension towards re-commencement – *In my end is my beginning*. Or it may be a liberating end, an end that renews because with it comes real re-generation.

Fifthly, there is that aspect of the myth of the Apocalypse that lays bare deep-rooted, timeless fears: the fear of the powers of Nature; the fear of separation and loneliness; the fear of death.

Sixthly, the Apocalypse functions internally rather than externally, as something close at hand rather than *other*, exciting a sentiment not unlike the kind of morbid fascination with which, in much contemporary science fiction, one contemplates the end of one's own life and world.

Finally, I believe we should remark, if only in passing, on the difference between what I would like to call the aesthetic of written destruction, an aesthetic rooted in the plastic power of the word, and that of the silver screen, the moving picture, an aesthetic of the imposing, dramatic power of the bigger-than-lifesize image, a world of superlatives and of special effects.[5]

The English *fin de siécle* gave us a particularly rich vein of anti-utopian novels from which none of the above ingredients of the apocalyptic paradigm has been left out, and in which the potent imagery of John the Evangelist is made to serve the purpose of representing the fear of the future that was rampant at the time.

The 1880s witnessed a deep crisis in England, one to which E. J. Hobsbawm gave the name 'Great Depression' – a fitting label for the general state of malaise and pessimism. The profound changes in the social structure, the violent process of urbanization, the effects of the Industrial Revolution on the countryside, the damage wrought on the ecology, the new means of production being implemented and, above all, the absolute triumph of technology – all of these played a part in creating a sense of unease and fear.

In this climate of profound uncertainty, of a loss of faith in the automatic progress that capitalism had been thought to guarantee, the myth of the Apocalype began to be re-thought and re-utilized: *News From Nowhere* by William Morris; *After London* by R. Jefferies; W. Hudson's *A Crystal Age*; *The Time Machine* by H. G. Wells and E. M. Forster's *The Machine Stops* all have this great myth as their backdrop. Moreover, all these works foreshadow the metamorphosis that the apocalyptic myth has undergone in our contemporary science fiction genre; this metamorphosis is discussed later in this essay with reference to the novels of John Wyndham, Brian Aldiss and J. G. Ballard.

In Morris's *News From Nowhere* (1890), the Apocalypse is evoked only to be exorcized by a total rebirth. Here what we are dealing with is a regenerative Apocalypse, one that has a profound cathartic significance: from the ruins of a civilization there arises a society that is renewed and purified of all past wrongs. Morris revisits the myth by means of paradigm of sin/punishment – expiation/rebirth. The society of the evil-doers, i.e. that of capitalism and the industrial society as a whole, is defeated by the proletarian class struggle. The prophetic vision, realized through dream, takes on a strong apocalyptic tint: the new world can come about only as a result of the revolution of the proletariat, a historical event that Morris, due to his own cultural background and reading, cannot help but translate into terms of Good vs Evil, the age-old struggle between the forces of Light and those of Darkness. It is sometimes overlooked that Morris included in his otherwise Edenic *News From Nowhere* a lengthy and quite tough-minded chapter dedicated to the history of the transition from Capitalism to the garden world of the future, including scenes of brutal massacres, paramilitary fascism, a great general strike, and the temporary break-down of civilization.[6] In Morris's utopian vision we get a clear sense of palingenesis, a messianic hope in salvation, in better times to come. To arrive at this better state, however, man must first return to his primitive beginnings – a return to a 'barbaric' state which, for Morris, carries the positive connotations of a civilization in its innocent infancy.

In *After London* (1885), Jefferies also re-thinks the apocalyptic myth, but the sense of regeneration and future aspiration found in Morris is absent. In this novel all progress towards a better world is missing, for man is no longer seen as capable of rebirth. Terrifying images inspired by the Bible – falling stars, monsters emerging from the deep, scourges that rain down upon the earth in the form of earthquakes, hail and fire – are employed to depict the progressive deterioration of England, and particularly London. The origin of the cataclysm is veiled in mystery, but its consequences are devastating: the physical and atmospheric condition of England is violently transformed, creating an immense forest in which ferocious beasts roam. From the earth arise yellow vapours and a noxious stench. London is deserted, its streets strewn with the skeletons of its past inhabitants. From stagnant, slimy waters monstrous amor-phous shapes emerge to lurk about in the night. *After London* records the progressive barbarization of the vegetable, animal and human kingdoms.

What we have in Jefferies' novel is a dark, obsessive, menacing Apocalypse that allows us to categorize *After London* as the first 'catastrophic' novel. This sub-category of science fiction was to prolifer-ate after the atom bomb was dropped on Hiroshima in 1945, and its main theme was the terror felt by those living on the eve of total destruction. In *After London* there is no palingenetic sense, and the cyclical historical process which humanity is made to undergo does not involve regener-ation. In contrast to Morris, for Jefferies the return to nature merely signifies a return to a wild, barbaric state. His portrait of the Dark Ages is violent and bloodthirsty; his creatures are deceitful and cruel.

Another text written in the 1880s which highlights this catastrophic premonition of the end of the world is Hudson's anti-utopian *A Crystal Age*, the crystal serving as a metaphor for the new world thus envisioned: coldly pure, perfect, hard and static. With this novel, Hudson proclaims his antagonism towards the violence and aggression that marked the industrial society of his times; he proposes instead a model agricultural community that has learned to do without technological 'progress', and which submits to Nature.

Yet the earthly paradise of *A Crystal Age* is ambiguous. No longer are we in the sun-baked and harmonic 'Garden Tree' of Morris, where languid idleness alternates with creative activity. In Hudson's utopia there is a stasis, an inactivity that tastes of death. From this cold and crystal-like stasis, all trace of passion and sexual attraction – considered an impetus to violence, disorder and unhappiness – have been eliminated.

In H. G. Wells's *The Time Machine* (1895) and E. M. Forster's *The Machine Stops* (1909), the apocalyptic vision does not serve to celebrate the end of the world, but rather functions as a sort of warning cry that is meant to force humanity to sit up and take notice of its self-destructive practices. Wells takes aim at the whole concept of evolution, paradoxically inverting the Darwinian theory into one of regression. The final pages of *The Time Machine* constitute a menacing threat, as well as a challenge, to the machine society. The apocalyptic scene is of a deserted beach that is occupied by the last survivor – a gigantic crab stretching out its claws against the bottom of a blood-red sea.

The Biblical myth of the Apocalypse also colours the conclusion to Forster's *The Machine Stops*, in which the Machine does just that – causing the underground mechanical city to explode. Yet from the ashes of the city and the violent demise of its inhabitants, their bodies torn and writhing in agony before the reader's eyes, humanity will once again rise up. The final words spoken by Kuno, the hero who rebels against the machine civilization and succeeds in escaping from this underground hell and reaching the starlit heavens, reveal the regenerative significance that the Apocalypse still has in Forster:[7]

'We have come back to our own. We die, but we have recaptured life, as it was in Wessex, when Ailfrid overthrew the Danes. We know what they know outside, they who dwelt in the cloud that is the colour of a pearl.'

'But, Kuno, is it true? Are there still men on the surface of the earth? Is this – this tunnel, this poisoned darkness – really not the end?'

He replied:

'I have seen them, spoken to them, loved them. They are hiding in the mist and the ferns until our civilization stops. To-day they are the Homeless – to-morrow –'

'Oh, to-morrow – some fool will start the Machine again, to-morrow.'

'Never,' said Kuno, 'never. Humanity has learnt its lesson.'

As he spoke the whole city was broken like a honey comb. An air-ship had sailed in through the vomitory into a ruined wharf. It crashed downwards, exploding as it went, rending gallery after gallery with its wings of steel. For a moment they saw the nations of the dead, and, before they joined them, scraps of the untainted sky.[8]

The Bible, then, was clearly a source of potent mythological imagery for the writers of the 1880s, and it continued to be mined by their 'descendants' – the science fiction writers of the 1960s and 1970s. These modern writers again employed the myth of the end of the world, but they were able to enrich it with references to the potential for self-destruction that man had perfected in the meantime.

Wyndham's works appear to be proof of how the apocalyptic myth, and particularly the 'catastrophic' side of it, has penetrated popular fiction. Wyndham too, following in the tracks of a good number of the Western World's eschatological movements, employs this Biblical imagery of destruction and plague, and even that of a new Leviathan rising up from the sea to swallow whole the paltry civilization of man.

In Wyndham, the cycle of death and rebirth, of destruction and regeneration (which is typical of the 'evolutionary utopias' modelled upon Olaf Stapledon's encyclopaedic *Last and First Man*) is represented as a tension towards, a search for, a new and better world. The idea of human perfectability has not yet vanished completely, and lives on in this search for utopia, a quest which informs both *The Day of the Triffids* (1951) and *The Chrysalids* (1955). In these novels the new, fictitious civilization serves as a parable for the real world, and suffers once again the catastrophic end that is the prerequisite of future regeneration. In Wyndham the notion of the palingenesis of a society – once it has been 'punished' and made to undergo overwhelming trials and tribulations in order to atone for its sins – is recuperated:

Tribulation wasn't just tempest, hurricanes, floods and fires like the things they had in the Bible. It was all of them together – and something a lot worse too.[9]

Thus it is that Wyndham's novels take on a warning function, a warning to humanity to repent, to mend its ways. At the same time, however, they reflect a firm belief in humanity's capacity for so doing, for being born again. Although the possibility that humanity could well come to the same end as the dinosaurs, that it too could find itself replaced with a 'superior' race, is always present, what ultimately triumphs in Wyndham is the positive apocalyptic vision, the new world now purified and regenerated. Man not only survives, he develops a new and more mature awareness of himself and his world. In any case, Wyndham's 'catastrophes' remain basically 'positive': his 'novels of survival' always afford a vision of a better future.

Such optimism rapidly loses ground in the work of the 'new wave' of science fiction writers, such as Aldiss and Ballard. In their novels the apocalyptic myth is progressively emptied of its full significance, of its cathartic and regenerative powers. The end of our civilization is portrayed as inevitable because of qualities inherent in human nature. The 'heroes' of these tales are dazzled creatures with one blinding ambition: destruction, if not self-destruction. As D. Ketterer has pointed out, here the subversion, the catastrophe, has truly become one of the mind.[10]

Brian Aldiss is one of the spokesmen for this new apocalyptic vision. In *Greybeard* (1964), the human race is bereft of its procreative capacity, and overcome with a monstrous and tragic impulse to murder its offspring; in his next novel, *Earthworks* (1965), the earth is conversely teeming with human beings and the planet, overrun, has been transformed into a veritable 'wasteland', stripped of all resources, having one, sole, paradoxical chance for survival: a nuclear holocaust. Aldiss's version of the Apocalypse is obsessive and menacing, and he develops a narrative technique that is capable of reflecting this terrifying vision. For instance, the narration is no longer linear. Instead, there is series of dislocated visions, indeed hallucinations, before which the reader is frankly disoriented, bewildered.

The metamorphosis of the Apocalypse reaches its climax, however, with the novels of J. G. Ballard, the writer who Robert Louit has acutely defined as 'le chirugien de l'Apocalypse'. All of his tales are marked by a horrifying admission that humanity essentially yearns for this Apocalypse, that it feeds upon disaster, that it actually pursues its own death, its total annihilation. In such a perspective, any argument for regeneration is quite clearly impossible, not least because Ballard's characters consciously deny the possibility. The Apocalypse is no longer feared; it is *desired*. It is no longer fought against; it is embraced. It has become a goal, an ambition, a means to fulfillment.[11]

Gone are the straight-thinking heroes who tirelessly and tenaciously struggle against all odds to create their future and that of their planet. Here we have men – almost always doctors, surgeons or bacteriologists – attracted by death, by cadavers, by corruption and decay. They are disturbingly passive creatures, engaged in an impossible search for some meaning to their existence in a world that becomes progressively more unreal. Their inability to act or react leads them, slowly but surely, to surrender to the haunting figments of their own imaginations; the final vision of this immobile and monadic world is one of total degradation, utter entropy, the negation of each and every energy.

Ballard's novels are a version of the Biblical myth that is now completely devoid of its cathartic, regenerative significance. The angels of the Apocalypse have been transformed into hideous lepers who perform their ecstatic and macabre dance in the crystallized forests of a hopeless world, pursuing a death with which their bodies are already clearly marked, but which remains an object of desire, indeed a necessity. No trace of palingenesis is to be found in Ballard. The waters of *The Drowned World* (1962) are not those of a baptism, leading to a new life, but rather those of the Biblical flood, bringing annihilation. In the face of death, however, humanity does not flee in terror. Rather it turns toward it yearningly, intent on embracing its end as one would a cherished lover that one cannot live without.

The metamorphosis that the myth undergoes in the transition that I have described in this essay is clearly remarkable. From the purifying function of the apocalyptic vision, as employed by authors such as Wyndham, who still believe in the regeneration of mankind, we pass to the terrifying utter hopelessness and nihilism of Ballard, in whose works we witness the climax, and closure, of the apocalyptic cycle – the total triumph of entropy, the unqualified negation of the possibility of motion in space or time. In the surreal world of Ballard, the terrible road to salvation is through stasis, crystallization:

And I am convinced, Paul, that the sun itself has begun to effloresce. At sunset, when its disc is veiled by the crimson dust, it seems to be crossed by a distinctive lattice-work, a vast portcullis that will one day spread outwards to the planets and the stars halting them in their courses [. . .] there is an immense reward to be found in that forest. There the transfiguration of all living and inanimate forms occurs before our eyes, the gift of immortality a direct consequence of the surrender by each of us of our own physical and temporal identities.[12]

7
'Politics Here is Death':
William Burroughs's Cities of the Red Night

DAVID AYERS

William Burroughs remains for most an icon rather than an author. His work challenges taste and, in its most experimental forms, patience. His celebration of homosexuality offends the right, while his hostility to women offends the left. His work has suffered academic neglect, yet he is an author's author whose impact on American and European writing has been marked. This essay is intended to place Burroughs in the context of utopian studies, through an analysis of his novel *Cities of the Red Night* (1981). The general background of this type of novel is outlined in Tom Moylan's *Demand the Impossible*, which analyses the genre of 'Critical Utopia' in the so-called 'post-SF' writing of the Seventies, although without specific reference to Burroughs.[1] This essay addresses itself primarily to the complex internal contours of the work, although some reference is made to the context of the work's genesis in the counter-culture. No attempt is made to accommodate the novel to a generic model of utopia, although the themes and modes of utopia are discovered throughout, revealing Burroughs to be as much a utopian fictionist as a novelist in any conventional sense.

The foreword to *Cities of the Red Night* is entitled simply 'Fore!', expressing the utopian impulse by suppressing the 'word' – which is both the medium of all utopian projection and the phantasmal essence of utopia itself. That 'foreword' becomes 'forward' in the economy of Burroughs's text precisely indicates the distinction between action and dream which is in many ways the subject – the productive dialectic – of the greater part of his work. This foreword is titled 'Fore' but stumbles in its own forward motion. Indeed, it might well be called 'Aft', as what it names is not a possible future, but an unrealized and now impossible present, extrapolated from a history that was never to be. This writing – the rewriting of history with the goal of postulating a more desirable outcome – is termed by Burroughs 'retroactive Utopia'.[2]

By situating utopia in the past, and emphasizing above all that the historic conditions for its realization have now passed and can never again return, Burroughs imbues the utopian with nostalgia at the same moment that he relegates it to daydreaming. Because utopia is thus not only unrealized, but unrealizable, he will concentrate less on the conditions of any projected utopia than on the conditions of the production of the utopian image in fantasy and writing, which become privileged themes in his work. While he demonstrates a sceptical awareness of the potential for corruption within any attempt to practice utopia, Burroughs is especially alert to the biological factors which may mitigate potential social perfectibility. So while the Burrovian ideal is often a type of Edenic primitive commune, from which women have been expunged and where sexuality is based on a type of communal free love, his 'Wild Boys' combine with their boyish liveliness and cleverness a cruelty and depravity which are seen as the inevitable features of man in a state of 'nature'. *Cities of the Red Night*, in one of its aspects, is an exploration of the ambiguous processes by which utopia is threatened in the very attempt to realize it, and the work serves as an oblique commentary on the aspirations of the Sixties counter-culture and the New Left.

Yet it is the fact of writing which is paramount over any actual utopian content. The conviction of Burroughs's earlier work was that individual existence is essentially generated by a predetermined 'reality script' which is the product of a non-human force, an abstract power sometimes represented as a failed or malevolent deity.[3] The stated objective of *The Ticket That Exploded* (1962) and *Nova Express* (1964) is to 'rub out the word', to achieve liberation by disrupting language to the point where its power to control is broken. In his later work, which almost entirely abandons the drastic 'cut-up' technique, this pessimistic perception of language is modified by an examination of the possibility that writing can equally be liberative in its capacity to rewrite the allegedly real. However, the vision of liberation is always deployed alongside a vision of total closure: there is no sense in which narrator, protagonist or reader can ever 'really' escape, and the view that reality is essentially 'pre-recorded' or 'pre-sent', a recurrent concept in the earlier work, remains dominant.

The retroactive utopia of *Cities of the Red Night* is an attempt to imagine a type of communism based on the traditional libertarian principles of revolutionary America.[4] It is argued that these principles had been put into practice a hundred years earlier by pirate communes.[5] Burroughs quotes a work on piracy, *Under the Black Flag* (1927) by Don Carlos Seitz, which outlines the story of the pirate Captain Mission.

Burroughs purports to take at face value Seitz's account of Mission, who allegedly established his ship as a kind of democratic and egalitarian 'republic of the sea', engaging in piracy for reasons of self-preservation, not massacring the crews of captured ships but inviting them to join the collective enterprise. Mission is then said to have founded a Republic in Madagascar, called Libertatia, with a constitution called the Articles which instituted democratic rule by referendum, the abolition of slavery and of the death penalty, and freedom of religion. This ideal commonwealth was too small to survive, but we are invited to contemplate what the survival of such a colony and others like it might have meant. Imitations would have sprung up throughout the colonized areas – South America, the West Indies, Africa and the Far East. These fortified colonies would form a loose federation drawing an ever increasing support from victims of the colonial powers throughout the world.[6] The new republics would have been opposed by the existing European powers, but would have survived through the use of guerrilla tactics: Vietnam and, implicitly, Mao are the contemporary analogues. The white man would be admitted as an equal, but never again as colonial master,[7] while the excesses of the industrial revolution would be reversed, as factory workers would abandon their cities and be welcomed in the 'Articulated areas', which are portrayed as a land of natural abundance.[8]

This 'retroactive Utopia' was a real possibility in terms of the available technology and social philosophy of the period, Burroughs notes, regretting that its moment is now passed.[9] While Burroughs seems genuinely to advance this proposal as an ideal, he does not reveal whether he knows the story of Mission to be in fact a plausible forgery. It is found in the second volume of Daniel Defoe's *A General History of the Pyrates* (1728), a fascinating work in its own right.[10] Alongside more or less factual accounts of piracy Defoe inserts this invented account of the Lockean Captain Mission. Mission's libertarianism is fuelled by a renegade priest, his constant companion, who educates him in Deism and egalitarianism. In Burroughs's novel, the story of Mission forms a credible historical overture which seems to ground the fictional elaborations that follow in some kind of reality. Yet in a subtle act of treachery which predicts one of the central themes of the narrative, this seeming history turns out to be just another piece of utopian forgery.[11]

The overt contention of the foreword to *Cities of the Red Night* is that the chance of establishing the libertarian and communistic utopia has passed, and that although writing can fancifully extrapolate from the past it is in the imagination rather than in any reality – the reality of the real being already in Burroughs *sous rature* – that Utopia exists. What Burroughs sets out to examine in the bulk of the narrative is the nature of this generative fantasy, and the narratives and situations that it generates.

It is not necessary here to outline every element of the multiple plots of *Cities of the Red Night*. Some of these plots develop intermittently over several chapters, while others are established in a single chapter and then discontinued. Each of the narratives is derived from one or other variety of popular fiction. At one point the library of Audrey – a protagonist and writer identified with Burroughs himself in a variety of manifestations – is introduced. Its contents include '*Amazing Stories*, *Weird Tales*, *Adventure Stories* and a stack of *Little Blue Books*',[12] and these are the ultimate sources of the genre fiction – detective, adventure, mystery, horror and science fiction – that sustains the narrative impulse of the Burrovian text.

It is however possible to identify three main threads and three main protagonists in *Cities of the Red Night*, as these are at first, to some extent, kept separate. One plot, set in 1702, concerns the fate of Noah Blake, the young son of a gunsmith who joins a strangely crewed ship which turns out to be part of a plot to establish a string of colonies on the model of Captain Mission. Generic adventure and pirate fiction underpin this strand. The second narrative concerns the private detective (or 'private asshole') Clem Snide, whose methods and interests are more magical than conventional. He stumbles across a bizarre (and ultimately incomprehensible) plot which evolves around the long lost Cities of the Red Night. These cities are known only in a magical book which is lost, although fragments of copies survive. Snide is hired to locate and ultimately to write the lost book (the slippage from writing history as discovery and transcription, to writing history as invention and forgery being a crucial one within the Burrovian economy). The third thread concerns the Cities themselves, and largely describes the activities of Audrey Carsons, a heroic and vicious Wild Boy who is engaged in a violent struggle. This struggle is at times no more than criminal and gratuitous, but at other times it becomes part of a boys' own fantasy of the righteous extermination of evil or inhuman enemies. To the interests of the various genres of boys' fiction, each of these narratives adds a liberal dose of the homoerotic fantasy for which Burroughs is famous.

The narratives are connected by the occurrence in each of mysterious figures: Nordenholz, the Iguana Twins, the Countess de Vile and the Countess de Gulpa. These characters appear in a variety of guises and seem to belong to a global conspiracy, the mechanics of which are never clearly articulated. The plots mutate from one genre to another, just as the characters at first allude to each other and then blend into each other. Not only these 'enemy' characters, but the protagonists themselves, become blended together. Noah Blake is entirely elided from the narrative, while Clem Snide, the writer of the book of the Cities of the Red Night, blends into Audrey Carsons, one of the characters in his own narrative.[13]

This folding and refolding of narrative levels might easily be adopted into general accounts of metafiction and the postmodern. However, it is worth pausing to disengage Burroughs's objectives and the specific effects obtained. Burroughs starts from the radical and seemingly mystical assumption that all 'reality' is in some sense 'written', that the present is the pre-recorded code of a malign and absent creator. Therefore to read/write the 'self' is at some level to reinscribe the real. Fantasies (particularly those of boyhood), and the reading which feeds them, are liberative precisely because they challenge the real of the malign creator. But in their turn they are or may be part of the pre-recorded script, and all such fantasies are demonstrated by Burroughs to be profoundly equivocal.

Those sections of the narrative that deal with Noah Blake negate the promise of the utopian speculation of the foreword. Blake and his young companions join a mysterious ship, *The Great White* commanded by Captain Jones, which is sailing out of Boston. Early on in the story, the connection with Captain Mission is implied by Captain Jones's reference to signing 'the Articles' before joining the ship. But Jones has a side to him that Mission lacked: he is known as 'Opium Jones' and pays double wages to his hands as unacknowledged compensation for the risk they run as smugglers. Once at sea, the crew of the ship is augmented by the appearance of two mysterious passengers: Juan and Maria Cocuera de Fuentes, twins with 'greenish complexions',[14] who are also known as the 'Iguana twins'. The nature and motivation of these figures is unstated. Their function is motivic: they recur in another guise in the Clem Snide narrative, but they also constitute a variation on the Venusian boy-girl motif of *The Ticket That Exploded*. The radically disjointed narrative of *The Ticket That Exploded* uses science fiction to construct a type of emblematic theology that explains the undermining of the human condition by an intergalactic conspiracy of parasitic alien beings known as the Nova Mob. One element of this conspiracy – and this is a theme to which Burroughs frequently returns – is the undermining of the human species through the introduction of sexuality in the so-called 'Operation Other-Half', conducted by 'Green Boy-Girls from the terminal sewers of Venus'.[15] Although the twins are never revealed to be part of the malign alien conspiracy, the sexual difference which they emblematize and embody – the ultimately alien division of flesh – is the original sin which has always already undermined the potential for perfectibility of the human species.

When *The Great White* is taken over by a pirate ship in a pre-arranged operation, the elision between the outlaw life and the alternative social project is made. The pirates and the smuggler have established a free republic like that of Captain Mission, based in 'Port Roger', Panama.

The outlaw commune anticipates a struggle against the imperial giant, Spain. Noah Blake is needed in his capacity as an arms manufacturer and designer, a profession with mystical and metaphysical dimensions: mystical in its cultivation of special knowledges which in turn have the magical and metaphysical power to alter reality by blowing a 'hole in time'.[16] As if to spark misgiving, Blake arrives in Port Roger on 1 April 1702. The aims of the new republic are outlined at a meeting of its leaders. Spain is the enemy, and the weapon that will destroy Spain is the very peoples that it has enslaved.[17] Their utopian project adopts the ideals of Captain Mission but differs in two important respects: its expansionism, based on guerrilla warfare and on an arms-development programme, and its farming of opium, not only for exploitation as an export crop alongside rum and sugar, but for its 'tranquilizing and stabilizing effect' on the population of the republic itself. Just as *The Naked Lunch* posited a society based on pyramids of control resembling those of drug pusher to addict,[18] so this seeming Utopia is predicated from the outset on the use of drugs and control: the leaders will control the opium and addict their own people, who will thereby become dependent on them.[19]

The Naked Lunch had already advanced a vision of social control based on drugs, and had postulated a type of 'control addiction' as powerful as any drug addiction; now Mission's utopia is thwarted and transformed to dystopia as the desire to control asserts itself over the desire to liberate. As the military fortunes of the republic advance, Noah Blake begins to treat captured Spanish NCOs and Inquisitors with a cruelty that is the mirror of their own,[20] and is shown to be completing the transformation from revolutionary into tyrant.

At this rather moralistic juncture in the tale, which reveals something like 'human nature' in its cruel and power addicted form, the Noah Blake narrative is broken off to make way for the fabulous transformation of the Snide/Carsons narrative; Burroughs, having developed the conventional narrative expectations of his reader, proceeds to dismantle them.

Burroughs's pessimism about human potential takes many forms, but usually identifies as a root factor addiction to sex or power, represented as being a kind of debilitating vampirism. While the Noah Blake narrative explores the corruption of power in terms that are (perhaps surprisingly) relatively conventional, the plots more directly concerned with the Cities of the Red Night – the Clem Snide and Audrey Carsons plots – advance Burroughs's own version of the myth of the Fall in the terms of science fiction. This suggests that Burroughs, who is often described as a Swiftian satirist,[21] might be more accurately compared to Nathaniel Hawthorne as a theological pessimist and a documenter of Original Sin. The Fall occupies a prime place in Burroughs's work, as it does in that of Hawthorne. Each tends to construct a narrative around an absent centre – that absent Original Sin which is never accessible as an event or meaning by narrative or other means, but the consequences of which play themselves out endlessly. Original Sin is, after all, the origin of narrative – as if narrative itself were sin – and the utopian impulse represents the drive to recreate the lost paradisal plenitude and to end narrative, to conclude history in regained stasis.

Burroughs perhaps plays Hawthorne to Marcuse's Emerson or Ginsberg's Whitman. While he revives Hawthorne's concern with Original Sin, he does so within a complex and evasive economy of narrative and ideas. He deploys a Gnostic conception of the human Fall, which preserves as its central ideal the escape of the spark of the human soul from the deadness of matter into which it has been treacherously thrown.[22] Elsewhere in Burroughs's work the escape from matter is posited as a mystical escape into the silence of space, a freedom from flesh and language, or even as a biological mutation which will take the human species into space, or into the Western Lands beyond death.[23] *Cities of the Red Night* hesitates to directly propose these far-fetched mystical or biological solutions, which in any case remain merely figures rather than the expression of anything which might be termed 'belief': utterances of an enigmatic and ironically detached Burroughs. But *Cities of the Red Night* does maintain, and indeed is maintained by, the framing figure of the Fall, which is represented both in terms of the Eden myth and in terms of Burroughs's own mythology of the B-23 virus and the Cities of the Red Night.

The B-23 virus is the central motif of the two Cities of the Red Night narratives, which are developed in Books Two and Three. It is introduced in Book One in two of the fragmentary and subsequently undeveloped narratives which preface the two main narratives, sketching the virulent recurrence of B-23 in the contemporary world. In 'Politics Here is Death' two doctors (favoured types in Burroughs's depiction of the modern scientific dystopia since his introduction of the Dr Benway character in *The Naked Lunch*) debate the nature and origins of B-23 and the fatal 'Red Fever' which it causes. B-23 is described as 'the virus of biological mutation', and is intimately connected with the evolution of the human species. Its symptoms are 'fever, rash, a characteristic odor, sexual frenzies, obsession with sex and death' – the symptoms of 'love'. The separation of Eve from Adam was akin to the separation of a virus from a healthy cell, and consequently 'we are all tainted with viral origins. The whole quality of human consciousness, as expressed in male and female, is basically a virus mechanism.'[24] B-23 is 'the *human virus*', and the result of its malignant outbreak is that the 'whole human position is no longer tenable'.[25] Burroughs's views, as advocated over a range of his work from *The Naked Lunch* through to *The Western Lands*, are complex and wilfully inconsistent. One of the most frequently recurring elements, however, is this view that the human species is biologically flawed, by sexual and other addictive vampirisms: or, as he controversially puts it elsewhere in terms that radically modernize the Eden myth, 'Women are a Biological mistake'.[26] This modernized, science fiction model of Original Sin underpins two areas of *Cities of the Red Night*: the description of the Cities of the Red Night themselves in both their fallen, dystopian state, and in their prelapsarian state; and the description of the all-male utopia which is realized in *The Wild Boys* (1971) in its most positive form, and which is reworked in the Noah Blake and Audrey Carsons narratives of *Cities of the Red Night*.

The Cities of the Red Night are depicted initially as being of a mysterious and magical origin, and it seems at first that they might have constituted some kind of prelapsarian utopia until they were beset by a now inadequately documented disaster: the Red Night, perhaps a nuclear fallout, which eliminated all trace of this original civilization. The possiblity of real knowledge of the Cities, and the validity of that knowledge which is available, is from the outset in some doubt. Clem Snide, the private investigator who adds an interest in magic to the conventional outlook of the private eye, is first introduced to the Cities in an arcane, parchment-bound pamphlet, which he is given to read at the end of Book One. Book Two opens with an explicative chapter called 'Cities of the Red Night' which presumably corresponds to this pamphlet. The pamphlet refers to a number of lost books which described the history of the Cities, but claims that they are 'flagrant falsifications'. Having read this scholarly pamphlet, Snide is presented with a set of pictorial, magical books like 'color comics', which are purported to be fragmentary copies of the original lost book. Snide is commissioned to recover this original, but sets out not to locate it, but to reconstruct it. To locate the origin – 'the truth, which these books cover with a surface so horrible and so nauseously prettified that it remains as impervious as a mirror'[27] – Snide must himself write the original book. The book which he sets out to forge will employ two of the most ancient languages, Ancient Egyptian and Mayan, utilizing the pictographic nature of the former in an attempt to approach the state of linguistic transparency which preceded Babel, 'a language . . . that was immediately comprehensible to anyone with a concept of language' – an objective recalling those ideals of Poundian Imagism which periodically surface in Burroughs's work.[28] As if to insist on the inaccessibility of the putative origin, the plot at this point mutates wildly, and Snide is left (in one short-lived metamorphosis) not as the inspired romantic author of the Book of Books, but as a Hollywood hack commissioned to produce a screenplay. The screenplay itself designates a whole unrealized subplot in which, following a global disaster, the world will be repopulated by Aryan youth, in a plan masterminded by the CIA. The 'screenplay' is not a work of fiction, but a 'reality script', like the pre-recordings which determine reality in *The Ticket That Exploded*. The shift from resistance to collaboration is easily made.

While such mutations of the plot conjure questions about the filmic/scriptive nature of reality – which Burroughs examines in more detail elsewhere[29] – here it is enough to note that any utopian vision will always be inscribed within the 'present' and can never transcend it. The writer as romantic genius is reduced to hired pen, mapping synecdochically the history of the conceptual and personal dilemma of the post-romantic writer from Poe through Fitzgerald to Burroughs himself;[30] it is a history in perpetual slippage from identity to *différance*, as writing repeatedly fails to make its mark on the absolute.

It comes as no surprise that the search for the original utopian condition should yield only another fallen world, that the Cities betray the expectation of perfection and stasis which builds up around them. The 'Cities of the Red Night' chapter blends a parody of the objective, scholarly, historical paper with elements of the characteristic Burrovian comic routine. The paper names the six Cities of the Red Night and locates them in the Gobi Desert 100,000 years in the past. This prehistoric civilization is presented as having reached peaks of artistic

and scientific attainment 'that have never before been equaled'.[31] In the
manner of Borges, whose spirit presides over much of *Cities of the Red
Night*, the narrative pretends to locate the Cities topographically and to
differentiate them socially and culturally. But the first false note in this
vignette of utopian perfection is sounded early, with the claim that the
level of population is entirely stable, as no-one is born unless someone
else dies.[32] A parody of the idealized binary class system of Plato's
Republic is invoked to explain this perfect stability. What follows is a tidy
illustration of one of Burroughs's favourite methods. He imitates the
distanced and objective tone of an anthropologist describing a social
system, transforming a nature characterized by vampiric need into neat,
systematic patterns: the Burrovian text will frequently dwell on invented
bodily and social economies, to satirical ends which are both devastating
and uncomfortable.[33] Burroughs mocks the denial of the biological,
need-driven basis of all society, whether in anthropological observation,
sentimentalization of the 'noble savage', or utopian projection.

The parodic Republic is introduced with mock-anthropological
neutrality. It is divided into two groups: an elite called 'Transmigrants'
and a majority called 'Receptacles'. By some unexplained mechanism, an
individual is not confined to one or other group but can act as either
Transmigrant or Receptacle.[34] There is no need to dwell on the feasibility
or otherwise of this classless class system. (Plato similarly allows for
movement between classes, but does not suggest a mechanism by which
this might take place.) The delicate social balance is already upset before
the Red Night, but changes stimulated by the Red Night unleash full-
scale biologically motivated warfare, setting the women against the men
and undermining the evolution of the race. The aspiration of the city had
been to create 'a race of supermen for the exploitation of space': the result
is 'races of ravening idiot vampires.'[35]

On the way to this apocalypse, which ends in the self-destruction of the
Cities and the dispersal of their populations, Burroughs concocts a
version of the Fall that links sex and death in the mechanics of
Transmigration. A dying Transmigrant summons the Receptacle parents,
who must copulate as he dies to conceive the receptacle of his soul,
'achieving orgasm just as the old Transmigrant dies so that his spirit
enters the womb to be reborn.'[36] This linking of sex and death recalls not
only the Fall, but also the image of the orgasm of the hanged man which
haunts *The Naked Lunch* and is found again in the 'The Double Gallows'
Club ('*the* late place in Tamaghis', the most degenerate of the Cities of the
Red Night).

Another surreal section of narrative terminates suddenly and place-lessly in a 'rubbly square' – one of the recurrent 'vacant lots' of Burroughs' poetics of the metaphysical insecurity of place. 'In the middle of the square is a platform built around a tree.'[37] (Hawthorne also set the encounter of his two sinners, Hester and Dimmesdale, on a gallows.) In a scene which plays on the myth that Eve was created from Adam's rib, violating the homosexual paradise, Audrey witnesses one male in a wig as Eve proffer a penis-like apple made of male flesh to a likeness of Audrey himself as Adam. As the Audrey on the platform bites into the apple, 'his face wearing an appalling expression of idiot ecstasy', the observing Audrey feels Eve/Arn tearing loose out of his side.[38] It is this rubbly square which is the real 'no-place' of the novel, the unrepresentable place in which the Fall has always already occurred: Audrey, who arrives at the square as if in a nightmare, tries to scream out to prevent the act, but finds himself 'without a throat, without a tongue', unable to intervene in the realm of the symbolic. This is the Original Sin which ties the human species to the world of matter, unable to step beyond death into space.

To ascribe this or that point of view to a notional Burroughs who transcends his own texts is always potentially misleading, even when Burroughs is seemingly at his most declarative. It is perhaps better to see Burroughs's work in terms of the intermittent taking up and pursuit of a number of possible scenarios; his work scorns the illusory totality often associated with the novel. More simply, an optimistic and a pessimistic Burroughs might be located. Alongside the ultimate pessimism about utopian social projections, Burroughs can be found offering a more positive, if still not entirely uplifting utopian vision.

Developed in the Noah Blake and Audrey Carsons narratives, Bur-roughs's portrayal of an idealized community of homosexual boys was first elaborated in *The Wild Boys* and *Port of Saints* (1973). If these works differ in mood from *Cities of the Red Night*, it is because the latter is a product of the Seventies, a period of retrenchment, while *The Wild Boys* and *Port of Saints* come out of the Sixties; the Wild Boys fantasy draws on the rise of youth, particularly in the Student Movement (anti-Vietnam protest reached a crescendo in these years[39]) and on the development of a widespread alternative culture and underground. But while the Sixties, as exemplified by Ginsberg, had spawned a search for the natural, for universal brotherhood and communal living, Burroughs steered a more equivocal course.

In Burroughs's fantasy, the Wild Boys' movement begins in North Africa, and rapidly spreads to offer an alternative to, and a resistance

to, Western culture and military hegemony – a theme taken up again in
the Noah Blake narrative of *Cities of the Red Night*. This movement is
an all-male youth cult which emphasizes vitality and grace, free
(homo)sexuality, a combination of magical and unobtrusive technological devices and weaponry, the sadistic treatment of all enemies of free
living, and the obviation of the need for women through the use of
magical birth and resurrection techniques. The rise of this movement is
seen in the United States as a Communist plot against middle America,
a threat to 'plain ordinary American folk, decent tax-paying citizens fed
up with Godless anarchy and vice'.[40] Thus the 'American Crusade' of
1976 is launched against the source of the revolution in Morocco, only
to be exterminated by the Wild Boys, who employ deception and
guerrilla tactics – traditional modes of anti-imperialist combat that
were contemporaneously employed in Vietnam. The failure of this
crusade leaves the movement free to spread, so that by 1988 vast
underground armies are operating throughout the Western World,
combatting the 'suppressive police states' that have been set up to
silence the counter-culture. In Mexico, Central and Southern America,
and Northern Africa, armies of liberation are assembled, 'to march on
the police machine everywhere':

We intend to destroy the police machine and all its records. We intend to destroy
all dogmatic verbal systems. The family unit and its cancerous expansion into
tribes, countries, nations we will eradicate at its vegetable roots. We don't want
to hear any more family talk, mother talk, father talk, cop talk, priest talk *or*
party talk. To put it country simple we have heard enough bullshit.[41]

Burroughs conflates his projection of the Wild Boys Utopia with the anti-
Western aspirations of the growing counter-culture, not in revolt against
scarcity, but seeking liberation through revolt from the deadening effects
of the end of scarcity. This revolutionary ideal does not emphasize arrival
at a well-defined goal, but insists on the primary importance of revolt
itself. Conceived at a time when the working-class was becoming
increasingly assimilated, and when Marxism seemed to be all but extinct
in the United States, the ideal is anarchic and anti-intellectual. The Wild
Boys function as a global political catalyst on the level of mythic
inspiration, not of rational politics, and they challenge an ill-defined
conspiracy of anonymous, bureaucratic power. The Wild Boys operate in
a context in which spontaneous 'mass' revolt substitutes itself for the
party discipline of the working-class revolution. A sentimentalized
notion of guerrilla warfare, modelled on the examples of Mao and Che,
inspires Sixties radical and Wild Boy alike, although in Burroughs's

version there is no emphasis on charismatic leadership. Instead, Burroughs is more interested to represent an achieved communism in the Wild Boy community, forged in struggle, which avoids all the tedious 'transitional stages' that are usually associated with Marxism.[42] Burroughs incorporates into this utopia his own misogyny, a nostalgia for a frustrated boyhood,[43] and his own Gnostic appropriation of the theology of the Fall. So the 'calm young faces' of the Wild Boys are 'washed in the dawn before creation':

Look at these faces that have never seen a woman's face nor heard a woman's voice. Look at the silence. The wild boys will defend their space. They are learning the old magic of wind and rain, the control of snakes and dogs and birds. . . . Calling all boys of the earth we will teach you the secrets of magic control of wind and rain. . . . We will free you forever from the womb.[44]

The Wild Boys' school oath runs: 'A Wild Boy is filthy, treacherous, dreamy, vicious and lustful.'[45] The Wild Boy state is one of harmony with nature, a transcendence of the womb and therefore of death, a realization of the silence beyond words (the Wild Boys employ a pictographic and universal language[46]) which is the goal of the experimentation of *The Ticket That Exploded*.[47] Yet these boys can be seen at the same time in terms of those negatives with which Western Romanticism has generally characterized and stigmatized 'pagan' and 'uncivilized' non-Western societies. And Burroughs explores at some length the Wild Boys' seemingly unlimited capacity for lustfulness and viciousness, providing numerous descriptions of their sex acts and of their ingenuity with respect to weapons and tactics.

In *Cities of the Red Night* the ambiguity of the utopian drive appears most clearly in the isolated chapter that portrays a group of boys who use hang-gliders to explore the Red Desert. This group of boys belongs to the achieved utopia of male youth (which, as *The Wild Boys* demonstrated, eliminates the need for the female); their exploring activities represent a male-bonding, scouting ideal, and an ideal of non-alienated labour, supplemented by the dream sex-fantasy activity of hang-gliding. These are 'migrants who move from settlement to settlement in the vast area now held by the Articulated', carrying few provisions because this woman-free, pre-industrial Paradise provides the roving hunter-gatherer with most of his necessary supplies. Where it does not, provisions are supplemented by an advanced but unobtrusive technology: powdered concentrates of essential nutrients.[48]

However, two ambiguous elements occur to cast doubt on this paradise. First, there is an encounter with the 'fruit-fish people', who diet

on huge fish which feed on the fruit that falls into the river from trees
planted on the banks. The adventurers sail:

> . . . past youths in the boughs of trees, masturbating and shaking the ripe fruit
> into the water with the spasms of their bodies as their sperm falls also to be
> devoured by the great green-blue fish.[49]

In this paradise, labour is unalienated, sexuality remains unrepressed.
Indeed, sex *is* labour: masturbation shakes the fruit into the river;
ejaculation supplements the diet of the fish; the fish and thus the
community thrive. However, as often in the depiction of his communities
of boys, Burroughs hints at the potential for depravity which is built into
this kind of utopia: at least, he fosters the awareness that what it would
mean to inhabit this prelapsarian world cannot be clear to the eyes of a
conditioned sexuality. There is an indication that utopia would be a
radical alterity not so much beyond good and evil as beyond conditioned
notions of shame and the propriety of the person, a drastic re-calculation
of the 'algebra of need',[50] of the whole bodily economy of labour and
desire.

The second incident, an encounter with another group of boys who
seem at first similar to themselves, is less ambiguous in its depiction of
sexuality. The adventurers see:

> . . . a gang of naked boys covered with erogenous sores. As they walk they giggle
> and stroke and scratch each other. From time to time they fuck each other in
> Hula-Hoops to idiot mambo.[51]

This incident, which closes the chapter, is a reminder that the human
virus or virus B-23 is an inevitable corruption in any Eden, returning the
body to death, disease and idiocy, and that it is only in the escape from
the body and from words, advocated in *The Ticket That Exploded* and
Nova Express, that liberation is possible.

Burroughs's pessimistic social and sexual prognostications are in sharp
contrast to those of Marcuse, one of the presiding spirits of the student
movement, yet are very much in line with the Freud of *Civilisation and its
Discontents*, whose most fundamental insights Marcuse in effect
reverses. Burroughs's concept of need, like Freud's drive, is fundamentally biological, and his view of civilization is always, in this sense,
pessimistic. While the 'Council' may have had high expectations of
creating a space-faring race, a race that would not transcend biological
essences but transform them, B-23 sabotages all such hopes. This
biological/genetic Fall introduces the sex/death nexus which, in a loose

fashion, parallels Freud's later suggestions about the nature of *eros* and *thanatos*. Freud emphasized the root conflict between *eros* and *thanatos*, and was unwilling to admit that they might, in origin at least, be identical. Maintaining a more rigorous pessimism, Burroughs, most famously in the images of the orgasm of the hanged man, insists on the ultimate identity of sex and death. Further, while figures such as Marcuse play down the importance of genital sexuality in favour of the possibility of a more general bodily 'sexuality' (which tends in the direction of the merely sensual), Burroughs privileges genital/anal sexuality in accounts of erection, masturbation and anal intercourse. The Wild Boys' version of liberated sexuality is, then, far from the 'polymorphous-perverse sexuality' which Marcuse celebrates in his reading of Freud.[52] If civilization is founded on repression, Burroughs like Marcuse is interested in what happens when that repression is removed. For Marcuse, the removal of 'surplus repression' and of excess labour will result in the satisfaction of deeper and more positive human needs, what he calls 'real needs'.[53] Burroughs's depiction of the City of Tamaghis in *Cities of the Red Night* forms a contrast to this, and offers a condensed version of much that is explored more expansively in *The Naked Lunch*. This city, where the climate forces retirement during the day, is the 'Nighttown' of a humanity at perpetual play, peopled by the addicts of sexual perversions and psychotropic substances; the citizens manoeuvre through an environment dominated by pushers, criminals and law enforcers – Sirens, Hanging Fathers, Painless Ones, Spermers, Dogcatchers – the litany of names suggesting an elaborate economy of desire and fulfillment amounting to an open black market. Desires are not modified by liberation, as Marcuse might have hoped, but multiply indefinitely into the Red Night, recalling the '*combinatoire*' of Barthes's Fourier,[54] as well as Poe's more sinister 'Masque of the Red Death' – which has underpinned this narrative from its outset.[54]

Death in a sense *enables* pleasure, and the structures of Burroughs's pessimism similarly enable optimism. As the basic vocabulary of *The Wild Boys* and *Port of Saints* is taken up and reconfigured in the more complex presentation of *Cities of the Red Night*, Burroughs foregrounds the partially autobiographical figure of Audrey Carsons, spurned St Louis misfit and would-be writer. Audrey is seen rampaging through the degenerate city of Tamaghis, and leading the attack from Ba'dan on the female stronghold of Yass Waddah.[55] His ingenuity in matters of violence identifies him with the Wild Boys, as does his opposition to representatives of the law and to the matriarchy of Yass Waddah. Yet the narrative framing devices employed in *Cities of the Red Night* serve to shift attention from the content of this gay version of boys' adventure fantasy to its sources and motivations. Event, character and place are all uncertain, temporarily conjured entities in Burroughs's surreal and shifting narratives. Thus the Casbah in Ba'dan is described as a multifaceted environment in which a gamut of the typical figures of adventure fiction can be found in circulation: Western gunmen, assassins, Mafiosi and so on.[56] When Audrey goes into battle against the forces of Yass Waddah, he too adopts a variety of roles, representing always the defenders of the oppressed fighting against oppressors from yet other historical time periods – thus he is a medieval knight charging down middle American matriarchs and lawmen, or a Western gunman 'leading the Wild Bunch to break up the auto-da-fé in Lima'.[57] Towards the close of the novel, after Audrey seemingly wakes up into a 'real time' that is set beyond the fantasies of the novel, the narrative is recapitulated as a series of scenes in a high school production called 'Cities of the Red Night', apparently identifying what has gone before as the product of the schoolboys' enthusiasm for adventure fiction.

The fluidity of Burroughs's utopian and dystopian environments, as of his narratives and characters, indicates a modernist apprehension of the utopian that is far from the representational stability of the Utopias of Plato, More or Wells. *Cities of the Red Night* aims not to negate the utopian impulse of adventure fiction, but to preserve it by seeming to negate it. As the first person singular of this novel shifts from one protagonist to another, it becomes increasingly clear that this 'I' is only realized through and across the narratives that it traverses. For this 'I' to be located always as outlaw and rebel, in roles drawn from 'genre' fiction, is to imply a thesis about the nature of the self and of the real; it is a thesis that conflates a (now) conventionally decentred concept of the self – 'we are the language'[58] – with a more traditional bourgeois faith in, or at least nostalgia for, the integrity of the individual.

This is most clearly realized in two of the most common strategies employed in *Cities of the Red Night*: the transition from one narrative to another by having a character wake up, or undergo visionary or ecstatic experience, and the foregrounding of the inability of the proper name to define a fixed character or personage. The former occurs for example when Audrey passes into his vision of the 'rubbly square', or when he wakes out of the Cities narrative into what is apparently 'real time'. The latter is exemplified by the shifting identity of the first person narrator; the recurrence, in seemingly separate plots, of the same villains – the

Countesses, the Iguana Twins, and others – and of the red-haired boy
with green eyes (who appears in a variety of guises); and by the plethora
of boy characters whose names multiply but whose identities remain
indistinguishable.

The self, no longer an identity but the product and producer of
language according to a model that Burroughs deployed in full-blown
form in *The Ticket That Exploded*, is simultaneously abolished and
enabled, in a transformation that will not capitulate to the materialist
determinism that is brutally advanced elsewhere in this text. A conflict
emerges. While there is one Burroughs who insists on the biological
rootedness of all life forms, and on the biological and evolutionary roots
of all conflict, there is another whose frequently repeated motto is
'nothing is true: everything is permitted'.[59] This Burroughs insists on the
primacy of the imagination.[60] While the other Burroughs rails against
language as a closed and repressive system, this Burroughs seeks to
recognize and restore what is liberative within the 'pre-sent' language,
using appropriation and irony, and hinting at a utopian transcendence
whether of a collective (*The Wild Boys*) or of an individual (*The Ticket
That Exploded*) nature. The biological pessimism, and the black humour
which it breeds, is, if we will, the transcendental signified of *Cities of the
Red Night*; yet the mood of abandon, associated with the simple moral
world of boys' adventure fiction (refracted through Burroughs's relentless revision of sentimentalized views of childhood), serves at least to
preserve the spirit of the utopian hopes which the narrative otherwise
negates.

8

Utopia the Good Breast:
Coming Home to Mother

JAN RELF

I think no one but one so unfortunate as to be early motherless can enter into the craving one has after the lost mother.[1] ELIZABETH GASKELL

It was like – coming home to mother. . . . I mean the feeling that a very little child would have, who had been lost – for ever so long. It was a sense of getting home; of being clean and rested; of safety and yet freedom; of love that was always there, warm like sunshine in May . . .[2] CHARLOTTE PERKINS GILMAN

The haunting figure of the lost mother is scarcely a new phenomenon in narrative fiction. She appears – and disappears – throughout the history of the world of once-upon-a-time, as a brief reconnaissance of that world, from fairy tales to the nineteenth-century novel, quickly makes clear.[3] She also appears, insistently and recurrently, in women's utopian fiction of recent years as an emblem of that feminist utopian desire which found its classic and most explicit expression in Charlotte Perkins Gilman's proto-feminist utopia, *Herland*.

The general context of this discussion, then, is the feminist utopias of the past two decades. My focus will be on the pervasive presence of, and desire for, the lost mother in these texts, and my purpose will be to determine the significance of that desire in the context of a broader concern, which has to do with the nature of the utopian impulse that drives the text. What will be of interest here is not so much the prescriptive or descriptive content of a written utopia, but the deeper impulse – the hidden agenda perhaps – which a deconstructive or psychoanalytic reading may reveal as a *progressive* or *regressive* impulse.

To that end, and with clarity as a consideration, I have organized these representations of the mother in women's utopias into five categories, each of which I shall discuss with reference to an exemplary text. The first of these is the *nurturing archetype* as she appears in Claudia McKay's *Promise of the Rose Stone* (1986). The second is the *goddess* – a representation of feminism's sporadic attempts to recuperate a female deity – and the exemplary text here is Joan Vinge's *The Snow Queen* (1980). I then move on to the third type, which I've identified as *earth mother* or *mother earth*, which makes a typical appearance in Sally Miller Gearhart's *The Wanderground* (1979); and the fourth type which, following Julia Kristeva, I've termed the *phallic mother*, appears as the founder of a race of Amazonian superwomen or as repository of the law, and here I shall refer to Suzy McKee Charnas's *Motherlines* (1978).

Finally I shall turn to Doris Lessing's *Memoirs of a Survivor* (1970). On the surface this is a pessimistic dystopia, but it is in fact, as I shall argue, a radically subversive and eutopian[4] text which deconstructs maternal iconography and opens up a way out of the quagmire of regress and sentimentality in which the less intelligent texts threaten to sink.

I shall be arguing that nostalgic valorization of the mother and desire for the lost homeland of maternality are actually counter-productive in the context of feminism's larger project which – I hope – is the utopian task of working for a better future state in which the family as we know it has been radically reconstructed, and constricting gender roles have been thoroughly challenged and possibly dissolved. The starting point for this discussion is that utopia is an image of desire, rooted in present dissatisfaction. Clearly this has political implications. If that image of desire manifests itself as a desire for the lost mother, then the question to be addressed to that maternal icon is, does that desire work to pull the present forward, progressively, towards the as-yet-inexpressible but hopefully better future state, located in what Ernst Bloch calls the *future* unconscious, or is it a regressive impulse, in search of some prelapsarian lost domain located in the *past* unconscious. This, expressed in psycho-analytic terms, might appear as the desire for the always already lost perfection of the mother/child dyad.

If the former, then – bringing Karl Mannheim's terms into play – we can locate Mother as a figure of utopia, which he defines as 'a complex of ideas directing activity towards the *changing* of the *status quo*'. If the latter, then she becomes a conservative figure of *nostalgia* in the service of an ideology, defined as 'a complex of ideas directing activity towards the *maintenance* of the *status quo*'.[5] Since a desire for the lost mother almost inevitably suggests the latter – conservatism and regressive desire – the starting point here will be to assume that the case *is* the latter unless the text yields evidence to the contrary.

As my title indicates, the theoretical approach employed here is grounded primarily in the work of Melanie Klein and Dorothy Dinnerstein. Psychoanalytic and object relations theory narrates and accounts for the way in which the mother is, for both girls and boys, the first love object. She – the good mother – is the all-enfolding, nurturing, ever-present figure who gratifies every desire and with whom there exists a perfect but illusory unity. It is this aspect of the mother which prompts separatist and lesbian feminism to posit woman as the original (and therefore supposedly natural) love object of women.[6]

The difficulty with this position is that it ignores several fundamental and related facts demonstrated by Freudian and post-Freudian accounts of the family. First, the infant's acquisition of language and mandatory entry to the symbolic order involve a permanent and unassuageable sense of loss for both sexes – specifically loss of the good mother and the sense of unity enjoyed with her. Second, the good mother is also, inevitably, the bad mother who withholds the breast, and towards whom – according to Klein – the infant experiences murderous rage and envy. Third, the sexual development and construction of gender for girls and boys is not symmetrical. If girls redirect their search and transfer their erotic allegiance to the father, they do so for reasons which are well accounted for in the psychoanalytic narrative of their development. What the girl continues to hold in common with her brother, however, is that driving sense of loss.

At this point I believe we must abandon – at least for a while – the Freudian and Lacanian position which identifies the phallus as the symbol of that which the girl does not have and which the boy fears to lose – in other words, penis envy and castration – and focus instead on the breast as the symbol of that which both sexes have lost, and as initiator of desire. The implications of this for textual practice are lucidly summarized by Robert Poole:

The withdrawal of the breast causes need and desperation in the baby, and longing for the breast becomes transformed into *the experience of desire*. The breast [is] an impossible object of desire, and hence has become the 'mark' of *the impossibility of satisfaction* in the chain of signifiers which makes up the child's new insertion into the public world. The search for this lost and impossible object of desire will . . . follow and torment the adult all his life.[7]

However, the asymmetry in the passage through the Oedipal crisis, and the consequent construction of gendered difference, indicate that girls and boys will not only occupy significantly different positions within the symbolic order, but that they will also construct significantly different narratives. As a generalization, when women embark on the search for what has been lost their heroines do not (as the male hero typically does)

engage in an active, externalized quest in the outer world of the fiction.
Rather, they tend to turn inward, into a metaphorical room of their own.
In utopia, women frequently retreat into the private, oneiric world of
separation from men, into fantastic pastoral enclosures, or walled-off
spaces in which they guard and protect a cluster of values perceived as
characteristically feminine. And within these spaces we find, more often
than not, Mother in one of her various guises. It is to those various
representations of the mother in women's utopias that I shall now turn.

I

Into the breast that gives the rose . . .
G. MEREDITH 'Ode to the Spirit of Earth in Autumn'

To say that utopia is 'about' an idealized society is self-evident. What
interests us here is, first, the somewhat more complex notion that it is *an
idealized image of desire*, and, second, the juxtaposition of that idea with
Klein's assertion that:

. . . idealization derives from the innate feeling that an extremely good breast
exists, a feeling which leads to the longing for the good object.[8]

Klein's formulation is, I suggest, one way of accounting for the paradox
of the utopian project. Utopian fiction, that is, narrates and stages
imaginary, fantastic solutions to an unassimilable contradiction in the
human condition; it strives to reconcile the knowledge that we inhabit an
irretrievably fallen and divided world in which the ideal state is
unattainable, with the irresistible and mysteriously present idea of
unified perfection (the good object) which we continue to desire.

One of the most bizarre images of the mother-as-breast-as-englobing-
totality occurs in Claudia McKay's *Promise of the Rose Stone*. Here the
figure of the mother is Olyeve, who combines the attributes of presiding
deity, the good, nurturing mother, and the terrible, phallic mother, from
whom, eventually, the heroine must escape. In the first of these roles, she is
the one from whom all gifts and blessings flow, and the embodiment of
'human virtues and strengths' which the dystopian and patriarchal
Federation has lost. She appears in their sky as a 'star', a celestial deity who
is also 'a whole living being'; and she figures in the children's dramatic
enactment of their revised myth of origin, fall and redemption, in which
man's greed for possession precipitates the modern version of the Fall. The
Fall is represented as the total degradation of a formerly paradisal planet

and the near annihilation of humanity through the making of war, which together constitute the post-catastrophe *donnée* of so many contemporary utopian novels by women. Olyeve, in this context, is both mother and daughter, a holy female duality in place of the orthodox (Christian) male trinity, who has helped her children to 'begin again'.

It is in the middle section of the text, however, that she appears most phantasmally and yet most clearly as the good breast. Isa, the heroine, finds herself 'encysted' in a dreamlike, all-female world of pregnant women which is both 'prison' and 'paradise'. She learns that she is now 'in Olyeve's belly': an interior of pulsating, 'responsive', fleshy cellular spaces. On the walls of these cells, Isa finds 'knobs or small bumps', which, when sucked, spurt life-sustaining streams of liquid 'broth'. Clearly this is not just a return to the pre-oedipal maternal space, but a deeper regress to a pre-natal retreat, where Olyeve is both the idealized image of desire of which Klein speaks – the 'inexhaustible and always present breast' – and the totally englobing mother who nurtures and protects.[9]

Olyeve is also, however, the object of the text's profound ambivalence. She *is* the all-wise, all-giving omnipotent mother, emphatically loved and revered by the inhabitants of *all* of the text's various spaces and settlements. But she also imprisons, and the 'encysted' space of mother-as-total-environment is *not* the privileged space of the text. It is, in fact, a space from which, having lived out her dream of total dependence and regress in the maternal space, Isa urgently desires to escape. She comes, that is, to experience Olyeve as the terrible mother, who imprisons and devours. This latter aspect of Olyeve is embodied in her horrible but necessary progeny – the 'eaters' – who devour civilization's garbage and anything else they can fasten their unpleasant blind mouths upon.

It has to be said that this is an extraordinarily muddled and badly written text, but it does appear to recognize, as Janet Sayers has argued, that:

. . . the phantasy of the positively fused mother and infant daughter is an illusory basis on which to found the unity and solidarity of women.[10]

It does not, in other words, advocate a simplistic regression to an idealized, pre-linguistic sphere of the mother-child relation. Rather, it narrates, in Kleinian terms, the infant's ambivalence in that relation; the process of splitting; and the eventual necessity of cutting oneself free from the hold of the terrible mother. This is accomplished, towards the end of the story, in quite shockingly literalistic terms:

Then Cleothe's sword was already making an ugly gash in the wall. Isa felt
Olyeve's scream of pain hit her, felt that it was her own body that was gashed,
and could not lift the staff. She watched the sword lift again and knew she
couldn't have made even that first cut. She was already too much a part of Olyeve
and she wept with the pain and wanted to tear the sword from Cleothe's grasp.
. . . Isa drew away from the self that defended against the cut and knew that she
too must strike with her staff. . . . Isa swung and Olyeve's delicate flesh
responded and began to assemble the new cyst that was to be their ship.[11]

The female child is thus twice split; first, as Cleothe who cuts the mother's
flesh and as Isa who feels the pain; and then Isa herself splits as she 'drew
away from the self that defended' and vents her pain and rage as the one
who also cuts the mother's flesh. Olyeve, the figure of the mother, is also
subjected to the primal division into the bad, hated object which must be
destroyed, and the good, empowering object whose flesh miraculously
shapes itself into the means of escape – the ship. But the description above
figures, in Kristevan terms, the abjection of, and breaking away from, the
'maternal entity' as 'a violent, clumsy breaking away, with the constant
risk of falling back under the sway of a power as securing as it is
stifling.'[12] Olyeve, as phallic mother and eternally lost object of desire,
has seduced with promises of plenitude and satisfaction, whilst actually,
symbolically, enchaining (encysting) and rendering impotently
dependent.

The two women duly make their escape, back to Isa's homeland,
taking with them Cleothe's baby daughter, but the text's ambivalence
about its own idealized image of desire is further revealed and confirmed
in its resolution. On the one hand, the narrative acknowledges the painful
loss of the mother, experienced as a longing for the good object: '[Isa] felt
the absence of Olyeve as a silent hunger, an ache.' On the other hand, the
narrative asserts the necessity of relinquishing the good object *and* of
liberating the mother herself:

Olyeve was trapped by the Agents. Isa knew deep inside, an ancient knowledge,
that she was to find a way to free her. Just as she knew that humans had to find a
way to live without Olyeve.[13]

So, in a text which reads somewhat like a naive and discontinuous
account of a dream, there is, it seems to me, an oddly sophisticated
awareness of primary processes,[14] and it is this incongruity which raises
such interesting questions. There is, in the passages just quoted, an
insight, not just that the child must free itself from the archaic mother,
but that the mother too must be set free from the paralytic hold of
iconography, mythologization, and the human desire for a return to

origins and/or final solutions. It attempts, that is, to name the unname-able of which Kristeva speaks. According to Noreen O'Connor:

Kristeva argues that analytic speech reveals the desire to return to the origin which she designates as the archaic mother. This desire subtends all speech. The archaic mother is resistant to meaning, she is unnameable.[15]

I suggest that this text, in spite of its surface naivety and clumsiness, reveals and names the archaic mother in her dual aspect, and exposes her as the phantasm who must be relinquished if her human children are ever to grow up.

II

I will go back to the great sweet mother,
Mother and lover of men, the sea
SWINBURNE 'The Triumph of Time'

Kristeva speaks directly of the need to challenge this myth of the archaic mother:

If the archetype of the belief in a good and pure substance, that of utopias, is the belief in the omnipotence of an archaic, full, total englobing mother with no frustration, no separation, with no break-producing symbolism (with no castration, in other words), then it becomes evident that we will never be able to defuse the violences mobilized through the counter-investment necessary to carrying out this phantasm, unless one challenges precisely this myth of the archaic mother.[16]

Carol Pearson suggests that feminist utopias 'challenge and correct biases about innate female "nature"'.[17] I suggest that, in discussing utopias which *deify* the figure of the mother – locating her as the Goddess or the Lady, and/or identifying her with the planet, the earth, or nature – and in suggesting that such representations have anything useful to tell us about 'innate female "nature"', Pearson's argument is far from helpful. It proposes, indeed, an essentialistic view of women which is profoundly *un*helpful. I further suggest that these deifications of the Mother perpetuate the problematic mythologization of woman; the identification of woman with nature, as opposed to that of man with culture – an opposition which I believe stands in dire need of demo-lition; and stereotypical and counterproductive images of women which actually reinforce (rather than correct) 'biases about innate female "nature"'. In Gilman's *Herland* – one of the utopias discussed by Pearson – the exaltation of motherhood can be seen to situate the figure of the mother as the archetype of the good mother; this contributes to and perpetuates the mythologization of woman as mother, an unhelpful process initiated and sustained by religious iconography and popular sentimentality.

The idea that, in some remote and probably matriarchal era of prehistory, some cultures worshipped a goddess, a female deity, has become a cliché of feminist consciousness raising, and has been sufficiently well-documented to have achieved some credibility and currency. Rosalind Miles notes, in her chapter on 'The Great Goddess', that:

Commentators stress the prominence and prevalence of the Great Mother Goddess as an essential element from the dawn of human life.[18]

but warns that:

Over-emphasis on the good mother, procreative and nurturing, also denies the bad mother, her dangerous, dark and destructive opposite.[19]

She also points to a problematic weakness in our contemporary understanding of the 'Great Mother':

In every culture, the Goddess has many lovers. . . . To the children of patriarchy, 'mother' always includes 'wife'; mother is the woman who is married to father. That puts a further constraint on the idea of the *good* mother. The good mother does not fuck around.[20]

The Great Mother of prehistory combines, in other words, the attributes of the *two opposed* role models available to women in Christian culture – the Madonna and the Magdalen, virgin-mother or whore. Her darker side, along with her insistent and often rampant sexuality, tends to be elided or conveniently forgotten in some of her recent literary appearances.

In one of those literary appearances – Joan Vinge's *The Snow Queen* – the Goddess is located in the sea, the source of life from which we all, supposedly, originated. Vulgar Freudianism clearly suggests the amniotic fluid – an image heightened by a number of incidents in the text, and by the name of the imagined planet – Tiamat – on which the story takes place. Tiamat signifies, in ancient creation myth, 'the great mother from whose formless saline body the universe was created'.[21] The mother in Vinge's novel is identified with earth and water. She is elemental; she is 'nature'. Here, the female deity is the repository of the sybilline wisdom supposedly needed to 'make the ideal real'.

The two opposed cultures on the planet of Tiamat, Winter and Summer, alternate in power every hundred years, but as the narrative gets under way, we find that Tiamat is a matriarchal utopia of process which has fallen on hard times, and is currently in the hands of Winter and the Snow Queen, who want to reign permanently and to arrest the necessary and dynamic rhythm of cyclical change. It is upon this that the plot turns. The privileged values of the text are located with the gynocentric, village-dwelling Summers, who worship the Goddess.

The figure of the Queen in her two aspects – Snow and Summer – clearly represents the dual aspect of the Mother as archetype. The Snow Queen is negatively valued, standing for darkness, and for predatory and rapacious sexuality, while the Summer Queen, called Moon, represents sunshine and roses, and monogamous 'true love'. The two value clusters represented are supposed, of course, to be complementary and to participate in a rhythmic alternation. But in the opposition which the plot sets up between them the Snow Queen is eventually vanquished and the triumph of Summer asserted. Conservative values (the good, faithful mother who does not fuck around) embodied in Moon's fidelity to her childhood sweetheart, Sparks, and in the pastoral pleasures of village life, are evidently privileged.

There is a further difficulty here. Moon, as her name indicates, is a symbol of feminine flux, cyclical change and intuitive wisdom. She is, in fact, one of the 'sybils', who believe that they are vehicles for the wisdom of the Mother Goddess. The suspicion that sybilline wisdom might be anything other than 'real' and of divine origin is initially expressed by the 'calculated' and textually degraded voice of the hegemonic Winters, whom we are naturally inclined to discredit. However, in Chapter 20 the myth of the Great Mother Goddess is at least partially dismantled, when we learn that the controlling intelligence of the Tiamatan world is not transmitted supernaturally, from the goddess to the sybils, but is actually located in a huge data bank created by a past, long-gone civilization. The Goddess, indeed, turns out to be a counterfeit construction, and the sybils are eventually revealed as human computer terminals – 'the sybil machine' – rather than magically gifted prophets empowered by a female deity.

We are told that the Snow Queen has lied to the Tiamatans about the Goddess, and that the reason she has done so is to keep the Tiamatans in a controllable state of unenlightened regress. And yet, at the end of the novel, we find their new and benevolent Summer Queen playing exactly the same game. Moon, in her new role as Queen, perpetuates the by now clearly spurious fiction of the Lady and the sybils, as the religious rhetoric of her speech to the people indicates:

People of Tiamat, the Lady has blessed me once, by giving me someone to share my life with me . . . She has blessed me twice, by making me a sibyl, and three times, by making me a Queen. . . . I've prayed that She will show me the way to do Her will and be Her living symbol. And She has answered me.[22]

It is tempting to speculate that this might be a profoundly ironic representation of the deity as a machine of social control and repression. Is the goddess finally exposed as a man-made construction because that is the way monotheistic male deities have historically appeared and been deployed? Is the great mother-goddess finally being routed and exposed as a fraudulent construction similar to that of father gods? Unfortunately, I do not think so. Astonishingly, Vinge's novel appears to endorse the use of religion – even a religion which has been exposed as fraudulent – as a necessary and legitimate opiate of the people. The Summer Queen's deception is textually legitimated and is designed to keep the Tiamatan community in a state of pseudo-utopian, pre-linguistic dependence and ignorance – the Winters '*speechless* with uncertainty' and the Summers '*speechless* with reverence' (emphasis added). That is, they are excluded from the new symbolic order, in which Moon rules and represents the new dispensation, the new law. Matriarchy rules – OK. But the law of the mother merely replaces the law of the father, and the new dispensation merely replaces the Good Mother-Goddess with the *phallic* mother who keeps her dependent children in silent ignorance. The text proposes two ultimately irreconcilable claims to 'truth' – divinely received wisdom and scientifically based knowledge – and in doing so creates a textual *aporia*; an epistemological impasse leading to the nowhere of illusion and ignorance, rather than to the now/here of a genuinely utopian, non-authoritarian discourse in which everyone has access to enlightenment, language and power.

There is, I suggest, a deep ambivalence underlying the confused representation of the mother-as-goddess in *The Snow Queen*. On the one hand, the text seems to want to discredit her, and to dismantle the myth of the archaic mother. On the other hand, it exhibits a reluctance to abandon her completely. If Moon needs the fiction of the Goddess as a power prop, the text seems to need it as a residual repository of desire, and the author seems worried that, by relocating the source of wisdom and power in the machine (identified with reason and the masculine principle), she has somehow betrayed her own feminist premise. So much for the Sea Mother: now for the Earth Mother.

III

And the earth helped the woman . . .
REVELATIONS: 12.16

Sally Miller Gearhart's *The Wanderground* – a separatist feminist eutopia which proposes a conflated identification of woman, earth, nature and the mother – opens with a vision of women and nature in harmonious alliance, enjoined in the struggle to save life on earth, once and for all, from the depredations of greedy, unreconstructed man. The precipitating action has been taken by the earth itself, in an event reverently referred to as 'the Revolt of the Mother'. Since this apocalyptic occurrence, men and their machines have been impotent – unable to function outside of the city in which they are safely contained. Women enjoy the safety and freedom of a pastoral world where they participate in a mystical and organicist relationship with the earth in its role as the protective, nurturing good mother.

Sybille Birkhauser-Oeri has written a Jungian-cum-Gravesian exploration of the meaning of the mother as an archetype in fairy tales. The ideas which she puts forward are a semi-theoretical version of the fictional electioneering on behalf of the female principle that informs so many feminist and lesbian utopias, where 'woman' and 'nature' are typically linked and envisioned as the persecuted objects of male greed and oppression, and as allied co-victims of literal and metaphorical rape. Birkhauser-Oeri advocates 'an attitude of service towards the Great Mother', and continues:

We go on exploiting nature until its gets its own back and takes away everything it has given us, including our humanity, and turns us into animals. The nature mother turns on those who are not aware of their limitations, particularly the limitations of the intellect, with which one so often identifies. In such a state of mind, one uses nature irresponsibly, for purely selfish ends. Then the Earth mother wreaks vengeance.[23]

This is a passage which could well stand as an epigraph to *The Wanderground*.

There are, I believe, two related causes for concern here, the first of which is the attribution of purposive action to the earth – a fantasy apparently shared by Birkhauser-Oeri. This seems to me like an unhelpful brand of green, fundamentalist theism which obscures the necessary distinction between natural laws, which are immutable, and social laws, which are human-made and can therefore be changed.

The second difficulty is the identification of the earth with the Mother.

At the conclusion of the novel we find that 'the task' still facing the women of the Wanderground is 'to work as if *the earth, the mother* can be saved' (emphasis added), and that the perceived difficulty and opposition to that task is still man, 'the slayer'. Of course, such tropes are a rhetorical strategy, and we might want to read the subversive, revolutionary energy attributed to Mother Earth in texts such as *The Wanderground* as a metaphor for women's revolutionary energy. What I would like to suggest, however, is that the persistent metaphorical association of these two overweighted signifiers, 'earth' and 'mother' (which has, of course, a long and respectable literary history), is profoundly unhelpful to women, and, moreover, that it is counterproductive in terms of the 'task' – that is, the saving of the earth and the admirably green politics which are evident throughout women's utopian literature.

Dorothy Dinnerstein has theorized and articulated precisely this problem. Her argument, in *The Rocking of the Cradle and the Ruling of the World*, helps to account both for the anxiety-producing (to me) linguistic conflation of the earth and mother, and for the potential problems arising out of that conflation in the context of the green task. She begins by acknowledging her dual premise, which is also the premise of most feminist utopias:

(a) that the prevailing mode of psychological interdependence between the sexes does in fact need to be changed, [and] (b) that there is in fact some basic pathology shaping our species' stance toward itself and nature, a pathology whose chances of killing us off quite soon, if we cannot manage to outgrow it first, are very good indeed.[24]

She assumes – as feminist utopias do not, since their rhetorical strategies are generally designed to convince the reader on both these points – that her reader is already convinced of the 'chronically uncomfortable' and 'life threatening' nature of the stance which humanity occupies in relation to itself and to nature.

Dinnerstein uses Melanie Klein's theoretical account of the infant's ambivalent experience of 'envy' and 'gratitude' at the mother's breast to demonstrate the way in which the mother is constructed as a representative of nature. Like nature, or the earth, the mother does not only offer the good breast. She also withholds it, leaving the despairing infant to suffer hunger pangs, cold, discomfort; she becomes the 'bad object' of the infant's destructive, envious impulses. Like nature, who sends blizzards and earthquakes to plague us as well as sunshine and roses to please us, the mother is the 'split' object of both gratitude and envy (the latter being

Klein's term for the infant's feelings of impotence, rage and 'persecutory anxiety'[25]). She appears to the naive and uncritical perceptions of the helpless infant to operate according to immutable but arbitrary – that is, *natural* – laws. In appearing thus, she becomes the first representative of nature, and retains more or less permanently this anomalous image, fluctuating between 'omniscient goddess' and 'dumb bitch', and associated with 'non-human' processes such as rain, seasonal change and vegetative growth and decay.[26]

The consequence of the early mother's apparent omnipotence and the ambivalent role which she shares with nature as the 'ultimate source of good and evil' lies, according to Dinnerstein, at the root of our chronically troubled human condition:

Both toward women and toward nature as a whole – as originally toward the mother, who was half human, half nature – we feel torn between two impulses: the impulse, on the one hand, to give free rein to the nursling's angry greed, its wild yearning to own, control, suck dry the source of good, its wish to avenge deprivation; and the impulse, on the other hand, to make reparation for these feelings, which threaten to destroy what is most precious and deeply needed.[27]

This need to make reparation is an important component of the Kleinian scheme, and it is upon this point that Dinnerstein constructs her account of difference in respect of the male and the female relation to nature. Women, she believes, have largely remained outside of the 'nature-assaulting parts of history' because their reparative feelings extend to nature as well as to women; whereas men's reparative feelings have a 'predominantly self-interested character'.[28] She continues:

Men's exploitation of Mother Nature has so far been kept in check largely by their conception of the practical risk they themselves ran in antagonizing, depleting, spoiling her. . . . As technology has advanced, and they have felt more powerful [this fear] has abated. A euphoric sense of conquest has replaced it: the son has set his foot on the mother's chest, he has harnessed her firmly to his uses, he has opened her body once and for all and may now help himself at will to its riches. What remains is the danger that she will be depleted, spoiled.[29]

Dinnerstein argues lucidly and passionately for a radical restructuring of parenting arrangements as a means of, firstly, changing the prevailing and unsatisfactory psychological relationship between the sexes and, secondly, of averting a global ecotastrophe. The problem with her text, as the above passage makes evident, is that the language in which it is couched perpetuates the *semantic* problem. Either there is some slippage here in Dinnerstein's own apparent conceptualization of nature as female, or her use of the term 'Mother Nature', and of the female pronoun in referring to nature, is ironic. If the latter, then the irony is insufficiently emphasized, too oblique. If we are seriously concerned to erase the identification of woman with nature, then we had better stop talking about 'Mother Earth', and we had better stop referring to the earth as a rapable female body. Dinnerstein's work, first published in 1976, is, I believe, an important one in the context of women's utopian writing and its concerted plea for the reconstruction of the family. Its weakness lies in its lack of attention to, and failure to account for, the symbolic function and paternal law. The point it does most usefully make is that present parenting arrangements are destructive and that they *can* be changed. In order to do this, however, I suggest that we have to be aware of linguistic complicity in a symbolic order which locates 'mother' as nature, as earth, as omnipotent deity or goddess; and which in so doing positions both women and the earth as potential or actual objects of male aggression.

In privileging the power of the mother, and/or in elevating the status of motherhood to a mystical – even sacramental – level, as *The Wander-ground* does, and as Gilman's proto-feminist utopia *Herland* did, these texts unfortunately perpetuate the idealization of the mother-child bond as a model of all future relationships. This idealized bond is, of course, irretrievable. And yet, as Dinnerstein says, 'Indefatigably we go on trying to recover what has been lost.'[30]

IV

Phallic mother, founder mother

One of the ways in which the search for the mother is narratologically resolved is to recuperate and reposition her – still omnipotent and still vested with magical powers – as the goddess or mother earth, as we have just seen. She also appears, similarly vested with authority and power, as the law-maker: the phallic mother. The question to be asked here is, does this matriarchal law routinely replicate that which it purports to subvert and ultimately replace – patriarchy – or does it actually propose something radically and authentically different?

There is plenty of evidence to support the argument that women's utopias are characterized, as Cora Kaplan suggests, by a dispersal or absence of paternal authority, and that this is indeed a significant reshaping of the 'imaginative landscape' of women's lives.[31] At the literal, surface level of the text, it is of course a simple matter to expel father from utopia. Yet, as Kaplan also notes, the 'shadow father' lingers on. He lurks, skulking like the serpent in Eden with its irresistible gifts of knowledge and power, disguised in a variety of phallic forms, or hidden in the body of the phallic mother. Women may be prepared to abandon their fathers as a prerequisite to the reconstruction of paradise, but it seems that we are now required to become symbolic orphans, since both Luce Irigaray and Julia Kristeva have spoken of the necessity of freeing oneself from the paralytic hold of the phallic mother, as Jane Gallop has noted:

The idyllic space of women together is supposed to exclude the phallus. The assumption that the 'phallus' is male expects that the exclusion of males be sufficient to make a non-phallic space. The threat represented by the mother to this feminine idyll might be understood through the notion that Mother, though female, is none the less phallic. So, as an afterthought, not only men, but Mother must be expelled from the innocent, non-phallic paradise.[32]

It is, I suggest, this phallic mother, represented as an aspect of the presiding deity, from whom the heroine of McKay's *Promise of the Rose Stone* wishes to free her people. The phallic mother, according to Gallop, is more dangerous than the father, since she is 'more veiled', less obvious.

Suzy McKee Charnas's *Motherlines*, as the title suggests, proposes a matrilineal community as a counter-society to the horrors of the dystopian Holdfast of her earlier novel, *Walk to the End of the World*. Like Gearhart's *Wanderground*, it excludes men from its privileged territory and similarly attempts to exclude the *symbolic* father – the phallus. It also revokes the goddess who presides over so many matriarchal or matrilineal eutopias, but I suggest that a suspicious reading may detect the veiled presence of the phallic mother – and that is my concern here.

The wilderness territory of *Motherlines* is inhabited by lines of 'Riding Women', descended from the founding mothers who escaped from the Holdfast of *Walk*. These transgressive heroines, who have broken free of the textual boundaries and scapegoat roles imposed upon them in the dystopian world of the first volume, have brought with them to the maternal space of *Motherlines* the secret of parthenogenetic reproduction, and pride themselves on the purity of their all-female 'lines'. There are, however, two ambiguous and problematic aspects to their situation.

First, 'motherlines' are clearly a feminist alternative to 'fatherlines' and to the entire apparatus of primogeniture, patriarchal succession, inheritance of authority and the law of the father. The women of the lines are, however, exclusive and resistant to change. They are also hostile to the different ways of other groups of escaped women, the 'free fems', who are constructed as Other, as the outsiders of this text. This situation is remedied by the transgressive action of Alldera, the text's liminal heroine, who provides a connecting link between the two groups as they eventually dissolve the boundaries which divide them and come to understand and accept each other. Thus, the phallic law of the mother is revised. The matrilineal tribes' initial resemblance to the patrilineal and phallocentric model of rigid exclusion and scapegoating is abandoned in favour of gynocentric flow and inclusivity.

The second difficulty is that the phallus seems to have a way of making its appearance in areas, textual or otherwise, designated as phallus-free zones. Here, in order to initiate the parthenogenetic process, the Riding Women mate with stallions. They require horse semen as the necessary catalyst, and they do not take the easier way of artificial insemination. The ceremony in which this extraordinary event takes place is 'the Gather', a carnivalesque and yet peculiarly decorous performance in which the entire female community participates, but in which the phallus is literally and unmistakably in evidence. (It is also tempting to speculate that there might be some associative slippage in the similarity of the signifiers, G/ather and F/ather.) The symbolic significance of this event may, however, be interpreted as something other than its literal representation would seem to indicate. When Alldera first learns 'what a Gather is all about', she responds with visceral revulsion and disbelief – much as the reader may do. What she realizes, upon reflection, is also shared by/with the reader:

Alldera sat silent, her hands on her knees, looking out at the shooting. She tried, but she could not make sense of what Nenisi said. This horse mating was like a river that Nenisi and the others had just crossed on an inexorable journey that they were making away from her into a mysterious and incomprehensible distance. And not the first river; there had been others, now she recognized them . . .[33]

This, I suggest, is a text which foregrounds and privileges transgressivity. Each of the symbolic rivers which the women cross is a threshold – a liminal point at which the conventional rules of structure no longer apply – signalling a new stage on the 'inexorable journey' that women are making in the course of their long revolution. It is a journey which patriarchy resists and, like Alldera, finds either unacceptable or incomprehensible. Charnas's project is to educate her reader by drawing her/ him along, in the company of Alldera, to cross those thresholds of unacceptability and to join the women in their new territory, beyond the law of the father. The phallus – here in the service of the Riding Women – makes its appearance, but is now subjected to the law of the mother.

Kristeva writes of this 'feminine power' which dissociates itself from the male:

This feminine power must have been experienced as denied power, more pleasant to seize because it was both archaic and secondary, a kind of substitute for effective power in the family and the city but no less authoritarian, the underhand double of explicit phallic power.[34]

Thus, the attempt to erase or obscure the phallus may be successful in so far as it removes *paternal* authority; but, as a mark of power and authority the phallus either becomes conspicuous by its absence, asserting *lack*, or finds its alternative location in the mother as representative of matriarchal law and female power. Whether or not the mother of *Motherlines* is phallic remains, I think, open to question.

V

The centre cannot hold / Mere anarchy is loosed upon the world
W. B. YEATS 'The Second Coming'

Doris Lessing's *Memoirs of a Survivor* decentres the figure of the mother, radically reconstructs the family, and anatomizes dystopia as process; a process which in her view has already begun, and for which, as she immediately makes clear, nostalgia – desire impelled by false mythologized memory – is not the remedy. 'Nostalgia' says the nameless female narrator, the survivor of the tale, is about 'craving' and 'regret'; it is a 'poisoned itch'.

It is a novel which also anatomizes, to use Nancy Chodorow's title phrase, the reproduction of mothering – specifically, bad mothering – demonstrating the way in which, as Chodorow says:

Women are prepared psychologically for mothering through the developmental situation in which they grow up, and in which women have mothered them.[35]

Kristeva tells us that 'this motherhood is the *fantasy* . . . of a lost territory',[36] and behind the dissolving wall of the narrator's apartment lie two very different and yet interconnected territories of motherhood. One of them is precisely the territory of the terrible mother, who presides over a dreadful, claustrophobic nursery world for which nostalgia and idealization are clearly totally inappropriate terms. The other is a more mysterious, ambiguous territory; potentially, but not yet, eutopia. It contains a shape-shifting, disorderly house of many mansions in which the narrator notes, so much 'work needed to be done' to make it 'habitable', but which nevertheless is 'full of possibilities, of alternatives'. Here, in the 'good' territory, the narrator moves dreamily yet purposefully, as if impelled by desire for something yet-to-be; but at the same time she experiences that sense of recognition and yearning – *heimlich* – associated with the longing for home:

> I did not go in, but stood there on the margin between the two worlds . . . I stood and looked, feeding with my eyes. I felt the most vivid expectancy, a longing: this place held what I needed, knew was there, had been waiting for – oh yes, all my life, all my life. I knew this place, recognized it . . .[37]

I want to focus on two closely connected points in this brief discussion of *Memoirs of a Survivor*. The first is the novel's concern with the idea of community, and with alternatives to the familial structures that presently exist; the second is the novel's representation of motherhood and of the reproduction of mothering.

The text contains several problematized representations of the human need and search for community. The one that concerns me here is the makeshift family of waifs and strays constructed by Emily and Gerald. It illustrates Emily's dismay at discovering that the children construct her as a mother and authority figure, and that it is apparently impossible 'not to have a pecking order'. But, as the narrator tells her, 'All that has happened is what always happens', since 'everybody has been taught to find a place in structure'. In other words, the communitarian spirit gives way, inevitably, to structure because we are conditioned to construct and locate ourselves within hierarchies – a pecking order. Moreover, this process, according to the narrator's account, is initiated in and by the presence of the mother, the first, omnipotent authority:

> It starts when you are born . . . She's a good girl. She's a bad girl. Have you been a good girl today? . . . We are all in it all our lives – you're a good little girl, you're a bad little girl. . . . It's a trap and we are all in it.[38]

This is the significant point of connection between the related themes of community and motherhood in *Memoirs*. It is the figure of the mother, in this account, who is doomed to frustrate our pathetic attempts to find true relationship in being and the utopian spirit of community.

In the bad place behind the wall, the narrator visits the world of childhood and the bad mother, where Emily is universalized as a daughter deprived of the good breast. The awful, omnipotent mother, 'that feared and powerful woman', gives her good breast to the baby boy, and rules despotically over the hot, airless world where 'nothing could change or move out of its order'. The painful process whereby this bad mother, arrested in her own primary narcissism, works to induce guilt and anxiety in her daughter – and husband – is emblematized in one particular scene of oppressive, familial interaction. For the narrator, however, these are 'real people', not ciphers, and the mother is 'one I had seen before, knew well'. She is, in other words, instantly recognizable as everybody's bad mother, the wicked step-mother of all the fairy tales. She is, indeed, her *own* bad mother. In a later scene, the narrator comes upon Emily's mother as a child, suffering the torments that she will in turn inevitably inflict upon her own daughter; the torments induced by a rigid nursery routine and the withholding of the good, nurturing breast:

The mother was elsewhere, it was not time to feed. The baby was desperate with hunger. Need clawed in her belly, she was being eaten alive by the need for food. . . . She twisted and fought and screamed. And screamed – for time must pass before she was fed, the strict order of the regime said it must be so: nothing could move that obdurate woman there, who had set her own needs and her relation with her baby according to some timetable alien to them both . . . I knew I was seeing an incident that was repeated again and again in Emily's? her mother's? early life.[39]

This, according to Lessing's narrator, is the way in which, under present conditions, motherhood is reproduced.

The good mother of *Memoirs* is harder to locate. Perhaps she is not there at all. The narrator, charged with the care of the child Emily, might have assumed the role of the good mother. It is, however, a role she explicitly rejects, along with the authority usually attached to that role. 'I had no authority', she says, 'She was not my child.' Indeed, there is no good mother for Emily. There is, however, the numenous 'Presence' of the good place behind the wall. It is indubitably female, as the consistent use of the female pronoun indicates, and when the narrator first encounters her she has a sense of 'welcome', of familiarity; and, as with the bad mother, a sense of someone known. She also knows that this is both the 'rightful' and the 'exiled' inhabitant of the protean mansion of alternative possibilities. I suggest that this shadowy but benign female presence is neither mother nor deity. I suggest further that she is, according to a Jungian rather than a Freudian *schema*, a representative of the female principle, perceived as exiled in the imbalanced world we currently inhabit, for which the disorderly mansion, on which so much work needs to be done, is a metaphor. It is time, Lessing is telling us in her didactic but supremely entertaining way, to put our house in order and to restore its exiled inhabitant – the female principle – to her rightful place.

At the end of the story, the reconstructed family group enters the world of the mansion to find the cosmic egg, a symbol which has appeared there several times already:

> . . . and on the lawn a giant black egg of pockmarked iron, but polished and glassy, around which, and reflected in the black shine, stood Emily, Hugo, Gerald, her officer father, her large, laughing, gallant mother, and little Denis, the four-year-old criminal, clinging to Gerald's hand . . .[40]

As they stand there, the 'force of their being' shatters the black, iron egg; shatters, that is, the symbol of iron-willed, fearsome maternality, and of the awesome power of the mother expressed in mythological terms as the cosmic egg. They break the chain of the reproduction of mothering, and in so doing they liberate the female principle, the Presence, who immediately appears and leads them forward 'out of this collapsed little world into another order of world altogether'. It is a world, however, which the text declines to describe; a world beyond the limits of the text that is located, perhaps, in Bloch's future unconscious.

As always in her novels, Lessing works to show how individual desire need not be incompatible with the greater, collective good; but at the same time she insists that the radical change and reconstruction of existing institutions – especially that of the family – are necessary. And again, as so often in Lessing's work, it is the vision of the lone, liminal soul – the narrator and survivor of the tale – whose forward-driving desire resists nostalgia; who moves beyond existing boundaries and value systems and in so doing makes the system grow, and indicates a possible way forward.

VI

From the foregoing, it has become evident that women writing about utopia, even while articulating, implicitly or explicitly, a desire to return to the mother, are urgently calling for the demolition of that most cherished of Western institutions, the family, in its bourgeois, traditional form.

Dorothy Dinnerstein believes that the family is based upon 'the infantile wish to *return* to an illusion of *oneness*', and that this desire is inimical to the well-being and survival of our social and natural environment.[41]

But, like romantic love, which in our culture is usually the prelude to the making of a family, the whole question of familial and gender relationships is entangled with the problem of women's complicity, as both Gallop and Dinnerstein have noted. That complicity, furthermore, is not always grounded in conscious, considered conservatism. Jane Gallop, in her discussion of Kristeva and Lacan, identifies 'two kinds of maternals', one conservative and one dissident. One of the dangers of Kristevan theory, as she sees it, is that whereas Kristeva urges a strengthening of the 'semiotic' – the pre-Oedipal, pre-linguistic maternal space – as that which breaks closure and disrupts the symbolic (the law of the father), the fall into the semiotic *may* be constructed as a return to the Lacanian 'imaginary' which, according to Gallop, is 'conservative and comforting' and 'tends towards closure'.[42]

Kristeva continues her discussion of female dissatisfaction with the conventional, constricting contextualization of female desire by saying:

We are not surprised, then, to read of women who proclaim another sort of love, whether for another woman or for children. This brings us into the obscure realm of primary narcissism or the archaic relationship which a woman has with her mother . . .[43]

That archaic relationship with the mother has been the chief subject of this discussion. My purpose has been, among other things, to expose the phallic mother, to unveil her as it were, and to point to the ways in which she may function as a representative of a fundamentally conservative ideology. I have tried to indicate how radical feminism's valorization of the mother and maternality risks, or may be impelled by, the regressive desire for fusion, and/or may be unwittingly seduced by the phallus as signifier of the law. Matriarchal law embodied in the mother may be just as phallic as the patriarchal law embodied in the father, and may constitute an unproductive replication of existing hierarchical models.

In unpacking the recurrent trope of coming home to mother in utopia, we have noted the way in which the heroine experiences a sense of recognition, a sense of having been there before, a sense of arrival. But we have also noted how, in the more complex and sophisticated texts, this is problematized. A precondition of coming home is, of course, to have been away. The *desire* to return can only be articulated from a position of being away, just as the desire for the semiotic space of the maternal *chora* can only articulate itself from a position of lack, within the symbolic order. But, having been away, and having taken up that position, the place/space to which one returns is familiar but – since now designated in and by the symbolic – it is, paradoxically, a place in which one has never been before. As the hero of Ursula Le Guin's *The Dispossessed* says: 'You can go home, so long as you realize it's a place you've never been'. The return, in other words, is to a place in the *future* unconscious, not to some prelapsarian garden or maternal breast of the past. The hero's words, as Tom Moylan points out, are 'an echo of Ernst Bloch's notion of *Heimat* and the forward pull of history'.[44] They become an expression of what Bloch calls 'the latency of being to come at work'.[45] Bloch fully recognizes the yearning of the human spirit, not just for something better than the radical insufficiency of the present, but for something ineffable, some impossible perfection. He warns, however, against memories, conscious or unconscious, which draw us back to the past as a retreat from the anxieties of the present, and speaks of the *novum* – the new which surprises, and pulls us forward into the as-yet-unrealized future – as the authentically utopian impulse.

Ernst Bloch has expressed as well as anyone this sense of coming home as an index, not of regress, but of utopian hope and fulfilment:

The real genesis is not at the beginning, but at the end, and it only begins when society and existence become radical, that is, grasp themselves at the root. The root of history, however, is the human being, working, producing, reforming and surpassing the givens around him or her. If human beings have grasped themselves and what is theirs, without depersonalization and alienation, founded in real democracy, *then something comes into being in the world that shines into everyone's childhood and where no one has yet been – home.*[46]

Like the hero Shevek in Le Guin's *The Dispossessed*, Bloch says that we can come home, but it must be to a place we have never been before, located in the *future* rather than the *past* unconscious. Only thus can the desire for utopia work progressively, to pull the present forward, towards the better future state.

9

McTopia: *Eating Time*

JOHN O'NEILL

The shortness of life is the length of the arts, especially of the art of utopia. I am going to start by defining a principal feature of *utopian bodies*, which I shall call *atresia*, in order to capture the utopian attempt to suture societies and bodies from time. Outside of utopia everything is eaten *by* time. This chronic state is the mark of all life and of every living thought, feeling and gesture. In view of the extraordinary literature[1] on the subject of utopian practices, it is inevitable that I shall fall into some conventional assumptions with regard to my topic. Indeed, it is necessary that I do so if I am to entertain any hope of focusing attention upon the device of *atresia*, through which I intend to draw together the following temporal phenomena that I consider constitutive of McTopia:

1. *Time as repetition*, that is, suturing the flow of corporeal time [McTaste]
2. The *mortification of objects* [The 'Square' Meal: Burger-Fries-Coke]
3. The *foreclosure* of the political history of fast-food by McTopia as the universal locus of the two phenomena cited immediately above

I begin with the final observation, inasmuch as I am anxious not to float McTopia outside of the geopolitics of fast food, despite employment of the tropes of semiology. Let us say, then, that I am employing an historical semiosis of structures that cannot avoid the fall into time, however much they struggle to achieve *atresia* in order to block time's passages. Therefore, despite my earlier fascination with Mary Douglas's unabashed claims for the universality of the structure of the meal,[2] I now see that this analysis must be modified by the history of the food industry and the forces of political economy that have so forcefully set the table at home and abroad. In the United States, as elsewhere, food production is an industry whose profitability to the larger holding companies involved in it results, for example, in the American beef complex:[3]

. . . the etic preference for beef over pork in the United States is of rather recent origin. The designation of beef as a symbol of wealth, generosity, and virility did not generate the ecological, technological, demographic and political ascendency of the beef industry; it was the ascendency of the industry as a result of those processes that has bestowed upon beef its special symbolic pre-eminence. It is not the magic of arbitrary symbols that restricts the composition of hamburgers to beef and only beef (and beef fat), but the beef industry's political clout in Congress and the Department of Agriculture.[4]

Although beef is less edible than pork, its by-products – fertilizers, soap, shoes and pharmaceuticals – are very profitable lines, and are exploitable by large corporations whose geopolitical clout has permitted them to colonize Central America for 'burger pasture'. The result is that Latin American exports of beef (best beef reclassified as US cow-meat) to the United States fast food industry acts to considerably dampen the impact of the US rate of inflation upon poorer families and individuals – a policy similar to that of England's importing of food from her colonies in the nineteenth century. Endemic to such a food policy is the increased nutritional deprivation of the 'third world', matched by the malnutrition in the 'first-world' itself that is caused by over-feeding on 'industrial-grade beef'.[5] The increase in pasture lands required for this process results in expanding deforestation, flooding, soil erosion, peasant dislocation and under-employment, while landholdings become larger and offer even greater collateral in the credit markets that fuel the burger economy and its new elites.

To the extent that the political economy of fast food is forgotten, then, McTopia appears to lie *between* the New World and the Old World – it is nowhere because it is everywhere. It is everywhere, because, wherever it is, it is always the place where the 'taste' is the same. The pleasure of McTopia resides in the 'play' between its 'McText', as advertised, and its McEvents as ruled by their McProcessing. So far from being a neutral (nowhere) organization, however, McTopia's M celebrates its relentless conquest of space-time by representing its open-endedness through its table of ever-mounting sales. There is no dialectical tension between the McConcept and McHistory. Time is eaten up relentlessly – the party is never over and there is no-place for critical indigestion or for *post festum* analysis of any other meal. McTopia must expand or, rather, the necessity of McTopia's expansion is given with the iterability of its *alimentary 'concept'*, whose ritual observance guarantees the colonization of its landscape. In McTopia, everything is fed into the process of entering and exiting from a meal that will not eat up time that is

minimally available as a release from socially committed time elsewhere. McTopia, however, is not a utopian place set apart from other social institutions. Whether McBurger is consumed in the automobile or in the 'restaurant', everything is timed to return the customer to the traffic flow to which s/he belongs and within which s/he will digest McMeal. The ubiquity of McSign signals the speed with which one can exit and return to the flow of society's traffic. All distances become distances between one McTopia and another, just as all times become times between one McMeal and another in McDay.

What, then, are we to make of the great golden fries in the sky? McArch symbolizes the dream of self-reliance – the body of *atresia* that can avoid or postpone the losses that it suffers in everyday life. McArch is both an opening and not an opening. It is a passage to a place where happiness is blocked by the removal of change, variety and imperfection through endless repetition. McFood fulfils the body's *dream of atresia* – its removal from the risk and revulsion in its own orifices. Just as Deleuze and Guattari remark that the 'body-without-organs' is never completely achieved,[6] the same must be said of 'the body-without-orifices'. Thus, what I am calling attention to in *atresia* is a form of the body-without-organs produced within the McTopian organization of fast-food. The body of *atresia* approximates the junkie's body as it is described in Burroughs's *Naked Lunch*:

The human body is scandalously inefficient. Instead of a mouth and an anus to get out of order why not have one all-purpose hole to eat *and* eliminate?[7]

McBody sacrifices itself to the collective circulation – '90 Billion Served' – of fast food, alcohol, drugs and perversion through which the economy achieves its double inscription of the body's passages within a commercial body. McTopia is an *alimentary utopia*. As Louis Marin has shown, in the design of the Abbey of Thélème the kitchens and the dining room are erased in favour of the text itself as food.[8] The body is only integrated mathematically with the Abbey, or through the Vitruvian grid that maps its navel to the Abbey's world. The orificial, sexual, alimentary and excretory body – the body of birth and death – is glossed over in favour of the abstract universality of Vitruvius's proportionate man. But, as Marin shows, it is the Rabelaisian text itself that performs the missing functions of the body (I have argued something similar in respect of Montaigne's *Essays*[9]). By contrast, in McTopia the excretory body is the 'body-in-line', moving forward, moving back, pausing at the bolted-down table to swallow the already dying burger/fries before garbaging the remains at the Thank You (trash can) and itself at the Exit. At the same time, the body is washed out with a frozen juice or an aroma-less coffee.

Everything conspires to render the alimentary Utopia uni-form. Thus the attendants themselves are dressed in uni-sex uniforms, they all offer the same greeting, and repeat the same inventory of questions to the answer (burger, fries, coke) already in wait for the customer. In no case does the customer choose or reject the items picked out of the assembly line. This is because the uniformity of the product-and-process rules out the arbitrary, the deviant, or the affectionate selection of the 'bigger' or 'nicest one', as might happen in an ordinary shop. While it is adamant about its status as a 'Family Restaurant', it is essential to McTopia that it does not surrender to the authority of the family body or to the familized eating pace of a restaurant. Thus there is never any evidence that anyone prepares McFood. Nor does anyone supervise its consumption. The absence of the mother-body is assured in the first place, as is the absence of the father-body in the second; and this double absence is triangulated by the child's decision to take the family to McTopia in the beginning because it is a 'restaurant' where a child can be sure to get a burger. Since McFood is neither prepared nor served, the parental bodies are themselves reduced to defamilized and desexualized bodies with nothing to say that hasn't already been said in McTopia's advertisements. Thus the defamilized child is the perfect inhabitant of McTopia. Admission nevertheless requires that the child be seen but not heard. McTopia favours children's birthday parties, of course, since this serves to recruit clients. Thereafter, children are frozen. They must not become teenagers since this would reintroduce the body with unpredictable controls, that is, the body that is noisy, dirty, sexual and languishing. Teenagers work at McTopia. But they do not linger or hang out there. Teenage culture belongs in McTopia advertisements but not in McTopia 'restaurants'. The absence of teenage or rock-age music in McTopia is more noticeable than the absence of dirt, of conversation and of the family. McTopia is the bastion of child labour – even when that labour is performed by recycled elders. Kids work in McTopia. They do not play there – although ideally all kids should play at going to McTopia. Between the fantasy and the reality lies the world of sweated labour at minimum wages. This is the young body that McTopia cannot hide, however much it may dress it up.[10] It is, therefore, especially horrendous for McTopia once any of its sites are contaminated by murder, homeless beggars, prostitutes and by drug dealers who can work out of the unsurveyed area between the street and the service counter of the 'restaurant'. Here the urbanization of McTopia brings it into contact with the economy from which it offers an escape that is increasingly precarious.

The counterpart of McTopia's sweated labour is the hurried McTopia consumer, whose total time in the restaurant can only exceed five to ten minutes if s/he is prepared to eat burgers/fries that have turned cold and gone to mush. Thus the artful McTopia consumer is pitted from the moment s/he leaves the counter against food that (never having been hot) is already beginning to turn cold and to decompose (nor can it be re-heated). A decision must be made to swallow fast – facilitated by meat and potatoes that in any case need no biting or chewing, and by condiments that soften them up even further – or else to garbage even before swallowing-and-garbaging! Because this alimentary behaviour is artful, it must be learned from infancy, if it is to be achieved readily – even though it tends to repeat on the elder stomach, yielding McBelch, the last gasp of McBody in its surrender to McMouth. McFood is fast because only you can slow it down. In other words, since you serve yourself – only you are responsible for how and what you eat. This is because, once you have paid for McFood, you are on your own. You serve the food; you seat yourself; you pace your meal; you clean up the remains. Fast-food not only recruits cheap labour on the production side, it relies on free labour donated as 'self-service' to complete its delivery and disposal. By the same token, fast-food is set in a panoptical and disciplinary culture that has its origins in the super-market, where customers allow themselves to be continuously surveyed by cameras that watch them working for no wages at all, lifting, carting and hauling on behalf of the market – not to mention gas-stations and large department stores.

Fast-food nevertheless imposes upon its casual communicants a strict order of service. Intolerant of fuzziness, the fast-food line requires that its customers flow towards their goal with the same precision that its supply lines move their contents towards the counter. To achieve this, the customer must be oriented from point of entry to the 'menu' above the pay counter. Choices are made on foot, while approaching a server who will register an order that must be paid for *before it is eaten*. (These two features already violate the restaurant code.) The next sequence involves turning to the 'service' area, counter (pail), where the customer condiments 'hir' meal. However, since this is a phase where there may occur inordinate expenditures of ketchup, mustard, onion and pickle in the personalization of the purchase, McTopia (unlike other outlets) controls the dispensation of these items at point of ordering and payment. It thereby restricts the 'service' area to a dispensary of paper and plastic products in the service of dirt control. (These McTopian features eliminate the restaurant functions of the waiter in the mediation/ recommendation of elements in the meal and its complements, as well as in clearing the table.) The next phase of the post-purchase period is involved with finding a seat or seats *after* the meal is served rather than before. Here the customer's allegiance to fast food is most in evidence, since it requires that previous communicants have disgorged themselves from McTopia in a continuous flow so that there is always a place for the next one (subject to the fast restriction that the furniture is bolted down and cannot be rearranged to correct seating imbalances). Once seated, the fast-food communicant proceeds to eat with 'hir' hands amidst the garbage that has been created by unwrapping the food – garbage that is carefully reserved in order to rewrap the remains for self-disposal, that is, for the climactic point of garbaging and exiting. (By now, any illusion of having eaten in a restaurant has faded.) Here the mortification of the fast-food communicant is at its highest point, whereafter it fades into (in)digestion off the premises, as the customer moves back into the flow of traffic. Some customers swallow their 'take-away' at the wheel, bringing life and death even closer.)

McCommunion

1. Get in line
2. Look up to the menu
3. Order food & drink & extra condiments
4. Pay when order is registered
5. Serve yourself napkins, straws and implements (no cutlery)

6. Seat yourself
7. Eat and drink
8. Clean away after yourself – Thank you
9. Exit
10. Steps (5–8) can be saved in Drive-Away and (5–6) in Drive-In, where the automobile *is* the restaurant.

What is achieved in the ritual order above is a momentary contact with a food that is completely uncontaminated by local cultures and customs:

The Bolshoi Mak will taste exactly the same as it does in Toronto, in Rio or in Des Moines, Iowa.[11]

The unfailing repetition of McTaste is paid for by ruling out any such incongruities as asking the servers what they recommend or of disprefer-ring the items that they pick from the rack – no next burger is any better than the previous one. Each item occasions no comment, anymore than it does while being consumed. McEating is thus, as nearly as possible, McFeeding. Conversation is as much a potential contaminant of the fast-food order as the dirt it is threatened with from its own garbage. It is similarly packaged:

'Hi, can I help you?'
'Quarter pounder with cheese, large fries, large coke.'
'Four fifty, please.'

Such conversational couplets are fed into the line, but are never allowed to expand lest the line be slowed down by them. The potential for such spills is, of course, very high from a youthful and familied clientele. A remarkable feature of McTopia is its elimination from its premises of the two sub-cultures it otherwise celebrates in its advertisements. The result is that McTopia operates more like a *mortuary-without-music!* than like the restaurants, cafés and diners from which it sets itself apart. McTopia caters to no other taste than McTaste even when it appears to add 'designer' or 'antique' elements to its decor, since these items are always subordinated to the exterior iconography of McTopia and its interior icon – the menu. At McTopia the menu is the venue.

My approach to the utopian idealization of place, then, differs from the earlier work of Louis Marin – and even from his more recent views – inasmuch as McTopia is neither a dystopia nor a degenerate utopia. McTopia is the temporally consistent achievement of its own presenta-tion of a mass-produced square meal, through its integration of the consumer's alimentary functions into the 'self-service' eating order of

'McRestaurant'. This is not to say that there are not signs of the degeneration of McRestaurant's fast-food concept, for these are evident in its contamination by nutritious food and menu supplements that threaten to slow McMeal into a time-consuming, profit-eating activity:

'Too many items slow the system down', he [Mr Richard McDonald] says. 'They should be very careful, or *fast food will be history*.'[12]

Mr McDonald's critical comment is interesting, as well as amusing, because it reveals that the concept of 'fast food' cannot in fact be frozen at a given historical juncture in the decline of family eating. The larger history of defamilization has so increased its pace that the family itself demands 'ever-faster-but-healthier' foods. Thus McTopia finds itself accommodating McFamily as each institution responds to the intensification of exploitable time in late capitalist society. The hamburger's fate has now taken a new turn with the greening of late capitalist consumption. The burger must learn to look lean and to share the 'plate' with more vegetables and fruits (a shift that might even reinvent the recycled paper-plate).

Yet, fast-food is not intelligible through its apparent abundance, nor even through the speed of its flow. Fast-food is what it is because food is *scarce* and the time needed to buy, prepare and eat it is scarce. Today, we not only work-against-the-clock – a highly stylized battle replayed in professional speed-sports – but we also 'consume-against-the-clock'.[13]

As I have argued elsewhere,[14] *consumption is work*, it takes time and it competes with itself since choosing, hauling, maintaining and repairing the things we buy is so time-consuming that we are forced to save time on eating, drinking, sex, dressing, sleeping, exercising and relaxing. The result is that Americans have taught us to eat standing, walking, running and driving – and, above all, never to finish a meal in favour of the endless snack (McSnack is literally the 'square' meal it momentarily replaces).[15] Thus the high-altar of the fast-food complex is the trash-can, the half-concealed garbage pail that offers us 'Thank you' or 'Service' as we struggle to fill it without spilling garbage over ourselves, or that functions as the table around which we eat, and in the belly of which previous deposits of garbage are held. For a while, the art of eating-on-the-run founded upon the McDrive-in complex appeared to have migrated from its burger-base to a doughnut-base – with doughnut shops opening where gas-stations closed. However, it now seems that gas-stations have found ways to reintegrate both functions, so that we can now pizza, burger, fry and coffee ourselves almost as quickly as we can gas our autos.

An added irony is that McFood teaches Americans how to eat poorly rather than how the poor would eat if they didn't increasingly eat McFood. What is involved here is the general de-skilling of the home, the kitchen, the cook and the consumer. McFamily Restaurant, of course, attempts to assuage the mother's guilt – guilt caused by her trying to buy a quick fix in the kitchen. The home cook has been seduced by defrosting and microwaving meals that again serve to speed-up the home-kitchen in order to release everyone for further consumption. The family meal, then, is destined to be eaten so fast that it has become too slow to cook. The result is that fathers can now share in the cooking of the meal that everyone can do without – even the kids, since they can all track through McTopia as soon as they leave home, and even on the way back. Defamilized meals – the ultimate goal of McTopia – constitute a further step in the democratization of American taste that begins with the infant addiction to sugary foods and 'soft' drinks (actually subject to the hardest sell in the world). The result of such gastronomic levelling is that America is the only country in the world where the rich eat as badly as the poor – a demonstration-effect that serves to underwrite the globalization of McTopia.

References

Introduction

1 The symposium, sponsored by the Centre for Modern Cultural Studies, took place on 8–9 November 1991.
   Louis Marin's *Utopiques, Jeux d'espace* (Paris, 1973) is also available in English, translated by Robert A. Vollrath: *Utopics: Spatial Play* (New Jersey, 1984). Marin's most recent work involving a section on 'Utopiques' is *Lectures traversières* (Paris, 1992): cf. pp. 35–125.
2 See Fredric Jameson, 'Of Islands and Trenches: Neutralization and the Production of Utopian Discourse' in *The Ideologies of Theory: Essays 1971–86* (London, 1988), I, pp. 80–81. I am indebted for this reference to Glenn Bowman, whose help in organizing the symposium is also gratefully acknowledged.
3 See Anthony Vidler, *Claude-Nicholas Ledoux: Architecture and Social Reform at the End of the Ancien Regime* (Cambridge, MA, 1990), p. 342.
4 Jean Baudrillard, *Cool Memories II, 1987–1990* (Paris, 1990), p. 47.
5 Andrew Ross, *Strange Weather: Culture, Science and Technology in the Age of Limits* (London and New York, 1991), p. 170.
6 Roland Barthes, *Sade, Fourier, Loyola* (Paris, 1971), p. 7.

2 J. C. Davis, Formal Utopia/Informal Millennium: The Struggle between Form and Substance as a Context for Seventeenth-century Utopianism

1 For examples of this line of criticism see Richard Sylvan and David Bennett, *Of Utopias, Tao and Deep Ecology*. Discussion Papers in Environmental Philosophy, no. 19 (Australian National University, Canberra, 1990) where Barbara Goodwin and I appear theoretically closer than either of us might find comfortable. Darko Suvin, 'Locus, Horizon and Orientation: The Concept of Possible Worlds as a Key to Utopian Studies', *Utopian Studies*, I/2 (1990), p. 76.
2 Suvin, 'Locus, Horizon and Orientation', pp. 79–80. For Suvin's definition see Ruth Levitas, 'Educated Hope: Ernst Bloch on Abstract and Concrete Utopia', *Utopian Studies*, I/2 (1990), p. 14. For my own grappling with the problem of definition, see J. C. Davis, *Utopia and the Ideal Society* (Cambridge, 1981), Ch. 1.
3 C. H. Firth and R. S. Rait, eds, *Acts and Ordinances of the Interregnum 1642–1660* (London, 1911), vol. II, pp. 409–10.
4 Blair Worden, *The Rump Parliament, 1648–53* (Cambridge, 1974).
5 My emphasis. See J. C. Davis, *Fear, Myth and History: The Ranters and the Historians* (Cambridge, 1986), pp. 101–102; *idem*, 'Fear, Myth and Furore: Reappraising the Ranters', *Past and Present*, 129 (1990), pp. 79–103.
6 J. C. Davis, 'Against Formality: One Aspect of the English Revolution', *Transactions of the Royal Historical Society* (forthcoming).

7 J. C. Davis, 'Cromwell's Religion', in John Morrill, ed., *Oliver Cromwell and the English Revolution* (London, 1990), pp. 202–3; Peter Sterry, *England's Deliverance from the Northern Presbytery compared with its Deliverance from the Roman Papacy* (Leith, 1652), pp. 6, 7, 18, 43.

8 C. H. Firth, ed., *Selections from the Papers of William Clarke, Secretary to the Council of the Army*, 4 vols (Camden Society, 1891–1901), vol. II, pp. 84–7, 119–20, 184–6. See also Blair Worden, 'Oliver Cromwell and the sin of Achan' in Derek Beales and Geoffrey Best, eds, *History, Society and the Churches* (Cambridge, 1985), pp. 125–45.

9 For a more detailed treatment of this theme see Davis, 'Against Formality'.

10 Natalie Zemon Davis, *Society and Culture in Early Modern France* (London, 1975); Barry Reay, ed., *Popular Culture in Early Modern England* (Oxford, 1985); Emmanuel Le Roy Ladurie, *Carnival in Romans* (London, 1981).

11 For one example of the formalities expected of victims see J. A. Sharpe, "'Last Dying Speeches" Religion, Ideology and Public Execution in Seventeenth Century England', *Past and Present*, 107 (1985), pp. 144–67.

12 G. Oestreich, *Neostoicism and the Early Modern State*, eds B. Oestreich and H. G. Koenigsberger, trans. D. McLintock (Cambridge, 1982); Peter Burke, 'Tacitism, Scepticism and Reason of State', in J. H. Burns, ed., *The Cambridge History of Political Thought 1450–1700* (Cambridge, 1991), pp. 491–5.

13 John Lilburne, *Strength out of Weaknesse* (1649), pp. 21–2. For the general argument summarized here, see J. C. Davis, 'Religion and the Struggle for Freedom in the English Revolution', *Historical Journal*, XXXV/3 (1992), pp. 507–30.

14 Joseph Salmon, *Heights in Depths* (1651). An Apologeticall Hint (my emphasis); see also pp. 4–5. See also Peter Toon, 'The Latter-Day Glory', in Peter Toon, ed., *The Millennium and the Future of Israel* (Cambridge, 1970), p. 38.

15 For an earlier statement of these ideal society typologies see J. C. Davis, *Utopia and the Ideal Society: A Study of English Utopian Writing 1516–1700* (Cambridge, 1981), Ch. 1.

16 Louis Marin, *Utopics: Spatial Play*, trans. Robert A. Vollrath (New Jersey, 1984), p. xxi.

17 James Harrington, *Aphorisms Political* (1659), in J. G. A. Pocock, ed., *The Political Works of James Harrington* (Cambridge, 1977), p. 763.

18 Cf., for example, Simon Berington, *The Memoirs of Sigr. Gaudentio di Lucca* (London, 1737), p. 202.

19 Yevgeny Zamyatin, *We* (Harmondsworth, 1972), p. 138.

20 Harrington, *A Discourse Upon this Saying* (1659), in Pocock, ed., *Political Works*, p. 744.

21 Barbara Goodwin, *Social Science and Utopia: Nineteenth Century Models of Social Harmony* (Hassocks, Sussex, 1981).

22 Gilles Lapouge, *Utopie et Civilisations* (Geneva, 1973), p. 13.

23 Marin, *Utopics*, p.xxv.

24 Krishan Kumar, *Utopianism* (Milton Keynes, 1991), p. 7.

25 Paul Foriers, 'Les Utopies et le Droit', in Jean Lameere, ed., *Les Utopies a la Renaissance* (Paris/Brussels, 1963), p. 234.

26 J. C. Davis, 'Science and Utopia: The History of a Dilemma', in Everett Mendelsohn and Helga Nowotny, eds, *Nineteen Eighty-Four: Science Between Utopia and Dystopia* (Dordrecht, 1984), pp. 21–48.

27 Ottavio Amaro, Maria Luisa Attardo and Giuliama de Fazio, *Ci Sare Una Volta un'Isola* (Vibo Valenzia, 1986): reviewed in *Utopian Studies*, I/1 (1990), p. 116.

28 *Annus Sophiae Jubilaeus* (1700), pp. 54–6. Cf. the formalization of landscape ('all trim and neat and pretty') in William Morris and in Aldous Huxley's *Island* ('Nature here

was no longer merely natural: the landscape has been composed, had been reduced to its geometrical essences . . .'). Kumar, *Utopianism*, p. 104; Aldous Huxley, *Island* (New York, 1963), p. 20.

29 *An Essay Concerning Adepts* (1698), p. 23.

30 J. C. Davis, 'Pocock's Harrington: Grace, Nature and Art in the Classical Republicanism of James Harrington', *The Historical Journal*, XXIV:3 (1981), pp. 683–97.

31 Thomas Campanella, *The City of the Sun*, trans. A. M. Elliott and K. Millner, introduced by A. L. Morton (London and New York, 1981), p. 32.

32 F. E. Held, ed., *Christianopolis: an Ideal State of the Seventeenth Century Translated from the Latin of Johann Valentin Andreae with an Historical Introduction* (New York, 1916), pp. 141, 158, 170.

33 Edward Surtz and J. H. Hexter, eds, *Utopia*, vol. IV of *The Complete Works of St Thomas More* (New Haven and London, 1965), p. 135.

34 Cited in Lise Leibacher-Ouvrard, *Libertinage et Utopies sous le Regne de Louis XIV* (Geneva, 1989), p. 41.

35 Huxley, *Island*, pp. 2–4.

36 J. C. Davis, 'Utopianism' in Burns, ed., *Cambridge History of Political Thought 1450–1700*, pp. 340–1.

37 Vivian Carol Fox, *Deviance in English Utopias in the Sixteenth, Seventeenth and Eighteenth Centuries*, unpublished PhD. thesis, Boston University, 1969.

38 For an example of the former influence see Luigi Firpo, 'Kaspar Stiblin, Utopiste', in Lameere, ed., *Les Utopies à la Renaissance*, pp. 107–33. For the latter, Frederic Lachevre, ed., *La Premiere Utopie Francaise: La Royaume D'Antangil* (Paris, 1933).

39 On this aspect of utopia generally see Bronislaw Baczko, *Utopia Lights: The Evolution of the Idea of Social Progress* (New York, 1989), Section V: Utopia and Festivals.

40 Francis Bacon, *New Atlantis: A Worke Unfinished* (1627), pp. 29–30.

41 *Ibid.*, pp. 44–7.

42 Paolo Paruta, *Politick Discourses*, trans. Henry, Earl of Monmouth (1657), pp. 1, 2, 11.

43 John Toland, ed., *The Oceana and other Works of James Harrington* (1771), pp. xv, 441, 445, 569.

44 It is noteworthy that Harrington's confidence in his republican institutions is such that he sees no need to exclude royalists from civic participation. Cf. Davis, *Utopia and the Ideal Society*, pp. 208–9.

45 George Psalmanazar, *An Historical and Geographical Description of Formosa* (1704), pp. 163–6.

46 Bulwer Lytton, *The Coming Race* (London, 1875), p. 23.

47 For a discussion in terms of 'system design' see Robert Boguslaw, *The New Utopians* (Englewood Cliffs, New Jersey, 1965).

48 Compare the discussion of Machiavelli's problem of the *buoni ordini* in an age of corruption in Nicolai Rubinstein, 'Italian Political Thought, 1450–1530', in Burns, ed., *Cambridge History of Political Thought 1450–1700*, pp. 51–4.

49 Lapouge, *Utopie et Civilisations*, p. 24.

50 Compare, Miriam Eliav-Feldon, *Realistic Utopias: The Ideal Imaginary Societies of the Renaissance 1516–1630* (Oxford, 1982), p. 45: '. . . no scope is left for spontaneity or chance.'

51 For a general treatment of this theme see Davis, 'Religion and the Struggle for Freedom'.

52 John Lilburne, *The Just Defence of John Lilburne* (1653) in David Wootton, ed., *Divine Right and Democracy: An Anthology of Political Writing in Stuart England* (Harmondsworth, 1986), p. 147.

53 *Ibid.*, p. 146.

54 Isaac Pennington Jr, *The Fundamental Right, Safety and Liberty of the People* (1651), To the present Parliament of England.
55 Davis, 'Religion and the Struggle for Freedom'.
56 In earlier writings I have stressed the impact of utopian modes in terms of a post-liberal perception of freedom. This still seems to me to be a valid stock-taking exercise, but we are beginning to recover the history of terms such as liberty/freedom and to understand their changing contexts across time. It is the historian's primary task to understand the past in its own terms. My own understanding of the meaning of 'freedom' in the seventeenth century has changed, and with it I must revise my perception of freedom in early modern utopias. Cf. Davis, *Utopia and the Ideal Society*, Conclusion.
57 Cf. John Locke, *The Second Treatise of Government*, Ch. IV.
58 Pennington, *The Fundamental Right*, To the present Parliament.
59 See the second collect for peace in the Order for Morning Prayer, The Book of Common Prayer. Cf. Joshua Sprigge and Captain Clarke at the Whitehall debates. Firth, ed., *Clarke Papers*, II, pp. 87, 93–5.
60 *Exodus*, 7:16 (see also 8:20, 9:11, 9:13, 10:3 and variants at 3:18, 5:1). The motif of Cromwell as Moses reinforced the use of these texts in the 1650s. The heart searching of that decade is not so much about liberation as an end in itself, as about service with liberation as purely preliminary, an enabling step.
61 For an example of the text's use see Pennington, *Fundamental Right*, To the present Parliament.
62 [Hezekiah Woodward], *Christmas Day* (1656), pp. 19–20, 25.
63 G. F. Nuttall, *The Puritan Spirit: Essays and Addresses* (London, 1967), p. 116; A. S. P. Woodhouse, ed., *Puritanism and Liberty*, 2nd edition (London, 1950), pp. [67–8].
64 C. H. Firth and R. S. Rait, eds, *Acts and Ordinances of the Interregnum* (London, 1911), I, 913–4.
65 Ibid., I, 1133–4.
66 Marjorie Reeves has pointed out that, in medieval millennial thought, *sub gratia* meant under the dynamic, providential-millennial activity of Christ. 'The Development of Apocalyptic Thought: Medieval Attitudes' in C. A. Patrides and Joseph Wittreich, eds, *The Apocalypse in English Renaissance Thought and Literature* (Manchester, 1984), p. 41.
67 William Walwyn, *A Pearle in a Dounghill* (1646), in A. L. Morton, ed., *Freedom in Arms: A Selection of Leveller Writings* (London, 1975), p. 81.
68 Gardiner, *Constitutional Documents*, p. 334. My emphasis.
69 Cf. J. C. Davis, *Utopia and the Ideal Society: A Study of English Utopian Writing 1516–1700* (Cambridge, 1981), pp. 178–9.
70 For Vane's views on conscience see Margaret Judson, *The Political Thought of Sir Henry Vane the Younger* (Philadelphia, 1969); Paul Harris, 'Young Sir Henry Vane's Arguments for Freedom of Conscience', *Political Science*, XL/1 (1988), pp. 34–48; 'A Digger Hymn of 1650' cited in R. C. Richardson and G. M. Ridden, 'Introduction', in Richardson and Ridden, eds, *Freedom and the English Revolution*, p. 3.
71 Joshua Sprigge at the Whitehall debates. Firth, ed., *Clarke Papers*, II, pp. 84–7. The quotation comes from p. 87.
72 Philip Nye at Whitehall, ibid., II, pp. 119–20.
73 John Goodwin, *Anti-Cavalierisme* (1642), p.8.
74 See, for example W[illiam] A[spinall], *Thunder from Heaven*, (1655); *The Work of the Age* (1655).
75 John Canne, *A Seasonable Word* (1959), p. 5.
76 Anon., *Certain Quaeres* (1648), pp. 3–7. The argument is also used against the adoption of *any* constitution in 1648–9, specifically *The Agreement of the People* at Whitehall. See Firth, ed., *Clarke Papers*, II, pp. 84–7, 108, 123–4.

77 See, for example, John Tillinghast, *Generation Work* (1653); John Rogers, *Sagrir* (1653) and *Dod* (1653); John Canne, *A Voice from the Temple* (1653) and *A Second Voyce* (1653).

78 Christopher Feake, *A Beam of Light Shining in the Midst of Much Darkness and Confusion* (1659), pp. 53–9.

79 Christopher Feake, *The Oppressed Close Prisoner in WINDSOR Castle* (1655), pp. 2–3, 10–11, 14–15.

80 [John Cook], *Monarchy No Creature of Gods Making* (Waterford, 1651). For Cook's providentialism see also *Unum Necessarium* (1648), p. 11.

81 *A Compleate Collection of the Lives Speeches Private Passages, Letters and Prayers of Those Persons lately Executed* (1661), pp. 55–6. Harrison justified his actions as service to 'a good Lord'; Carew justified his as bearing witness to 'the true Magistracy, that Magistracy that is in the Word of the Lord'. Colonel Axtell insisted that the Bible 'hath the whole cause in it'. Ibid., pp. 21, 37, 169.

82 Richard Coppin, *A Hint of the Glorious Mystery of Divine Teachings* (1649), p. 2; *Saul Smitten for Not Smiting Amale* (1653), pp. 6, 17–18; *A Man-Child Born* (1654), p. 114.

3 *Louis James, From Robinson to Robina, and Beyond: Robinson Crusoe as a Utopian Concept*

1 A. L. Morton, *The English Utopia* (London, 1952), p. 89.

2 Karl Marx, *Grundrisse.* [1853] (Harmondsworth, 1939), p. 83.

3 Ruth Levitas, *The Concept of Utopia* (Hemel Hempstead, 1990), pp. 175–200.

4 Diane Macdonell, *Theories of Discourse: An Introduction* (Oxford, 1986), p. 45.

5 Michael McKeon, *The Origins of the English Novel, 1600–1740* (New York, 1987), pp. 1–4, 423.

6 Ian Watt, *The Rise of the Novel* (Harmondsworth, 1963; 1st ed. 1957), passim. All references are to this Peregrine edition.

7 McKeon, op. cit., p. 7.

8 John Richetti, *Popular Fiction before Richardson* (Oxford, 1969), especially Chapters III and IV.

9 Richetti, op. cit., p. 133.

10 McKeon, op. cit., pp. 112–13.

11 Morton, op. cit., p. 96.

12 See M. M. Bakhtin, trans. Michael Holquist, *The Dialogic Imagination* (Austin, 1981), pp. 3, 83.

13 Daniel Defoe, *Robinson Crusoe* [1719] (Harmondsworth, 1965), pp. 65–88. All references to *Robinson Crusoe* are to this Penguin edition.

14 Charles Gildon, ed. Paul Dottin, *The Life and Strange Surprising Adventures of Mr. D- de F-* [1719] (London and Paris, 1923).

15 Watt, op. cit., pp. 65–88.15.

16 McKeon, op. cit., p. 319.

17 Defoe, op. cit., p. 129.

18 Ibid., p. 157.

19 Ibid., p. 159.

20 Ibid., p. 130.

21 Ibid., p. 130.

22 F. Brueggemann, *Utopia und Robinsonnade. Untersuchen zu Schanbel's 'Insel Felsenberg'*, 1731–43 (Berlin, 1914), passim.

23 Kevin Carpenter and Bernt Steinbrink, *Ausbruch und Abentuer* (Oldenburg, 1984), pp. 89–96.

24 James Fennimore Cooper, *Mark's Reef, or the Crater. A Tale of the Pacific* (London, 1847), I, p. 92.
25 Ibid., III, p. 257.
26 Jules Verne, Preface to *The Second Fatherland* (1900), quoted by Kenneth Allott, *Jules Verne* (Port Washington and London, 1970), p. 78.
27 Jules Verne, trans. W. H. G. Kingston, *The Mysterious Island* (London, 1879), I, p. 64.
28 See Martin Green, *The Robinson Crusoe Story* (University Park and London, 1990), pp. 33–47.
29 Jean-Jacques Rousseau, trans. Barbara Foxley, *Emile* [1762] (London, 1911), p. 147.
30 Rousseau, op. cit., p. 147.
31 Rousseau, op. cit., pp. 147–8.
32 Jean-Jacques Rousseau, trans. J. G. Fletcher, *The Reveries of a Solitary* [1778] (New York, 1927), p. 115.
33 Bernadin de St. Pierre, anonymous translator, *Paul et Virginie* [1788] (London, 1839), p. 101.
34 Rousseau, *Emile*, p. 148.
35 Kevin Carpenter, *Desert Isles and Pirate Islands* (privately printed, Frankfurt am Main, 1984), p. 163.
36 Lesley Stephen, 'De Foe's Novels', *Hours in a Library* (rev. ed. 1907), I, pp. 62–3; quoted in Carpenter, *Desert Isles*, p. 21. The passage is not present in the original *Cornhill Magazine* version of 1868.
37 [Bracebridge Hemyng], *Jack Harkaway after Schooldays*, London, 1878). See Louis James, 'Tom Brown's Imperialist Sons', *Victorian Studies*, III (September, 1973), p. 98.
38 Karl Marx, *Grundrisse* [1853] (London, 1939), p. 83.
39 See Green, op. cit., pp. 169–73.
40 Adrian Mitchell, *'Man Friday' and Other Plays* (London, 1974), p. 8.
41 Derek Walcott, *The Castaway* (London, 1965), pp. 51–7.
42 Derek Walcott, *'Remembrance' and 'Pantomime'* (New York, 1980), pp. 92–170.
43 J. M. Coetzee, *Foe* (London, 1986), p. 141.
44 Green, op. cit., p. 205; Patrick Parrinder, *Science Fiction: Its Criticism and Teaching* (London, 1980), p. 108.

4 *Gregory Claeys, Utopianism, Property and The French Revolution Debate in Britain*

1 Paul Langford, *A Polite and Commercial People. England 1727–83* (Oxford, 1989), p. 685.
2 On the conservative English enlightenment see J. G. A. Pocock, 'The Conservative Enlightenment' in *l'Eta dei lumi: studi storici sul Settecento europeo in onore di Franco Venturi* (Naples, 1985). The more radical English enlightenment is analysed in Margaret Jacob, *The Radical Enlightenment: Pantheists, Freemasons and Republicans* (London, 1981).
3 On which, most recently, see David Spadafora, *The Idea of Progress in Eighteenth Century Britain* (New Haven, 1990).
4 A. L. Morton's *The English Utopia* (London, 1952), discusses only four British works written in the eighteenth century. My forthcoming edition, *Eighteenth Century British Utopias*, describes about fifteen more, and reprints some of the texts discussed here.
5 On the background to this debate, see my *Thomas Paine: Social and Political Thought* (London, 1989).
6 E.g. Jean-Jacques Rousseau, *The Basic Political Writings* (Indianapolis, 1988), p. 180.

7 Reprinted in my *Eighteenth Century British Utopias* (forthcoming).

8 See Thomas Paine, *Rights of Man*, ed. G. Claeys (Indianapolis, 1992).

9 E.g. Thomas Spence, 'A Supplement to the History of Robinson Crusoe', in *The Political Works of Thomas Spence*, ed. H. T. Dickinson (Newcastle-upon-Tyne, 1982), p. 11.

10 Richard Price, *Additional Observations on the Nature and Value of Civil Liberty, and the War with America* (London, 1777), pp. 89–147.

11 William Godwin, *Enquiry Concerning Political Justice* (1793; last reprinted, ed. Isaac Kramnick, London, 1976).

12 On its republican roots, see my 'William Godwin's Critique of Democracy and Republicanism and Its Sources', *History of European Ideas*, VII/3 (Spring 1986), pp. 253–69, and more generally my 'Republicanism, Commerce and the Origins of Modern Social Theory in Britain, 1796–1805', *Journal of Modern History* (forthcoming). On Godwin's 'anarchism' see in particular John Clark, *The Philosophical Anarchism of William Godwin* (Princeton, 1969). On his philosophy generally, see Mark Philp, *Godwin's Political Justice* (London, 1986).

13 See my *Thomas Paine: Social and Political Thought*, Chapters 5 and 6.

14 Ibid., pp. 157–9.

15 A brief account of these is given in Lyman Tower Sargent, *British and American Utopian Literature, 1516–1985. An Annotated Chronological Bibliography* (New York, 1988), pp. 31–4.

16 Thomas Northmore, *Memoirs of Planetes; or, a Sketch of the Laws and Manners of Makar* (1795), pp. v, 25, 35, 41, 43, 80, 92, 124–5, 129.

17 A.D.R.S., *An Essay on Civil Government, or Society Restored* (1793), pp. 121, 82, 85–6, 93, 125, 153, 176.

18 On the authorship of *Equality*, see Michael Durey's forthcoming article in the *William and Mary Quarterly* (October 1992).

19 [John Lithgow], *Equality – A Political Romance* (1837 edn), pp. 2–7. On the origins of Owenite politics, see my *Citizens and Saints. Politics and Anti-Politics in Early British Socialism* (Cambridge, 1989).

20 [John Lithgow], *Equality – A Political Romance*, pp. 8–10, 17–22.

21 On the development of the utopian tradition to the early eighteenth century, see especially J. C. Davis, *Utopia and the Ideal Society. A Study of English Utopian Writing, 1516–1700* (Cambridge, 1981).

22 Thomas Spence, *The Political Works of Thomas Spence*, ed. H. T. Dickinson (Newcastle-upon-Tyne, 1982), pp. 104–18.

23 William Hodgson, *The Commonwealth of Reason* (London, 1795), p. 17, reprinted in my *Eighteenth Century British Utopias* (forthcoming). On Hodgson see Nicholas Hans, 'Franklin, Jefferson, and the English Radicals at the End of the Eighteenth Century', *Proceedings of the American Philosophical Society*, XCVIII (1954), 406–26.

24 William Hodgson, *The Commonwealth of Reason* (London, 1795), pp. 18, 21, 23, 64, 74, 77–8, 81, 91–3, 96, 99–100.

25 'Aratus', *A Voyage to the Moon Strongly Recommended to All Lovers of Real Freedom* (London, 1793), pp. 6, 8, 20, 22, 26.

26 *Modern Gulliver's Travels* (1796), pp. 14, 35–40, 145–73, 195–207.

27 Thomas Paine, *Agrarian Justice* (London, 1796); John Thelwall, *The Rights of Nature against the Usurpations of Establishments* (London, 1796), reprinted in my *John Thelwall: Political Writings* (University Park, Pennsylvania, forthcoming).

28 E.g. Robert Owen, *A New View of Society and Other Writings*, ed. G. Claeys (London, 1991), p. 194; John Gray, *The Social System* (London, 1831).

29 Karl Marx, *Selected Writings*, ed.David McLellan (Oxford, 1977), p. 237.

5 *Krishan Kumar, The End of Socialism? The End of Utopia? The End of History?*

1 Speech to a meeting of 'Democratic Russia', Moscow, June 1, 1991.
2 The Times Higher Education Supplement, December 27, 1991.
3 Geopolitics and Geoculture (Cambridge, 1991), p. 96.
4 For the millennial expectations at the end of the first millennium, see Henri Focillon, *The Year 1000*, trans. Fred D. Wieck (New York, 1969). An early indication of those at the end of the second millennium was the Channel 4 series on British television, *Fin de Siècle*, broadcast in February 1992 (summary booklet: London, Broadcasting Support Services, 1992); for other indications see Martin Jay, 'Apocalypse and the Inability to Mourn' in *Force Fields: Between Intellectual History and Cultural Criticism* (London, 1992).

There is, of course, as Focillon himself admits, no intrinsic or necessary relationship between the ordinary calendrical millennium and the millennial hopes and strivings born of the prophecies of the Book of Revelation (the Apocalypse of St John of Patmos). The reason why the year 1000 carried a millennial charge was that thinkers such as St Augustine identified the millennium of Revelations with the first thousand years of the Christian era. Thus as the year 1000 approached people were seized with the expectation that the vividly-portrayed events of the Apocalypse were imminent. The disconfirmation of this did nothing to still millennial hopes in future centuries: indeed the 11th-16th centuries were the period of the most intense millennialism in Europe. See Norman Cohn, *The Pursuit of the Millennium* (London, 1962). On Joachim, see Marjorie Reeves, *Joachim of Fiore and the Prophetic Future* (London, 1976). A compelling interpretation of the millennial impulse in literature is Frank Kermode, *The Sense of An Ending: Studies in the Theory of Fiction* (New York, 1968).

Calendrical endings – such as the end of a century – undoubtedly do stimulate millennial-type prophecies of death and rebirth, of endings and new beginnings. See Hillel Schwartz, *Century's End: A Cultural History of the Fin de Siècle from the 990s to the 1990s* (New York, 1990); for the celebrated case of the last century, see Mikulas Teich and Roy Porter, eds, *Fin de Siècle and Its Legacy* (Cambridge, 1991).

5 See especially Francis Fukuyama, *The End of History and the Last Man* (New York, 1992), pp.287–339. The sense of unease is particularly marked in the book, as compared to the more light-hearted treatment of Fukuyama's original article, 'The End of History?', *The National Interest*, Summer 1989, pp. 3–18.
6 See my 'The Revolutions of 1989: Socialism, Capitalism and Democracy', forthcoming in *Theory and Society*, Fall 1992.
7 See my *Utopia and Anti-Utopia in Modern Times* (Oxford, 1987), pp. 380–88; also my *Utopianism* (Milton Keynes, 1991), pp. 90–95.
8 Anthony Sampson, 'The Need for Utopias', *The Independent Magazine*, 21 September 1991, p. 14. Cf. also Norberto Bobbio, reflecting on the collapse of communism in Central and Eastern Europe in 1989: '. . . in a seemingly irreversible way, the greatest political utopia in history . . . has been completely upturned into its exact opposite.' 'The Upturned Utopia', in Robin Blackburn, ed., *After the Fall: The Failure of Communism and the Future of Socialism* (London, 1991), p. 3.
9 For a good study of this way of thinking, see David Caute, *The Fellow-Travellers: Intellectual Friends of Communism*, revised and updated edition (New Haven, 1988). For subsequent defections, see Richard Crossman, ed., *The God that Failed* (1950; New York, 1965).
10 On the utopian elements in Fascism, see Zeev Sternhell, 'Fascist Ideology', in Walter Lacquer, ed., *Fascism: A Reader's Guide* (Harmondsworth, 1979), esp. pp. 354–64. For Soviet Communism, see Jerome Gilison, *The Soviet Image of Utopia* (Baltimore, 1975). And cf. Joe Bailey: 'The most dramatic test of socialist utopianism has been the

experience of its actual practice in the Soviet Union or in China, where it is irredeemably tainted with, and condemned by, its totalitarian formation.' *Pessimism* (London, 1988), p. 69.

11 For the contemporary reception and interpretation of *Nineteen Eighty-Four*, see Bernard Crick's 'Introduction' to his edition of George Orwell, *Nineteen Eighty-Four* (Oxford, 1984).

12 *We*, written in Russia in 1920, was first published in English in New York in 1924, but for long remained a rarity. It was translated into various languages thereafter; Orwell reviewed a French edition in 1946. It was not published in the original Russian (again in New York) until 1952; and it was not available in Russia itself until the Khruschev thaw of the 1960s. See Christopher Collins, *Evgenij Zamyatin: An Interpretive Study* (The Hague, 1973).

13 On Koestler's 'lost weekend in Utopia', see his contribution to *The God That Failed*, pp. 11–66.

14 They belong to a whole 'literature of disillusionment' that runs from Zamyatin to Pasternak and Solzhenitsyn, and includes both fictional and non-fictional works. For some of the former, see Alan Swingewood, *The Novel and Revolution* (London, 1975); Paul N. Siegel, *Revolution and the Twentieth-Century Novel* (New York, 1979).

15 K. R. Popper, *The Open Society and Its Enemies*, 2 vols, 4th ed. (London, 1962), I, p. viii.

16 Ibid., I, p. 168; and generally, pp. 157–68. This criticism is substantially repeated in Popper's essay, 'Utopia and Violence' (1948) in *Conjectures and Refutations*, 2nd ed. (London, 1965), pp. 355–63.

17 George Kateb calls *The Open Society and its Enemies* 'the most inclusive book' of the anti-utopian critique: *Utopia and Its Enemies* (New York, 1972), p. 19. Kateb's study gives an excellent account of twentieth-century anti-utopianism.

18 The inquiry was continued in two other books, *Political Messianism: The Romantic Phase* (London, 1960), and *The Myth of The Nation and the Vision of Revolution* (London, 1980). Talmon was born in Poland.

19 Cohn, *The Pursuit of the Millennium*, p. vi. Cohn's book was first published, in London, in 1957.

20 Isaiah Berlin, *The Crooked Timber of Humanity: Chapters in the History of Ideas* (London, 1990), p. 68. For Berlin's other attacks on utopian forms of thinking, see his *Four Essays on Liberty* (London, 1969); see also 'Philosophy and Life', an interview with Berlin by Ramin Jahanbegloo, *New York Review of Books*, 28 May 1992, pp. 46–54.

21 Berlin's pessimism comes out in his comment that the 'liberal sermon which recommends machinery designed to prevent people from doing each other too much harm, giving each human group sufficient room to realise its own idiosyncratic, unique particular ends without too much interference with the ends of others' – his own creed – 'is not a passionate battle-cry to inspire men to sacrifice and martyrdom and heroic feats.' *The Crooked Timber of Humanity*, p. 47. This strikingly echoes Fukuyama's melancholy (see note 5).

22 Leszek Kolakowski, 'The Death of Utopia Reconsidered', in Sterlin M. McMurrin, ed., *The Tanner Lectures on Human Values IV* (Cambridge, 1983), pp. 229, 237–8, 242. Kolakowski earlier took a more benevolent view of Utopia, in 'The Concept of the Left' in *Toward a Marxist Humanism*, trans. from the Polish by J. Z. Peel (New York, 1969), pp. 67–83. What he regards as the most pernicious aspects of the Marxist utopia are discussed in vol. III of his *Main Currents of Marxism*, 3 vols, trans. from the Polish by P. S. Falla (Oxford, 1981). For Kolakowski's reflections – by no means entirely triumphalist – on the collapse of this utopia, in Poland and elsewhere, see 'Amidst Moving Ruins', *Daedalus* (Spring 1992), pp. 43–56.

23 Kolakowski, 'The Death of Utopia Reconsidered', p. 229.

24 Popper, 'Utopia and Violence', p. 360.

25 See my *Utopianism*, pp 86–99. I leave out here myths of Arcadia, Paradise or the Golden Age, as well as fantasies of the Blessed Isles or the Land of Cockaygne. For these see ibid., pp. 3–19.

26 My *Utopianism*, pp. 64–73, pursues this topic.

27 See Nicholas Berdyaev, 'Democracy, Socialism and Theocracy', in *The End of Time*, trans. D. Attwater (London, 1935), pp. 187–8. Utopia, for Berdyaev, largely meant the socialist utopia, and he warned: 'Socialism is no longer an utopia or a dream: it is an objective threat.' The threat consisted in the denial of 'the right to imperfection' which is the cardinal requirement of freedom: ibid., pp. 188, 192. Kateb calls this objection to utopia 'the essence of modern anti-utopianism' in *Utopia and Its Enemies*, p. 13.

28 See Chad Walsh, *From Utopia to Nightmare* (London, 1962), p. 25; Elaine Hoffman Baruch, 'Dystopia Now', *Alternative Futures*, II/3 (1979), p. 56.

29 Gellner's remarks are in the report on the symposium on Fukuyama's *The End of History and the Last Man*, *The Times Higher Education Supplement*, 20 March 1992, p. 17. And cf. Peter Beilharz: '. . . it can today be argued that the real ideological locus of the capitalist utopia is not market so much as *consumption*.' *Labour's Utopias: Bolshevism, Fabianism, Social Democracy* (London, 1992), p. 126. See also note 40, below.

30 Alexander Solzhenitsyn, 'How We Are To Rebuild Russia', translated and reprinted from *Komsomolskaya Pravda*, in *The Independent on Sunday*, 23 September 1990. See also Vladimir Tismaneanu, *The Crisis of Marxist Ideology in Eastern Europe: The Poverty of Utopia* (London and New York, 1988), esp. pp. 91–107; Alex Kozinski, 'The Dark Lessons of Utopia', *University of Chicago Law Review*, LVIII/2 (1991), pp. 575–94.

For the anti-utopianism and 'anti-politics' of the East European dissidents, see my 'The Revolutions of 1989'; see also Tony Judt, 'The Dilemmas of Dissidence: The Politics of Opposition in East-Central Europe', *Eastern European Politics and Societies*, II/2 (1988), pp. 191–9; Timothy Garton Ash, 'Does Central Europe Exist?', in *The Uses of Adversity* (Cambridge, 1989), pp. 161–91. Fredric Jameson notes the 'canonical anti-utopianism' of the East, and observes that 'for Eastern intellectuals, the word "utopia" has become as automatically stigmatized as the words "totality" and "totalization" are for us.' 'Conversations on the New World Order', in Blackburn, ed., *After the Fall*, pp. 261–2.

Those, incidentally, who think that Vaclav Havel has given up his 'anti-political politics' when faced with the 'realities' of Presidential office are roundly rebutted by Havel himself. See his 'Paradise Lost', *New York Review of Books*, 9 April 1992, pp. 6–8.

31 Milan Simecka, 'A World With Utopias or Without Them?', in Peter Alexander and Roger Gill, eds, *Utopias* (London, 1984), p. 171. And cf. Milan Kundera: 'The paradise of political utopia is based on the belief in man. That is why it ends in massacres.' 'An Interview with Milan Kundera', *Granta*, XI (1984), p. 29.

32 Simecka, 'A World With Utopias or Without Them?', pp. 173–4. For the popularity of Orwell in Eastern Europe, see Jacques Rupnik, 'Totalitarianism Revisited', in John Keane, ed., *Civil Society and the State: New European Perspectives* (London, 1988), pp. 263–89.

33 Hans Magnus Enzensberger, 'Ways of Walking: A Postscript to Utopia', in Blackburn ed., *After the Fall*, p. 20. By contrast Enzensberger praises present-day Germans, both East and West, for their devotion to 'ordinariness' and 'everyday normality': ibid., p. 24.

34 Jürgen Habermas, 'The New Obscurity: The Crisis of the Welfare State and the

Exhaustion of Utopian Energies', in *The New Conservatism*, edited and translated by
Shierry Weber Nicholsen (Cambridge, MA, 1989), pp. 48–69.

35 For a discussion of the nineteenth-century American communities, see my *Utopia and
Anti-Utopia in Modern Times*, ch. 3; for some of the varieties of socialism, see
Beilharz, *Labour's Utopias*.

36 Andre Gunder Frank, 'Revolution in Eastern Europe: Lessons for Democratic Social
Movements (and Socialists?)', *Third World Quarterly*, XII/2 (1990), p. 50. Frank
equally dismisses the alternative of 'world socialism' as unreal 'for any foreseeable
future.' Moreover, 'it is difficult to imagine what this might ever mean. What could
distinguish this world socialism from world capitalism, so long as competition reigns
as a fact of life in the future as it has for millennia in the past?' He concludes gloomily
that 'things will, and will have to, get worse before they get better' (ibid., pp. 51–2).
And cf. Robin Blackburn: 'As we enter the last decade of the twentieth century the ruin
of "Marxist-Leninist" communism has been sufficiently comprehensive to eliminate it
as an alternative to capitalism and to compromise the very idea of socialism.' 'Fin de
Siècle: Socialism After the Crash', in Blackburn, ed., *After the Fall*, p. 173.

37 André Gorz, *Critique of Economic Reason*, trans. Gillian Handyside and Chris Turner
(London, 1989), p. 183. See also the earlier essay, *Farewell to the Working Class: An
Essay on Post-Industrial Socialism*, trans. Michael Sonenscher (London, 1982). 'If one
understands socialism as a form of society in which the demands deriving from
[economic] rationality are subordinated to social and cultural goals, then socialism
remains more relevant than ever.' Gorz, 'The New Agenda', in Blackburn, ed., *After
the Fall*, p. 289.

38 For the eco-socialists, see Andrew Dobson, *Green Political Thought: An Introduction*
(London, 1990); for market socialism, Robin Blackburn, 'Fin de Siècle: Socialism
After the Crash', in Blackburn, ed., *After the Fall*, pp. 218–27; David Miller, *Market,
State and Community: Theoretical Foundations of Market Socialism* (Oxford, 1990).
See also Jon Elster and Karl Ove Moene, eds, *Alternatives to Capitalism* (Cambridge,
1989).

39 On socialism as the 'counter-culture' of capitalism, see Zygmunt Bauman, *Socialism:
The Active Utopia* (London, 1976); see also Beilharz, *Labour's Utopias*, p. 15. For the
persisting relevance of socialism, variously defined, see the essays in Part II of
Blackburn, ed., *After the Fall*, pp. 173–325; see also Ralph Miliband and Leo Panitch,
'The New World Order and the Socialist Agenda', in R. Miliband and L. Panitch, eds,
Socialist Register 1992: New World Order? (London, 1992); Lucio Magri, 'The
European Left Between Crisis and Refoundation', *New Left Review*, no. 189 (Sept./
Oct. 1991), pp. 1–18; Christiane Lemke and Gary Marks, eds, *The Crisis of Socialism
in Europe* (Durham, NC, 1992); Paul Auerbach, 'On Socialist Optimism', *New Left
Review*, no. 192 (March/April 1992), pp. 5–35.

40 George Steiner, 'The State of Europe: Christmas Eve 1989', *Granta 30: New Europe!*
(Harmondsworth, 1990), p. 130. Steiner has developed this idea in his story 'Proofs', a
dialogue about Marxism and capitalism, in *Proofs and Three Parables* (London,
1992), pp. 3–75. Cf. Erazim Kohak, a Czech philosopher who has lived in America for
many years: 'The unfortunate truth is that as the former subjects of the Soviet empire
dream it, the American dream has very little to do with liberty and justice for all and a
great deal to do with soap operas and the Sears catalogue.' 'Ashes, Ashes . . . Central
Europe after Forty Years', *Daedalus* (Spring 1992), p. 209. See also Noel Annan, on
consumerism as the cause of the 1989 revolutions, 'The State of Europe', *Granta 30*,
p. 160; similarly Zygmunt Bauman, 'Communism: A Post-Mortem', in *Intimations of
Postmodernity* (London, 1992), p. 171. For the contrary view, that the 1989
revolutions were driven by the non-material demand for 'recognition', see Fukuyama,
The End of History and the Last Man, pp. 177–80.

41 See, for example, John Kenneth Galbraith, 'Revolt in our Time: The Triumph of Simplistic Ideology', in Gwyn Prins, ed., *Spring in Winter: The 1989 Revolutions* (Manchester, 1990), pp. 1–11; see also Eric Hobsbawm, 'The Crisis of Today's Ideologies', *New Left Review*, no. 192 (March/April 1992), p. 61. Hobsbawm also points to a different kind of misperception, a blindness to capitalism's deepening problems: 'What confronts the ruins of the Eastern socialist economies today is not a triumphant capitalism but a global capitalist economy in trouble, and recognizing that it is in trouble.' *Ibid.*, p. 59.

42 See Ivan and Szonja Szelenyi, 'The Vacuum in Hungarian Politics: Classes and Parties', *New Left Review*, no. 187 (May/June 1991), pp. 121–37. On 'the recurrence of political apathy' in the region, see Mihaly Simai, 'Hungarian Problems', *Government and Opposition*, XXVII/1 (1992), p. 55; see also Piotr Sztompka, 'The Intangibles and the Imponderables of the Transition to Democracy', *Studies in Comparative Communism*, XXIV/3 (1991), p. 304.

43 It is undeniable, of course, that a revived socialism in East-Central Europe could take on authoritarian forms. See Martin Malia, 'Leninist Endgame', *Daedalus*, Spring 1992, pp. 73–5; Ken Jowitt, 'The Leninist Legacy', in Ivo Banac, ed., *Eastern Europe in Revolution* (Ithaca and London, 1992), pp. 207–24. And cf. Bauman: 'East-Central European societies have victoriously accomplished their February revolution. The dangers of an October one are, as yet, far from being excluded.' 'Communism: A Post-Mortem', p. 172.

44 Gorz, 'The New Agenda', p. 293; see also Hobsbawm, 'The Crisis of Today's Ideologies', p. 59.

45 R. W. Johnson, 'Ahead lies – what?', *London Review of Books*, 12 March 1992, p. 5. A similar point is made by Jürgen Habermas, 'What Does Socialism Mean Today? The Revolutions of Recuperation and the Need for New Thinking', in Blackburn, ed., *After the Fall*, p. 45. The general point holds, I think, despite the poor performance of the French socialists in the regional elections of March 1992 and the British Labour Party in the general election of April 1992. For the view that these elections are further evidence of the 'terminal decline' of socialism in Europe, see Peter Jenkins, 'Goodbye to All That', *New York Review of Books*, 14 May 1992, pp. 16–17; Stanley Hoffman, 'France Self-Destructs', *New York Review of Books*, 28 May 1992, pp. 25–30.

It has been fascinating, incidentally, to see the growing acclaim on the contemporary left for the social democratic legacy of Bernstein and Kautsky, as critics of Bolshevism and advocates of socialist democracy: see, for example, Blackburn, 'Fin de Siècle', pp. 175–89; Beilharz, *Labour's Utopias*, pp. xi, 93–124.

46 Frank Manuel, 'A Requiem for Karl Marx', *Daedalus* (Spring 1992), p. 18. Manuel is too readily dismissive of Marxism as a theory. For whatever the fate of so-called Marxist societies, Marxism as a theory should surely have no difficulty in explaining the current predicament of communists. As Fredric Jameson says: 'It does not seem to make much sense to talk about the bankruptcy of Marxism, when Marxism is very precisely the science and study of just that capitalism whose global triumph is affirmed in talk of Marxism's demise.' 'Conversations on the New World Order', p. 255. See also Immanuel Wallerstein, 'Marx, Marxism-Leninism, and Socialist Experiences in the Modern World-System', in *Geopolitics and Geoculture: Essays on the Changing World-System* (Cambridge, 1991), pp. 85, 96–7.

47 Kohak, 'Ashes, Ashes . . . Central Europe after Forty Years', pp. 203–4.

48 Simecka, 'A World With Utopias or Without Them?', pp. 175–6. A similar claim, that we cannot do without a 'concrete utopia', a coherent vision to oppose to the 'irrational forces' current in the world today, is made by a veteran Trotskyist reflecting on the fall of 'real socialism': Yvan Craipeau, 'L'Implosion du "Socialisme Réel": Une Nouvelle Période de l'histoire', *Les Temps Modernes*, no. 544 (November 1991), p. 80.

49 For the ecological and the feminist utopia, see my *Utopianism*, pp. 101–6.

50 See Richard Rorty, *Contingency, Irony, and Solidarity* (Cambridge, 1989). The consequence of this conception of utopia, Rorty points out, is that 'it would regard the realization of utopias, and the envisaging of still further utopias, as an endless process – an endless, proliferating realization of Freedom, rather than a convergence toward an already existing Truth.' Ibid., p. xvi. For a somewhat similar conception of utopia as 'metautopia', a 'framework' for the further realization of diverse utopias, see Robert Nozick, *Anarchy, State and Utopia* (New York, 1974), pp. 297–334.

51 It is idle to pretend that there is any agreement on the meaning of postmodernism. For a helpful guide, see Margaret A. Rose, *The Post-Modern and the Post-Industrial: A Critical Analysis* (Cambridge, 1991). Postmodernism's rejection of Utopia has some similarities to its rejection by Popper et al. – but they get there by very different routes; and postmodernists would have no truck with 'social engineering' as the solution.

52 Scott Lash and Jonathan Friedman, 'Introduction: Subjectivity and Modernity', in S. Lash and J. Friedman, eds, *Modernity and Identity* (Oxford, 1992), p. 1. Cf. Robert Venturi, the postmodernist American architect and author of *Learning from Las Vegas* (Cambridge, Mass., 1972): 'Disney World is nearer to what people want than what architects have ever given them.' Disneyland is 'the symbolic American utopia'. Quoted in David Harvey, *The Condition of Postmodernity* (Oxford, 1989), p. 60.

53 Fredric Jameson, *Postmodernism or, The Cultural Logic of Late Capitalism* (London, 1991), pp. 160, 180.

54 Berlin, *The Cooked Timber of Humanity*, p. 24.

55 Fukuyama, *The End of History and the Last Man*, p. 42. For the 'worldwide democratic revolution', see Dankwart A. Rustow, 'Democracy: A Global Revolution?', *Foreign Affairs*, LXIX/4 (1990), pp. 75–91.

56 Piotr Sztompka, *Society in Action: The Theory of Social Becoming* (Cambridge, 1991), p. 20. Cf. also Zygmunt Bauman, 'Living Without an Alternative', in *Intimations of Postmodernity*, p. 183. Fukuyama himself comments: 'One of the most striking facts about the original debate on "The End of History?" was that not one single critic put forward the vision of a society fundamentally different from contemporary liberal democracy and at the same time better.' 'The End of History is Still Nigh', *The Independent*, 3 March 1992.

   For some typically bad-tempered reviews of Fukuyama's book, though often making some telling points, see Alan Ryan, 'Professor Hegel Goes to Washington', *New York Review of Books*, 26 March 1992, pp. 7–13; John Dunn, 'In the Glare of Recognition', *Times Literary Supplement*, 24 April 1992, p. 6. A more balanced review is Steven Lukes, 'Hegel's Recurrence', *New Statesman and Society*, 6 March 1992, p. 44. There is no room to consider here the striking view of Immanuel Wallerstein that the 1989 revolutions mark the end of *liberalism* as much as socialism – his argument being that the two were but varieties of the same thing, and both had been steadily undermined since the '1968 revolution' against the state and bureaucracy. See 'The Collapse of Liberalism', in Miliband and Panitch, eds., *The Socialist Register 1992*; see also 'The Lessons of the 1980s' and '1968, Revolution in the World-System', in *Geopolitics and Geoculture*, pp. 1–15, 65–83.

57 Ryan, 'Professor Hegel Goes to Washington', p. 12; see also Hobsbawm, 'The Crisis of Today's Ideologies', pp. 60–61.

58 The victory of capitalism is seen as the result of the worldwide recognition that the free market is the best institution for realizing the full potential of modern science and technology. The victory of liberal democracy is attributed to the growing force of the 'thymotic' factor in human history – the desire and struggle for recognition of our innate worth and dignity as equal human beings. *The End of History and the Last Man*, pp. xiii–xix.

59 See Dietrich Rueschmeyer, Evelyne Huber Stephens and John D. Stephens, *Capitalist Development and Democracy* (Cambridge, 1992). For the contrary view, see Samuel Bowles and Herbert Gintis, *Democracy and Capitalism: Property, Community and the Contradictions of Modern Social Thought* (New York, 1987).

60 Fukuyama, *The End of History and the Last Man*, p. 46 (his emphasis).

61 Fukuyama, 'The End of History is Still Nigh'.

62 Fukuyama, *The End of History and the Last Man*, pp. 288–9, 326–39.

63 On the destructive consequences of Macdonald et al., see Peter Singer, 'Bandit and Friends', *New York Review of Books*, 9 April 1992, pp. 9–13; Joseph K. Skinner, 'Big Mac and the Tropical Forests', *Monthly Review*, December 1985, pp. 25–32.

64 Many of these points were powerfully made some years ago by Fred Hirsch, *Social Limits to Growth* (London, 1977). See also Adrian Ellis and Krishan Kumar, eds, *Dilemmas of Liberal Democracies: Studies in Fred Hirsch's Social Limits to Growth* (London, 1983). And cf. Paul Auerbach, 'On Socialist Optimism', pp. 20, 33–4. Of course, ecological movements have in most cases already adopted religious language and religious concepts, often from Eastern religions. For this and other elements of the 'Green utopia', see Dobson, *Green Political Thought*; Adrian Atkinson, *Principles of Political Ecology* (London, 1991), esp. pp. 169–219. On the need for a religious – 'theistic' – dimension to our thinking about our predicament, see also Charles Taylor, *Sources of the Self: The Making of the Modern Identity* (Cambridge, 1989); a robust rebuttal of this is Quentin Skinner, 'Who Are "We"? Ambiguities of the Modern Self', *Inquiry*, XXXIV (1991), pp. 145–50.

65 See, for example, R. E. Pahl, 'The Search for Social Cohesion: from Durkheim to the European Commission', *European Journal of Sociology*, XXXII (1991), pp. 345–60.

66 See, for example, Kohak, 'Ashes, Ashes . . . Central Europe after Forty Years', p. 208.

67 A point forcibly put by Sztompka, 'The Intangibles and Imponderables of the Transition to Democracy'; see also Jowitt, 'The Leninist Legacy'; Edmund Mokrzycki, 'The Legacy of Real Socialism and Western Democracy', *Studies in Comparative Communism*, XXIV/2 (1991), pp.211–17. A contrary view, that communism has left virtually no legacy in Eastern Europe, has engagingly been argued by Stephen Howe, 'Hiccup in the Long March of History', *New Statesman and Society*, 6 March 1992, pp. 12–14.

6 *Vita Fortunati, The Metamorphosis of the Apocalyptic Myth: From Utopia to Science Fiction*

1 Cf. P. Boyer, *When Time Shall Be No More* (Cambridge, Massachusetts, 1991).

2 F. E. Manuel and F. P. Manuel, *Utopian Thought in the Western World* (Cambridge, Mass., 1979), p. 15.

3 T. Boman, *Hebrew Thought Compared With Greek* (London, 1960), particularly the first two chapters.

4 M. H. Abrams, 'Apocalypse, Theme and Variation' in *The Apocalypse in English Renaissance Thought and Literature*, ed. C. A. Patrides and J. Wittrech (Manchester, 1971), pp. 345 ff.

5 Cf. S. Sontag, 'The Imagination of Disaster' in S. Sontag, *Against Interpretation and Other Essays* (London, 1987).

6 Cf. W. Warren Wagan, *Terminal Visions* (Bloomington, Indiana, 1982), p. 112.

7 U. Eco, 'Introduzione' to E. Bay, *Apocalypse* (Milan, 1979), p. 7.

8 E. M. Forster, *The Machine Stops* (1909), *Collected Short Stories* (Harmondsworth, 1947), pp. 148–9.

9 J. Wyndham, *The Chrysalids* (1955, rpt Harmondsworth, 1984), p. 78.

10 D. Ketterer, *New World For Old* (Bloomington, Indiana, 1974), especially the first two chapters.
11 R. Louit, 'Le chirugien de l'Apocalypse' in *Le livre d'or de la science-fiction* (Paris, 1980), pp. 17 ff.
12 J. G. Ballard, *The Crystal World* (London, 1966), pp.212–13.

7 *David Ayers, 'Politics Here is Death': William Burroughs's Cities of the Red Night*

1 Tom Moylan, *Demand the Impossible: Science Fiction and the Utopian Imagination* (New York and London, 1986).
2 *Cities of the Red Night* (London, 1981), p. 11.
3 On the 'God that failed', see for example William S. Burroughs and Brion Gysin, *The Third Mind* (London, 1979), p. 97. I give further consideration to presence and writing in Burroughs's work in my 'The Long Last Goodbye: Control and Resistance in the Work of William Burroughs' (forthcoming in the *Journal of American Studies*).
4 The conflation that takes place here, between communism and bourgeois libertarianism, is typical not only of Burroughs but of a generation in the 1960s – a generation that was able to see a figure such as Thoreau as 'progressive' – and would require a full-length commentary in its own right.
5 *Cities of the Red Night*, p. 9.
6 Ibid., p. 10.
7 Ibid., p. 11.
8 Ibid., p. 11.
9 Ibid., p. 12.
10 Daniel Defoe, *A General History of the Pyrates*, ed. M. Schonhorn (Columbia, 1972), pp. 383–418. Mission's colony is here called Libertalia.
11 This is not to say that the element of utopianism amongst pirates is an invention. Marcus Rediker's *Between the Devil and the Deep Blue Sea: Merchant Seamen, Pirates, and the Anglo-American Maritime World, 1700–1750* (Cambridge, 1987), pp. 254–87, emphasizes the orientation of pirates towards egalitarianism, democracy and justice; their constitutionalism which often involved 'articles'; and their deep-seated and politically conscious hostility to the existing powers. Rediker's account is scrupulously researched, but it needs always to be borne in mind that Defoe's work remains one of the primary sources for all accounts of piracy. In his account of Mission, Defoe seems to have simply extended the politics of the pirate ship, as he understood them, to a land-based and potentially more viable community.
12 *Cities of the Red Night*, p. 284.
13 Ibid., p. 238.
14 Ibid., p. 62.
15 *The Ticket That Exploded* (London, 1987), pp. 43–6.
16 *Cities of the Red Night*, p. 287.
17 Ibid., p. 100.
18 See, for example, *The Naked Lunch* (London, 1986), pp. 9–10.
19 *Cities of the Red Night*, p. 100.
20 Ibid., p. 170.
21 See the remarks in Calder's defence of Burroughs in the *Times Literary Supplement*, reprinted in *The Naked Lunch*, pp. 208–10, and Burroughs's own comments, *The Naked Lunch*, pp. 241–2.
22 Compare Bloch, who discusses Gnosticism in *The Principle of Hope*, vol. III, translated by Neville Plaice, Stephen Plaice and Paul Knight (Oxford, 1986), pp. 1241–9.
23 On space and silence see for example *The Ticket That Exploded*, pp. 43–4; on the

evolutionary goal of space travel see the epigraph to *The Place of Dead Roads* (London, 1976), p. 7, and compare 'Here to Go' on Burroughs's recording, *Dead City Radio* (New York: Island Records, 1990), where he asks 'What are we here for?' and replies: 'We're here to go. Into space'; on death as the final frontier see *The Western Lands* (London, 1987), passim.

24 *Cities of the Red Night*, p. 36.
25 Ibid., p. 36.
26 *The Adding Machine: Collected Essays* (London, 1985), p. 124.
27 *Cities of the Red Night*, p. 152.
28 I discuss this connection in '"It's a sick picture, B.J.": Imagism Regurgitated', in *Parataxis: Modernism and Modern Writing*, no. 1 (Spring 1991), pp. 51–66.
29 See for example *The Ticket That Exploded*, pp. 133–4, and my discussion in 'The Long Last Goodbye'.
30 *Cities of the Red Night*, p. 182.
31 Ibid., p. 141.
32 Ibid., p. 141.
33 See also Burroughs's parody of an American Express travelogue which portrays an essentially barbaric race as 'a simple happy people' (*Cities of the Red Night*, pp. 209–10); compare Freud's strictures in 'Civilisation and its Discontents', where he employs a similar expression: *Group Psychology, Civilisation and its Discontents and Other Works*, The Penguin Freud Library Volume 12, trans. from the German under the general editorship of James Strachey and edited by Albert Dickson (London, 1991), p. 275.
34 *Cities of the Red Night*, p. 141.
35 Ibid., p. 144.
36 Ibid., p. 142.
37 Ibid., p. 264.
38 Ibid., p. 265.
39 On Burroughs's experience of protest see Ted Morgan, *Literary Outlaw: The Life and Times of William S. Burroughs* (London, 1991), p. 446.
40 *The Wild Boys: A Book of the Dead* (London, 1982), p. 123.
41 Ibid., pp. 139–40.
42 On the New Left see, for example, Herbert Marcuse, 'The Problem of Violence and the Radical Opposition', in *Five Lectures: Psychoanalysis, Politics and Utopia*, trans. by Jeremy J. Shapiro and Shierry M. Weber (London, 1970), pp. 83–108, and (*contra*) Irving Louis Horowitz, 'American Radicalism and the Revolt against Reason' (1968) in *Ideology and Utopia in the United States 1956–1976* (Cambridge and New York, 1977), pp. 180–93.
43 See Morgan, pp. 35–6, 50–2.
44 *The Wild Boys*, pp. 93, 94.
45 *Port of Saints* (London, 1983), p. 135.
46 Ibid., pp. 71–2.
47 Jan Relf, in her 'Utopia the Good Breast' (in this volume), identifies the 'recurrent trope of coming home to mother' in feminist utopian writing, arguing that the genuinely utopian should posit a more fundamental reordering of the economy of desire. Burroughs, arriving at the problem from the opposite direction as it were, goes some way toward doing this by substituting magical birth for physical birth in the utopia of the Wild Boys, thereby eliminating the traditional family and cancelling matriarchy and patriarchy alike at the symbolic level. On the symbolic in Burroughs, see Wayne Pounds, 'The Postmodern Anus: Parody and Utopia in Two Recent Novels by William Burroughs', *Poetics Today*, VIII (1987), 611–29.
48 *Cities of the Red Night*, p. 194.

49 Ibid., p. 196.
50 See *The Naked Lunch*, p. 10: 'Junk yields a basic form of "evil" virus. *The Algebra of Need*. The face of "evil" is always the face of total need.'
51 *Cities of the Red Night*, p. 197.
52 *Five Lectures*, p. 8.
53 Eros and Civilisation (New York, 1962), p. 34.
54 Roland Barthes, *Sade, Fourier, Loyola* (Paris, 1971), especially pp. 114–20.
55 *Cities of the Red Night*, pp. 158–64, 203–7, 256–68.
56 Ibid., p. 243.
57 Ibid., p. 262.
58 Ibid., p. 151.
59 For example, *Cities of the Red Night*, p. 13.
60 Compare 'Apocalypse' on *Dead City Radio*.

8 *Jan Relf, Utopia the Good Breast: Coming Home to Mother*

1 J. A. Chapple and A. Pollard, eds, *The Letters of Mrs. Gaskell* (Manchester, 1966), p. 614.
2 Charlotte Perkins Gilman, *Herland* (London, 1979), p. 142.
3 Motherless heroines abound in fairy tales and folk literature, and the nineteenth-century novel is remarkable for its lost mothers, as Jean Pfaelzer has also noted. In her unpublished paper, 'Utopia the mother', she observes that: 'Sandra Gilbert and Susan Gubar have argued that motherlessness becomes a textual emblem for female powerlessness. The maternal absence denies the daughter a role model which can facilitate her passage into womanhood . . .'; but on the other hand, 'Adrienne Rich argues that motherlessness frees Victorian heroines from a model of female subservience.' In women's utopias, this lost mother has, in many cases, become the object of the heroine's search, or quest. (J. Pfaelzer, 'Utopia the Mother', unpublished conference paper presented at the University of Exeter, March 1990).
4 On the question of definitions I follow Lyman Tower Sargent (*British and American Utopian Literature, 1516–1985: an Annotated, Chronological Bibliography*, New York and London, 1988). 'Utopia' is used as a generic term to denote novels which depict a fictitious or fantastic society. 'Dystopia' refers to the fictitious 'bad' place which extrapolates from the contemporaneous reader's present to serve as an awful warning of what the probable future, towards which that present is tending, may be like. 'Eutopia', in contrast, denotes the idealized 'good' place. The reader is implicitly or explicitly invited to compare it with, and find it infinitely superior to, the 'real' society in which that reader lives.
5 T. Moylan, *Demand the Impossible* (London, 1986), p. 18.
6 Adrienne Rich, a representatively lesbian voice on this subject, asserts that: 'If women are the earliest sources of emotional caring and physical nurture for both female and male children, it would seem logical, from a feminist perspective at least, to pose the following questions: whether the search for love and tenderness in both sexes does not originally lead toward women; why in fact women would ever redirect that search . . . ?' 'Compulsory Heterosexuality and Lesbian Existence', *Desire*, eds A. Snitow, C. Stansell and S. Thompson (London, 1984), p. 217.
7 R. Poole, 'Psychoanalytic Theory', *Literary Theory at Work*, ed. D. Tallack (London, 1987), p. 185.
8 M. Klein, 'A Study of Envy and Gratitude', *The Selected Melanie Klein*, ed. J. Mitchell (London, 1986), p. 217.
9 Ibid., p. 212.

10 J. Sayers, 'Feminism and Mothering', *cit.* P. Waugh, *Feminine Fictions* (London, 1989), p. 63.

11 C. McKay, *Promise of the Rose Stone* (Vermont, 1986), p. 233.

12 J. Kristeva, *Powers of Horror* (New York, 1982), p. 13.

13 C. McKay, *op. cit.*, p. 238.

14 In psychoanalytic theory, the primary processes are conceptualized as unconscious, irrational, ignorant of time and space, and as being governed by the pleasure principle, which according to Freud seeks to avoid tension and to restore to an earlier state of things.

15 N. O'Connor, 'The An-Arche of Psychotherapy', *Abjection, Melancholia and Love*, eds J. Fletcher and A. Benjamin (Warwick, 1990), pp. 44–5.

16 J. Kristeva, 'Women's Time', *The Kristeva Reader*, ed. T. Moi (Oxford, 1986), p. 205.

17 C. Pearson, 'Coming Home: Four Feminist Ueopias and Patriarchal Experience', *Future Females*, ed. M. Barr (Ohio, 1981), p. 64.

18 R. Miles, *The Women's History of the World* (London, 1988), p. 37.

19 Ibid., p. 40.

20 Ibid., p. 41.

21 D. Bird, 'Gynocentric Mythmaking in Joan Vinge's *The Snow Queen*', *Extrapolations* (Autumn 1986), p. 237.

22 J. Vinge, *The Snow Queen* (New York, 1980), pp. 454–5.

23 S. Birkhauser-Oeri, *The Mother: Archetype Image in Fairy Tales* (Toronto, 1988), p. 154.

24 D. Dinnerstein, *The Rocking of the Cradle and the Ruling of the World* (London, 1987), p. 4.

25 M. Klein, 'A Study of Envy and Gratitude', *The Selected Melanie Klein*, ed. J. Mitchell (London, 1986), p. 212.

26 D. Dinnerstein, *The Rocking of the Cradle and the Ruling of the World* (London, 1987), p. 104.

27 Ibid., p. 100.

28 Ibid., pp. 103–4.

29 Ibid., p. 104.

30 Ibid., p. 61.

31 C. Kaplan, 'Wicked fathers', *Sea Changes* (London, 1986), p. 210.

32 J. Gallop, *Feminism and Psychoanalysis* (London, 1982), p. 118.

33 S. McKee Charnas, *Motherlines* (London, 1980), p. 296.

34 J. Kristeva, 'Stabat Mater', *The Kristeva Reader*, ed. Toril Moi (Oxford, 1986), p. 170.

35 N. Chodorow, *The Reproduction of Mothering* (Berkeley and London, 1978), p. 39.

36 J. Kristeva, 'Stabat Mater', *The Kristeva Reader*, ed. T. Moi (Oxford, 1986), p. 161.

37 D. Lessing, *Memoirs of a Survivor* (London, 1976), p. 15.

38 Ibid., p. 118.

39 Ibid., p. 135.

40 Ibid., p. 189.

41 V. Bar, 'Introduction', D. Dinnerstein, *The Rocking of the Cradle and the Ruling of the World* (London, 1987), p. xiii.

42 J. Gallop, *Feminism and Pychoanalysis* (London, 1982), pp. 124–5.

43 J. Kristeva, 'Talking about Polylogue', *French Feminist Thought*, ed. Toril Moi (Oxford, 1987), p. 112.

44 T. Moylan, *Demand the Impossible* (London, 1986), p. 116.

45 E. Bloch, *On Karl Marx* (New York, 1971), p. 172.

46 E. Bloch, *cit.* Jack Zipes, *Breaking the Magic Spell* (London, 1979), p. 129 (emphasis added).

9 *John O'Neill, McTopia: Eating Time*

1 L. T. Sargent, *British and American Utopian Literature 1516–1985* (New York, 1988).
2 Mary Douglas, 'Standard Social Uses of Food: Introduction' in *Food in the Social Order: Studies of Food and Festivities in Three American Communities*, ed. Mary Douglas (New York, 1984), pp. 1–39; John O'Neill, *Five Bodies: The Human Shape of Modern Society* (Ithaca, 1985), Ch. 2; Eric B. Ross, 'An Overview of Trends in Dietary Variation from Hunter-Gatherer to Modern Capitalist Societies' in *Food and Evolution: Towards a Theory of Human Food Habits*, eds Marvin Harris and Eric B. Ross (Philadelphia, 1987).
3 Eric B. Ross, 'Patterns of Diet and Forces of Production: An Economic and Ecological History of the Ascendency of Beef in the United States Diet' in *Beyond the Myths of Culture: Essays in Cultural Materialism*, ed. Eric B. Ross (New York, 1980), pp. 181–225.
4 *Food and Evolution*, p. 61.
5 Mark Edelman, 'From Costa Rican Pasture to North American Hamburger' in *Food and Evolution*, p. 544; Norman Meyers, 'The Hamburger Connection: How Central America's Forests Become North America's Hamburgers', *Ambio: A Journal of the Human Environment*, X/1 (1981), pp. 3–8.
6 Gilles Deleuze and Félix Guattari, *A Thousand Plateaus: Capitalism and Schizophrenia* (Minneapolis, 1987), Ch. 6.
7 William Burroughs, *The Naked Lunch* (New York, 1966), p. 131.
8 Louis Marin, *Food for Thought* (Baltimore, 1989), p. 97. See also: Richard Halpern, *The Poetics of Primitive Accumulation: English Renaissance Culture and the Genealogy of Capital* (Ithaca, 1991), Ch. 4.
9 John O'Neill, *Essaying Montaigne: A Study of the Renaissance Arts of Writing and Reading* (London, 1982).
10 Marcus Mabry, 'Inside the Golden Arches', *Newsweek*, 18 December 1989, pp. 46–7.
11 Chris Wood with Anthony Wilson-Smith, 'A "Bolshoi Mak" attack', *Maclean's*, 16 May 1988, p. 30.
12 Ellen Graham, 'This McDonald is the real McCoy', *The Globe and Mail*, 26 August 1991, p. 136.
13 Stalfan B. Linder, *The Harried Leisure Class* (New York, 1970); Jeremy Rifkin, *Time Wars: The Primary Conflict in Human History* (New York, 1987).
14 John O'Neill, *Five Bodies: The Human Shape of Modern Society* (Ithaca, 1985), Ch. IV.
15 John L. Hess and Karen Hess, *The Taste of America* (New York, 1977), p. 7.

Select Bibliography

This bibliography is drawn partly from the works referred to in this volume; we have also added other works relating to the general topics of utopias and the millennium.

Albinski, N. B., *Women's Utopias in British and American Fiction*, London: Routledge, 1988.

Alexander, P. and Gill, R., eds, *Utopias*, London: Duckworth, 1984.

Baczko, B., *Utopian Lights: The Evolution of the Idea of Social Progress*, New York: Paragon Press, 1989.

Bailey, J., *Pessimism*, London: Routledge, 1988.

Barr, M., ed., *Future Females*, Ohio: Bowling Green State University Popular Press, 1981.

Barthes, R., *Sade, Fourier, Loyola*, Paris: Seuil, 1971.

Baudrillard, J., *Cool Memories II 1987–1990*, Paris: Seuil, 1990.

Bauman, Z., *Socialism: The Active Utopia*, London: Allen and Unwin, 1976.

Beilharz, P., *Labour's Utopias: Bolshevism, Fabianism, Social Democracy*, London: Routledge, 1992.

Berdyaev, N., *The End of Time*, trans. D. Attwater, London: Sheed and Ward, 1935.

Berlin, I., *The Crooked Timber of Humanity*, London: Fontana Press, 1990.

Berneri, M.-L., *Journey Through Utopia*, London: Freedom Press, 1982.

Blackburn, R., ed., *After the Fall: The Failure of Communism and the Future of Socialism*, London: Verso, 1991.

Blaim, A., *Early English Utopian Fiction: A Study of a Literary Genre*, Lublin: Uniwersytet Marii Curie-Sklodowskiej, 1984.

Bloch, E., *The Principle of Hope*, 3 vols, Oxford: Basil Blackwell, 1986.

Boyer, P., *When Time Shall Be No More*, Cambridge, Mass.: Harvard University Press, 1991.

Buber, M., *Paths in Utopia*, Boston: Beacon Press, 1958.

Ciorenescu, A., *L'Avenir du Passé: Utopie et Littérature*, Paris: Gallimard, 1972.

Claeys, G., ed., *Eighteenth Century British Utopias*, Cambridge: Cambridge University Press, 1993.

Cohn, N., *The Pursuit of the Millennium*, London: Mercury Books, 1962.

Davis, J. C., *Utopia and the Ideal Society: A Study of English Utopian Writing 1516–1700*, Cambridge: Cambridge University Press, 1983.

Dinnerstein, D., *The Rocking of the Cradle and the Ruling of the World*, London: The Women's Press, 1987.

Eliav-Feldon, M., *Realistic Utopias: The Ideal Imaginary Societies of the Renaissance 1516–1630*, Oxford: Clarendon Press, 1982.

Elliot, R. C., *The Shape of Utopia: Studies in a Literary Genre*, Chicago: Chicago University Press, 1970.

Ferguson, J., *Utopias of the Classical World*, London: Thames and Hudson, 1975.

Fishman, R., *Urban Utopias of the Twentieth Century: Ebenezer Howard, Frank Lloyd Wright and Le Corbusier*, New York: Basic Books, 1977.

Fortunati, V., *La Letteratura Utopica Inglese*, Ravenna; Longo Editore, 1979.

Frankel, B., *The Post-Industrial Utopians*, Cambridge: Polity Press, 1987.

Friedman, Y., *Utopias Réalisables*, Paris: Union Générale d'Editions, 1975.

Frye, N., *The Great Code: The Bible and Literature*, London: Routledge, 1982.

Fukuyama, F., *The End of History and the Last Man*, New York: The Free Press, 1992.

Geoghegan, V., *Utopianism and Marxism*, London: Methuen, 1987.

Gerber, R., *Utopian Fantasy: A Study of English Utopian Fiction Since the End of the Nineteenth Century*, London: Routledge and Kegan Paul, 1955.

Goodwin, B. and Taylor, K., *The Politics of Utopia*, London: Hutchinson, 1982.

Green, M., *The Robinson Crusoe Story*, Philadelphia: Pennsylvania State University Press, 1990.

Hall, P., *Cities of Tomorrow*, Oxford: Basil Blackwell, 1988.

Hansot, E., *Perfection and Progress: Two Modes of Utopian Thought*, Cambridge, Mass.: MIT Press, 1974.

Harrison, J. F. C., *Robert Owen and the Owenites in Britain and America: The Quest for the New Moral World*, London: Routledge and Kegan Paul, 1969.

Hayek, F. A., *The Road to Serfdom*, London: Routledge and Kegan Paul, 1944.

Hill, C., *The World Turned Upside Down*, London: Temple Smith, 1972.

Jameson, F., 'Of Islands and Trenches: Neutralization and the Production of Utopian Discourse', in *The Ideologies of Theory: Essays 1971–86*, London: Routledge, 1988, vol. I.

Kaleb, G., *Utopia and Its Enemies*, New York: Schocken Books, 1972.

Kermode, F., *The Sense of an Ending: Studies in the Theory of Fiction*, New York: Oxford University Press, 1968.

Ketterer, D., *New Worlds for Old*, Bloomington: Indiana University Press, 1974.

Kolakowski, L., 'The Death of Utopia Reconsidered', in Sterling M. McMurrin, ed., *The Tanner Lectures on Human Values IV*, Cambridge: Cambridge University Press, 1983.

Kumar, K., *Utopia and Anti-Utopia in Modern Times*, Oxford: Basil Blackwell, 1987.

Kumar, K., *Utopianism*, Milton Keynes: Open University Press, 1991.

Lasky, M., *Utopia and Revolution*, London: Macmillan, 1976.

Levitas, R., *The Concept of Utopia*, London: Philip Allan, 1990.

Mannheim, K., *Ideology and Utopia*, London: Routledge and Kegan Paul, 1960.

Manuel, F. E., ed., *Utopias and Utopian Thought*, London: Souvenir Press, 1973.

Manuel, F. E. and Manuel, F. P., *Utopian Thought in the Modern World*, Oxford: Basil Blackwell, 1979.

Marin, L., *Lectures traversières*, Paris: Albin Michel, 1992.

Marin, L., *Utopics: Spatial Plays*, trans. R. Vollrath, Atlantic City, N.J.: Humanities Press, 1984.

McCord, W., *Voyages to Utopia: Visions and Realities*, New York: Norton, 1990.

McKean, M., *The Origins of the English Novel 1600–1740*, New York: John Hopkins Press, 1987.

Morton, A. L., *The English Utopia*, London: Lawrence and Wishart, 1969.

Moylan, T., *Demand the Impossible: Science Fiction and the Utopian Imagination*, New York and London: Methuen, 1986.

Mumford, L., *The Story of Utopias: Ideal Commonwealths and Social Myths*, London: Harrap, 1923.

Negley, G. and Patrick, J. M., eds, *The Quest for Utopia: An Anthology of Imaginary Societies*, College Park, Maryland: McGrath, 1971.

Olson, T., *Millennialism, Utopianism and Progress*, Toronto: Toronto University Press, 1982.

Passmore, J., *The Perfectibility of Man*, London: Duckworth, 1972.

Popper, K., *The Open Society and Its Enemies*, 2 vols, 4th ed., London: Routledge and Kegan Paul, 1962.

Richetti, J., *Popular Fiction Before Richardson*, Oxford: Clarendon Press, 1969.

Ricoeur, P., *Lectures on Ideology and Utopia*, New York: Columbia University Press, 1986.

Rosenau, H., *The Ideal City: Its Architectural Evolution in Europe*, London: Methuen, 1983.

Ross, A., *Strange Weather: Culture, Science and Technology in the Age of Limits*, London and New York: Verso, 1991.

Sargent, L. T., *British and American Utopian Literature 1516–1985: An Annotated Chronological Bibliography*, New York: Garland Publishing, 1988.

Schwartz, H., *Century's End: A Cultural History of the Fin de Siècle from the 990s to the 1990s*, New York: Collier-Macmillan, 1990.

Seidel, M., *Robinson Crusoe: Island Myths and the Novel*, Boston: Twayne Publishers, 1991.

Seligman, A. B., ed., *Order and Transcendence: The Role of Utopias and the Dynamics of Civilizations*, Leiden: E. J. Brill, 1989.

Shklar, J., *After Utopia: The Decline of Political Faith*, Princeton: Princeton University Press, 1957.

Steiner, G., *Proofs and Three Parables*, London: Faber and Faber, 1992.

Suvin, D., *Metamorphoses of Science Fiction: On the Politics and History of a Literary Genre*, New Haven: Yale University Press, 1979.

Taylor, B., *Eve and the New Jerusalem*, London: Virago, 1983.

Teich, M. and Porter, R., eds, *Fin de Siècle and Its Legacy*, Cambridge: Cambridge University Press, 1991.

Thrupp, S., ed., *Millennial Dreams in Action*, New York: Schocken Books, 1970.

Toon, P., ed., *The Millennium and the Future of Israel*, Cambridge: Cambridge University Press, 1970.

Tuveson, E. L., *Millennium and Utopia: A Study in the Background of the Idea of Progress*, New York: Harper Torchbooks, 1964.

Vidler, A., *Claude-Nicholas Ledoux: Architecture and Social Reform at the End of the Ancien Regime*, Cambridge, Mass.: MIT Press, 1990.

Wagar, W. W., *Terminal Visions*, Bloomington: Indiana University Press, 1982.

Walsh, C., *From Utopia to Nightmare*, London: Geoffrey Bles, 1962.

Index

'A.D.R.S.' (*pseud.*) 56
Abrams, M.H. 83
Aldiss, Brian 88
America 51, 65, 78–80, 91, 101, 109–37; American beef complex 109; eating habits in 137
see also Soviet Union
Andreae, Johann Valentin 24
Apocalypse 82–3, 117, 141
see also millennium
Arcadia 11
Augustine, St 63, 145
Ayers, David 5

Bacon, Francis 25, 65
Ballantine, R.M. 42–3
Ballard, J.G. 4, 88–9
Barrie, J.M. 43
Barthes, Roland 6, 104
Baudrillard, Jean 1, 4
Baxter, Richard 30
Behn, Aphra 35
Bellamy, Edward 69, 72
Berdyaev, Nicholas 70, 147
Berlin, Isaiah 67, 77, 146
Berrington, Simon 47
Birkhauser-Oeri, Sybille 117
Blackburn, Robin 148
Bloch, Ernst 13, 108, 126, 128
Bobbio, Norberto 145
Boman, T. 82
Boyer, Paul 82
Brett, Edwin J. 43
Bunyan, John, 34
Burgh, James 49, 60
Burke, Edmund 46, 51, 54, 60
Burroughs, William 5, 90–105, 152–3; (*Cities of the Red Night*) 90–105; (*Port of Saints*) 100; (*The Naked Lunch*) 95, 104, 131; (*The Ticket That Exploded*) 94, 98, 102; (*The Wild Boys*) 100

Callenbach, Ernest 76
Campanella, Tommaso 24–5
Campe, J. Johann Heinrich 39, 41
Canne, John 31
capitalism 5, 73, 136, 147, 150
Carey, Henry, Earl of Monmouth 26
Carpenter, Kevin 39
Certeau, Michel de 13–14
Charles I, King of England 17, 28
Charmas, Suzy McKee 123
Chodorow, Nancy 108, 121–3
Claeys, Gregory 5
Coetzee, J.M. 44–5
Cohn, Norman 67
communism 49, 91
see also capitalism, Marxism, socialism
Condorcet, Antoine de 47
Cook, Captain James 34
Cook, John 31–2
Cooper, James Fenimore 37
Coppin, Richard 32
Cromwell, Oliver 18–19, 141

Davis, J.C. 3–4
Day, Thomas 41–2
Defoe, Daniel 33, 152; (*A General History of the Pyrates*) 92; (*Robinson Crusoe*) 3, 33–45, 58; 'Robinsonnade' 37
Deleuze, Gilles 131
Descartes, René 24
Deutscher, Isaac 65
Diggers 31
Dinnerstein, Dorothy 108–9, 118–20, 126

Disneyland 2, 76, 150
Douglas, Mary 129
dystopia, *see* utopia

Eastern Europe 5, 11, 68, 74
   see also Soviet Union
'Endism', *see* apocalypse, millennium
Engels, Friedrich 61
English Revolution 18, 20
   see also Glorious Revolution
Enlightenment 5, 46
Enzensberger, Hans Magnus 71, 147

Fairfax, Sir Thomas 18
Feake, Christopher 31
Focillon, Henri 145
Forster, E.M. 84, 86–7
Fortunati, Vita 4
Fourier, Charles 6, 104
Fowkes, Ben 32
Frank, Andre Gunder 72, 148
French Revolution 5, 46–62, 66, 79
Freud, Sigmund 103–4, 125, 153
   see also psychoanalysis
Fukuyama, Francis 6, 77–9, 145, 148, 150

Galbraith, John Kenneth 74, 149
Gallop, Jane 121, 127
Gaskell, Elizabeth 107
Gearheart, Sally Miller 108, 117–20
Gellner, Ernest 70
Gildon, Charles 35
Gilman, Charlotte Perkins 107, 113–6,
   120
Giraudoux, Jean 43
Glorious Revolution 33, 36
Godwin, William 48–9, 52, 55–6, 61,
   144
Golding, William (*Lord of the Flies*) 38,
   42–4
Goodwin, John 31
Gorz, André 73–4
Gray, John 61
Green, Martin 39, 45
'Green' movement 5, 62, 73, 79–80, 117,
   148, 151
Guattari, Félix 131

Habermas, Jürgen 71, 147, 149
Hall, Charles 52–3
Harrington, James 22, 25, 26–7;
   (*Oceana*) 22–3

Harrison, Thomas 18
Hayek, Friedrich von, 67
History, end of 11, 77–80, 150; fast food
   as 136; redefinition of liberty in
   Western 29
Hobsbawm, Eric 84, 149
Hodgson, William 58–9
Hudson, W. 84–6
Hugo, Victor 7–8
Huxley, Aldous 76; (*Brave New World*)
   70

Irigaray, Luce 121
island stories 39; utopia as 11, 41; *Ile des
faisans* 9–10

James, Louis 3
James II, King of England 36
Jameson, Fredric 2, 77, 147
Jefferies, R. 84–5
Joachim of Fiore 63
Johnson, R.W. 75
Judaeo-Christian tradition 4, 46, 82

Kant, Immanuel 12, 67
Kaplan, Cora 120–2
Kermode, Frank 81
Klein, Melanie 108–10, 118–9; 'Bad
   Object' in 118
Koestler, Arthur 66
Kohák, Erazim 75
Kolakowski, Leszek 67–8, 146
Kristeva, Julia 108, 112–3, 121, 123,
   127; on feminine power 123
Kumar, Krishan 5, 22–3

Lacan, Jacques 127
Lapouge, Gilles 22
Le Brun, Charles 9
Ledoux, Claude-Nicholas 2
Le Goff, Jacques 81
Le Guin, Ursula 76, 128
Lepenies, Wolf 63
Lessing, Doris 5, 108, 123–6
Levellers 18
Levitas, Ruth 33
Lilburne, John 21, 28
Lithgow, John 57
Locke, John 29
Lytton, Edward Bulwer 27

McKay, Claudia 107, 110–3
McKeon, Michael 34
Malthus, Thomas Robert 50, 60–1
Manley, Mary de la Rivière 35
Mannheim, Karl 108
Marcuse, Herbert 4, 103, 153
Marin, Louis 1, 4, 6, 22, 132, 135; (*Utopiques*) 1
Marryat, Captain Frederick 42
Marx, Karl 43, 61, 71, 72–3, 78
    see also Marxism
Marxism 5, 63, 75, 101–2, 149
    see also socialism
Messiah, the 63
Miles, Rosalind 114
Mills, John Stuart 67
millennium 3, 20–21, 63, 81, 143
Mitchell, Adrian 44
More, Sir Thomas 1, 8, 11–12, 14–16, 24, 50, 76, 103; (*Utopia*) 8, 11, 15, 24, 27, 33–4, 58
Morgan, John Minter, 61
Morris, William 61, 69, 72, 76, 84–5
Morton, A.L. 33, 35, 143
Moylan, Tom 128

narrative 14; Bakhtinian 35
    see also travel narrative
Neville, John 34–5
Nietzsche, Friedrich 79
Northmore, Thomas 49, 55, 60
Nye, Philip 18

O'Connor, Noreen 113
O'Neill, John 2
Orwell, George 65; (*1984*) 65–6, 71, 146
Owen, Robert 56–7, 61, 69

Paine, Thomas 60; (*Rights of Man*) 48–9, 51, 53, 54
Paley, William 56
Paltock, Robert 47
Parrinder, Patrick 45
Paruta, Paolo 26
Pearson, Carol 113
Pennington, Isaac 28–9
Pirates 43, 92–5, 152
    see also Defoe, Daniel
Plato 14, 56, 65, 82, 105; compared to Hebrew thought 82, *Republic* parodied 99

Poe, Edgar Allan 104
Poole, Robert 109
Popper, Karl 66, 68, 71
Price, Richard 51–2
Psalmanazar, George 27
psychoanalysis 5, 109, 155

Reeves, John 53
Relf, Jan 4, 153
revolution: *see* English Revolution, Glorious Revolution, French Revolution
Reynolds, James 57
Rich, Adrienne 154
Richetti, John 34–5
Robinson Crusoe: as natural man 37
'Robinsonnade', *see* Defoe, Daniel
Rorty, Richard 150
Rose, Margaret A. 150
Ross, Andrew 5
Rousseau, Jean-Jacques 2, 3, 39–40, 46, 48

Saint-Pierre, Bernardin de 40
Salmon, Joseph 21
Sampson, Anthony 64
Schnabel, J.C. 37
science fiction 5, 84–9
Scotland 50–1
Scott, Sarah 47
Seitz, Don Carlos 91–2
sexuality 4, 5, 57, 94–106
    see also utopia, sexual
Showalter, Elaine 4
Simecka, Milan 71, 75
socialism 5, 64, 69, 75, 147, 149
    see also capitalism, Marxism, Soviet Union
Solzhenitsyn, Alexander 71
Soviet Union 64–9, 72
Spence, Thomas 51, 58
Sprigge, Joshua 18
Stapledon, Olaf 87
Steffens, Lincoln 64
Steiner, George 5, 6, 73, 148
Stephen, Leslie 42
Stevenson, Robert Louis 43
Strickland, Agnes 41
Suvin, Darko 17
Swift, Jonathan 3, 35, 59, 65, 96; (*Gulliver's Travels*) 35
Sztompka, Piotr 77–8

Talmon, Jacob 67
Thelwall, John 60
Time, notions of 4, 129
  see also millennium
Tocqueville, Alexis de 67
Tournier, Michel 44
travel 7, 13–14; narrative 34, 94–5

United States *see* America
utopia: and dystopia 43, 154; and
    education 24; and feminism 4, 76,
    107–28; and formality 17, 19; and
    freedom 141; and history 6, 77; and
    Marxism 5; and neutrality 2, 11; and
    postmodernism 76, 150; and
    republicanism 50, 55; and socialism
    70–7; and time 129; and
    totalitarianism 65; architecture of 2;
    as horizon 11–12; as ideology 13, as
    image of desire 108; as narrative
    form 34; assault on 64–70;
    definitions of 8; end of 1, 4, 63–4;
    frontiers of 7–16; garden as 2; in
    eighteenth century 47, 144; sexuality

and 4–5, 24, 94–106; (utopian)
    tracts 60

Vane, Sir Henry 17, 30
Verne, Jules 38
Vespucci, Amerigo 15
Vidler, Anthony 4–5
Vinge, Joan 108, 114–6

Walcott, Derek 44
Wallerstein, Immanuel 63, 150
Walwyn, William 30
Watt, Ian 34, 36
Weber, Max 36
Wells, H.G. 86, 103
Whittaker, Elizabeth 42
Winstanley, Gerrard 30
Wyndham, John 4, 87
Wyss, Johann David 41

Yeltsin, Boris 63, 74

Zamyatin, Yevgeny 22, 66